# ❧ *Heartwood* ❧

# ❧ *Heartwood* ❧

## THE FIRST GENERATION OF THERAVADA
## BUDDHISM IN AMERICA

## Wendy Cadge

The University of Chicago Press  CHICAGO & LONDON

WENDY CADGE is assistant professor of sociology at Bowdoin College.

The University of Chicago Press, Chicago 60637
The University of Chicago Press, Ltd., London
© 2005 by The University of Chicago
All rights reserved. Published 2005
Printed in the United States of America
14 13 12 11 10 09 08 07 06 05      1 2 3 4 5

ISBN: 0-226-08899-5 (cloth)
ISBN: 0-226-08900-2 (paper)

Cadge, Wendy.
    Heartwood : the first generation of Theravada Buddhism in America / Wendy Cadge.
        p. cm. — (Morality and society series)
    Includes bibliographical references.
    ISBN 0-226-08899-5 (cloth : alk. paper) — ISBN 0-226-08900-2 (pbk. : alk. paper)
        1. Theravada Buddhism—United States—History—20th century.   2. Southeast
Asian Americans—United States—Religious life.   3. Buddhist converts—United
States—Religious life.   4. Buddhist centers—United States—History.   5. Asia,
Southeastern—Religion.   I. Title.   II. Morality and society.
BQ734.C33 2004
294.3'91'0973—dc22
2005000207

# CONTENTS

# NOTE ON TERMINOLOGY

A number of non-English words appear in this book. Buddhist words included are in Pali, the scriptural language of Theravada Buddhism. Commonly used Pali words like "dhamma, dukkha, kamma, mettā, nibbāna, saṃsāra, saṅgha, sutta," and "vipassanā" are not placed in italics, while less commonly used Pali words are. Many of these words are spelled with diacritical marks (as above), but I omit those marks for ease of reading for an English-language audience. I also omit the diacritical marks on honorific titles for the same reason. When I use the word "dhamma" to refer to the teachings of the Buddha, I use the Pali form of the word. The teachers and practitioners at the Cambridge Insight Meditation Center, however, use the Sanskrit version of the word, "dharma," when they describe their weekly talks as "dharma talks." Thus, when quoting the teachers or practitioners at CIMC or describing these talks, I use the Sanskrit form of the word. Thai words included here are transliterated according to the Library of Congress system and placed in italics. Some organizations and people, however, have their own transliterations and when appropriate I use those rather than my own.

# ACKNOWLEDGMENTS

The sound of monks and lay people chanting was one of the most soothing aspects of this research. Their undulating tones continually calmed and quieted me. In the last few months of writing, I often found myself at the computer in the late afternoon chanting, "metta, karuna, mudita, upekkha." These are the four sublime states taught by the Buddha, translated roughly as loving-kindness, compassion, sympathetic joy, and equanimity. These states describe the ways the Buddha said we should conduct ourselves toward all other beings. I was blessed in this research and writing by many people with deep understandings of these states who taught me, in word and by example.

First, I want to thank the monks, teachers, and practitioners at Wat Mongkoltepmunee (Wat Phila) and the Cambridge Insight Meditation Center (CIMC) who welcomed me and shared their stories. I appreciate their welcome, their time, and their trust. At Wat Phila, I am particularly grateful to the monks for their support, particularly the late Taan Chaokuhn Rattanamēthē. I dedicate any merit that may come from these words to him. Many thanks also to Taan Nom Kalasang, Taan Charin Waisurasingha, Taan Laothong Puenpa, and especially to Taan Supichaya Esawanish for answering my many questions. Deep thanks also to Supranee and Sompoppol "Tang" Jampathom, Rani and Thira Thiramongkol, Boonchuay and Nantipha "Maeo" Ieamniramit, Khunakorn "Tim" Jamavan, and Agung "Ming" Fu for their friendship. At CIMC, I thank Larry Rosenberg, Narayan Liebenson Grady, and Michael Liebenson Grady for welcoming me and for their teachings. Center staff Maddy Klyne, Meg Hobbs, Pash Voynow, and Jef Weisel went out of their way in so many ways for me, and I thank them for their friendship. Much metta also to Ruth Nelson for welcoming me into her home in Watertown, Massachusetts, during my research at CIMC and to Margo McLoughlin for her kindness. A special thanks to the many other teachers, monastics, lay leaders, and administrators, listed in Appendix A, who spoke with me and provided me with newsletters and data. I am especially grateful to Edwin Kelly for giving me access to the history closet at the Insight Meditation Society.

Second, I have been particularly blessed by teachers at Swarthmore College and Princeton University. My thanks to Donald Swearer and Steven Hopkins, who independently suggested I pursue this line of research, and to Donald Swearer for introducing me to Wat Mongkoltepmunee and guiding me in many ways. Thanks to Joy Charlton, who taught me how to do fieldwork in her course at Swarthmore College in 1995 and has been a source of support and guidance since. Deep thanks to Robert Wuthnow, who taught me, in word and by example, how to be a sociologist and who supported me in this project and throughout my time in graduate school. I am also deeply grateful to Sara Curran, Miguel Centeno, Paul DiMaggio, and Stanley Katz at Princeton University for their feedback and support of this project and of me more generally. Anita Kline at the Center for the Study of Religion helped in more ways than she knows. The financial support of Princeton University, the Center for the Study of Religion at Princeton University, the Princeton University Center for Human Values, the Society of Fellows of the Woodrow Wilson Foundation at Princeton University, and the Society for the Scientific Study of Religion made this project possible.

Third, I want to thank colleagues and friends who provided field contacts, offered guidance, accompanied me on visits to organizations, and read drafts of chapters, and in several cases, the entire manuscript. My dissertation writing group of Leslie Callahan, Elaine Howard Ecklund, Jenny Wiley Legath, and Tisa Wenger deserves special mention, as do Nick Guyatt, Katie Klingensmith, and Fred Wherry. Thank you also to Ajahn Amaro, Debbie Becher, Courtney Bender, Sylvie Bertrand, Anne Blackburn, Ron Browning, Amy Cadge, Linda Callahan, Jake Carbine, Rosemary Polanin Carbine, Marion Carter, Joseph Cheah, Carolyn Chen, Lynn Davidman, Sara Davis, Jennifer Eichman, Paula England, John Evans, Gil Fronsdal, Genelle Geertz-Robinson, Gretchen Gignac, Lisa Ginsburg, R. Marie Griffith, Eszter Hargittai, Kristen Harknett, Scott Hoffman, Pawn Kanmoung, Kenneth Kraft, Prema Kurien, Peggy Levitt, Paul Lichterman, Sumi Loundon, Tania Rands Lyon, Margo McLoughlin, Margarita Mooney, Ann Morning, Ruth Nelson, Paul Numrich, Andrew Olendzki, Laura Olson, Todd Perreira, Charles Prebish, Stephen Prothero, Christopher Queen, Lynn Robinson, Kyoko Sato, Barton Sensening, Lisa Simons, Brian Steensland, Jacqueline Stone, Anna Xiao Dong Sun, Gaspar Taroncher-Oldenburg, Stephen Teiser, Thanissaro Bhikkhu, Craig Upright, R. Stephen Warner, John Wilson, Alan Wolfe, and Daniel Zelinski.

A special thank-you to Nongpoth Sternstein, for teaching me Thai language and for her help with many aspects of this research. Thanks to Sidhorn Sangdhanoo for collecting data about Thai temples and helping with Thai transliterations, Siam Sukumvanich and Poonsiri Trujillo for help with Thai translations, and Margo McLoughlin for help with Pali romanization. Thank you also to social science reference librarian Linda Oppenheim, data services reference librarian Ann Gray, and Paul Bern and Dan Edelstein at Data and Statistical Services at Princeton University. And thanks to Chrissy Bell, Jacqueline Chew, Anissa Graham, Natania Kremer, Michelle Owens, and Cherie Potts for help with transcription. I am grateful also to Natalie Searl for her help locating Thai temples and thinking about interview techniques. Portions of this research were presented at the Religion and Culture Workshop, the Center for Human Values, the Woodrow Wilson Society, and the Buddhist Studies Workshop, all at Princeton University. Chapters were also presented at meetings of the American Sociological Association, American Academy of Religion, Eastern Sociological Association, Midwest American Academy of Religion, and Society for the Scientific Study of Religion. Questions I was asked in each of these settings furthered my thinking in important ways.

Alan Wolfe, series editor, and Douglas Mitchell, Tim McGovern, Matt Avery, and others at the University of Chicago Press have been wonderful in making the transition from dissertation to book go smoothly. A special thank-you to Carol Saller for her fine editorial eye. I am grateful to all of these people for their guidance. I reserve my final and deepest thanks for my parents and sisters, Amy Cadge, Barbara and Donald Cadge, Laura Cadge, and Nancy and David Walls, and my grandparents Arthur Griffith, Elizabeth Hemminger, Phyllis and Ran Lyon, Doris and Arthur Stettler, and Mary Walls for their support. The encouragement of my friends, especially Katie Klingensmith, has been a deep source of strength. And to my partner, Nina Paynter, who was with me in Sri Lanka when this idea took root and has visited Buddhist centers, read chapters, talked with me about all of the ideas presented here, and put up with the many challenges of fieldwork, I am deeply grateful—for your patience, your love, your compassion, and your joy. You eased this journey in many ways and made the excitement of discovery sweet.

*Chapter 1*

## ARRIVALS AND A MAP
## OF THE JOURNEY

I talk with Mai,[1] a forty-six-year-old Thai woman, in her florist shop in Center City Philadelphia about what it was like to grow up in Thailand, meet her husband, and come to the United States. I had met Mai several months earlier at Wat Mongkoltepmunee (also called Wat Phila), a Thai Buddhist temple about thirty minutes outside Philadelphia. Mai tells me that her father-in-law was involved with the founding of Wat Phila in the 1980s, but that she and her husband Sing rarely made it to any of the festivals that Wat Phila holds seven or eight times a year.[2] Sing was diagnosed with cancer in the early 1990s, and it was not until shortly after his death that Mai woke up one morning knowing that she needed to go to the temple. "I was seeking something," she explains, "some peacefulness because I was in a terrible state. People do lots of things to deal with loss, like becoming compulsive gamblers, compulsive shoppers, or eating to death. I chose the temple. I chose religion to soothe me. I didn't know what I was looking for but I knew I was looking for something."[3] Reflecting on her choice now, Mai says, "I took Buddhism for granted because I was born with it. I was not really paying full attention . . . but I can tell you now that what I thought I knew [about Buddhism] was not true. Now I know more. . . . I corrected some of the understandings I had since I was little."

During the first year that she went to Wat Phila, Mai remembers spending a lot of time just watching the people there. "I was new and I didn't really know how to deal with everyone. I just wanted to go to the temple to do something good. I didn't really know anyone or have any friends, but I observed what people did and what people said. Later on I moved out of my shadow, little by little," she remembers. "During that period of time, I heard a lot of things. You judge for yourself what you want to believe." When she first started going to Wat Phila, Mai wanted to "make merit" by making donations to the monks to dedicate to her deceased husband. "I wanted to give him more than what I had given him. I love him so much," she explains. By meditating and making offerings to the monks, Mai thought she could help Si*ng* be reborn in a better life. As she talks, Mai closes up her shop and we walk to her car. On our way to her home in a northeast suburb of the city, Mai tells me that although she initially went to Wat Phila to make merit for Si*ng*, now she thinks she gained more than he did.

As we enter Mai's house, she motions for me to leave my shoes at the door and introduces me to the two cats that run to greet her. She asks if I would like to see her Buddha room and then shows me to a small bedroom on the second floor of the house. A low teakwood table with a gold Buddha image at the center sits against one wall. Votive candles and photos of orange-clad monks are carefully arranged below the Buddha image, and an artistic rendering of a standing Buddha hangs behind the table. As we enter the room, Mai kneels down on a cushion in front of this altar, and I quietly kneel at her side. She lights the candles and three sticks of incense and bows deeply to the Buddha, placing her forehead and the palms of her hands and her elbows on the floor with each bow. She turns to a photo of a monk named Luāngphō Sot and bows three times. Mai then takes one stick of incense from a box under the table, lights it, and places it in a bowl in front of a photograph of her late husband. Mai gently strokes an urn there that holds his ashes, in greeting. As I watch Mai, I think about how she described her daily Buddhist practices when we were talking at her shop. "As soon as I get home, I pick up the mail and I go upstairs because I have an altar set. . . . I light the candles and do my worshiping and light a candle and incense for my husband. . . . At night I pray before I go to sleep. Some nights I would get to do meditation but [other nights] I'm too tired, too sleepy, procrastinating, maybe tomorrow. From being around people and friends, they just keep pushing. They say, 'Don't wait, do it now. We don't know how much time we have so today, present, is the best.' It sticks in here," Mai said, motioning to her heart. "You choose to do it or you don't. So now, as soon as I get home, I meditate. I try." Mai finishes her worshiping and as I follow her downstairs, we start to talk about what we will have for dinner.

Several weeks later, I stand over a sink at Wat Phila with Mai washing and drying the huge pots and pans used to prepare the food for the festival today. As we wash, we listen through an intercom to the talk that Maha Nom, one of the monks, is giving to the one hundred and fifty people seated in the next room. He concludes and Mai and I say "sāthu," raising our soapy hands to our foreheads and gently bowing our heads in thanks.[4] Going to Wat Phila over the past few years, Mai tells me as we wash, has changed her attitude about what it means to be a Buddhist. "Being Buddhist means trying to be a better person. . . . You can't save the world but you do the best you can." She mentions a little tip given one Sunday by Maha Nom: "Don't worry about what other people say," Mai remembers. "Worry about your ears. Worry about what you hear, because people tend to hear what they want to hear. So be conscious of that." Mai liked that and jotted it in a small notebook in the purse she takes to the temple. Occasionally Mai visits other Thai temples in New York and North Carolina but tells me that really it does not matter what temple you go to. "We all have the same final destination. It's just a different practice."

※ ※ ※

Several months later, I talk with Becky, a sixty-year-old white American-born woman, in her living room in the Boston area about how she came to Buddhism and how she practices daily.[5] A standing Buddha image is on a sideboard across from where Becky sits on the couch, and a seated Buddha image is on the mantle over the fireplace. After watching some TV in the evening, Becky tells me, she normally goes into her bedroom and sits on the floor on two round cushions facing a seated Buddha image. "It's a really simple rule that I have," she says. "I sit before I go to bed no matter what else I have done that day, sitting or not sitting, and there is no minimum time limit. So sometimes it is as short as ten or fifteen minutes and sometimes it's an hour." Before we sat down in the living room, Becky showed me the place in her bedroom where she meditates. On a low table next to her bed a statue of a seated Buddha is surrounded by candles, incense, and a few amulets that depict the Buddha or monks. She described sitting down to meditate on the cushions in front of the Buddha, wrapping a shawl around her shoulders if it is a chilly evening, closing her eyes, and bringing her attention to her breath. Some nights she meditates by focusing on the in-and-out flow of her breath and other nights she watches the thoughts and sensations that move through her mind and body without judging or commenting on them.[6]

Becky moved to Boston from Philadelphia in 1959, she tells me, and went to college and graduate school at the Massachusetts Institute of Technology (MIT). She was married in 1962 and bought this house in 1971 with her husband. After she and her husband were divorced and her two children had moved out of the house, Becky began to hike and to exercise at an athletic club. She was concerned about her physical balance, and on the advice of one of the trainers at the club, signed up for a tai chi class at the Cambridge Center for Adult Education in 1990. She remembers her second tai chi class. "It was a really unpleasant day. . . . It was slushy and horrible and I was not in a good mood and I had to take a night plane down to Baltimore [for a business meeting]. Anyway, I went to the class and I couldn't figure out anything. It was really hard." After the class, Becky remembers walking in Harvard Square and suddenly, everything was different. "The weather had not changed, but I had, and everything was just fine. I took a cab and totally enjoyed the ride to the airport. And I'm sitting there waiting for the plane, which was an hour late, no problem. And I kind of got it that there was something about this that was quite strong." Becky continued tai chi and, on the advice of another teacher, began a form of standing meditation. "I set my timer in the kitchen and tried it," Becky tells me, "and that was the beginning of a daily meditation practice that hasn't stopped."

When I ask Becky how she first came to the Cambridge Insight Meditation Center (CIMC), she mentions her successful career in computer network security research and says that she occasionally compared notes about tai chi, yoga, and meditation with one of her coworkers. One evening, she visited a meditation class with this coworker and heard about CIMC from his teacher. Before going to CIMC for the first time, Becky told me she had been clear with herself that her meditation practice was not "spiritual." She was born into a Jewish family and at the time she first went to CIMC remembers that "there was no spiritual practice in my life." Going to CIMC was a big step for her because it was officially a Buddhist center. On her first visit, Becky says, "I was completely freaked because the cushions were all lined up and they were all the same color and then I saw the big altar and was almost out of there. But I was too far in the door and somebody was behind me and she was also confused and new so we sat next to each other." Then, Becky remembers, "this guy comes in and starts fiddling with the light switches and I thought, 'He is either the teacher or the janitor.' . . . And then he sits up in front and starts talking in this wonderful Brooklyn accent and I knew I was home. That was how I first met Larry [Rosenberg]. And he gave me this wonderful teaching right at the beginning because he kept using the word 'spiritual.'" Becky was clear that she did not want to hear anything "spiritual" and when she said that to Larry, he responded saying, "Maybe it's time to let that one go." Becky went home and sat with that teaching in her daily meditation practice. The next week when she went back to CIMC, Larry's use of the word "spiritual" did not bother her anymore.

After her initial visit to CIMC, Becky began to devote a large amount of time to meditation practice and to ten-day silent retreats at the Insight Meditation Society (IMS) in Barre, Massachusetts. In 1993, she retired from her career and attended IMS's yearly three-month retreat. She has continued to do many retreats and was part of the volunteer staff at IMS for about a year. She has taken classes at the Barre Center for Buddhist Studies, read hundreds of books about Buddhist teachings and practices, and when we talked, had recently returned from Sharpham College in England, where she was taking a course about Buddhism. I spoke with Becky often during the time I spent at CIMC, where she regularly takes classes, leads meditation sessions, and cooks for retreats. She calls herself a Buddhist "to stretch people's ideas about what is possible." "The heart of the practice," she tells me as our conversation in her living room concludes, "is opening to things."

Mai and Becky are two of an estimated two to three million women and men who practice Buddhism in the United States.[7] While Mai was born in Thailand and Becky in the United States, both made deliberate choices to get involved with Buddhist groups in the United States and both see their personal practices and involvement in these groups as central parts of who they are. As they sit before their Buddha images every evening, Mai and Becky draw guidance and inspiration from the Buddha. Quotes from the Dalai Lama and Buddhist texts hang on both of their refrigerators, and they each told me stories about how they draw from the Buddha's teachings in their daily lives. Both describe Buddhism as a religious or spiritual path and describe themselves as Buddhists. In addition to practicing Buddhism privately in their homes, Mai and Becky gather with others at Wat Phila and CIMC and rely on the practical and spiritual support they get from people in these centers. Both Mai and Becky currently share their homes with students they met through Buddhist organizations, and regularly practice Buddhism in speaking and silent groups at Wat Phila and CIMC.

While Buddhists have been in the United States for more than one hundred years, public interest in Buddhism has increased dramatically in the past thirty years.[8] Between 1970 and 2000 the number of books published about Buddhism more than tripled.[9] Articles have been written about Buddhism in *Time, Newsweek, Harper's,* and *Maclean's* magazines as well as the *New York Times Magazine,* the *New York Times,* and *USA Today.*[10] In addition to books and magazines, Buddhist-themed movies like *Kundun, Seven Years in Tibet, Little Buddha, The Golden Child, The Razor's Edge,* and *The Cup* have shown in major U.S. theaters, grossing more than 135 million dollars from U.S. box offices.[11] Buddhist words like "karma" and "nirvana" have even begun to enter the national vocabulary, as evident in Pepsi's recent advertising campaign for the drink Sobe Zen Blend and in the names of stores and boutiques across the country. In the 1990s, the Dalai Lama became something of a household name, speaking to thousands of people in New York's Central Park in 1999. The number of Buddhist meditation centers in the United States also more than doubled between 1987 and 1997, and companies devoted to meditation cushions and Buddhist art emerged.[12] In a recent national survey, one American in seven claimed to have a fair amount of contact with Buddhists and close to one-third said they were very or somewhat familiar with Buddhist teachings.[13] This growing interest in Buddhism, particularly since 1990, has led some people to describe the 1990s as something of a "Buddhism boom."

The dramatic growth of Buddhism in America in the past thirty years results from increased immigration from a number of Buddhist countries and the interest and conversion of native-born Americans.[14] The Immigration Act of 1965 ended country-of-origin quotas in immigration, leading to increased ethnic and religious diversification of the U.S. population, in part through the immigration of a number of Buddhists, Hindus, Muslims, and practitioners of other non-Western religious traditions.[15] This diversification in immigration began at the same time in the 1960s that many non-Asians in the United States were becoming interested in Buddhism. As a result, Buddhists in America at the end of the twentieth century included people born in Asia, people born in Asian families in the United States, and people born in non-Asian families in the United States, many of whom came to Buddhism as teenagers or adults.

This book examines how Buddhism arrived in the United States and is changing and adapting in this new context. I ask how Mai and other immigrants and Becky and other converts understand and practice the Buddhist tradition here, and what this suggests more generally about the processes through which religions new to the United States adapt and change in the American religious context.

Recent research about Buddhism in America by Charles Prebish, Richard Seager, Duncan Ryūken Williams, Christopher Queen, James Coleman, and others also asks questions about Buddhist adaptation.[16] My approach to the issue differs from their research in two main ways.

First, despite the fact that immigrants and converts are involved in all three main branches of Buddhism in the United States, researchers have not systematically compared communities of immigrant and convert Buddhists, as opposed to studying only one group or the other.[17] This comparison allows me to address broader sociological questions about how immigrant and convert groups that are, on the face of it, quite different, have simultaneously devel-

oped organizations, identities, and communities and negotiated gender relations in and through the same religious tradition in the United States. These
broader questions should be of interest theoretically even to people who are
not interested in the empirical case of Buddhism in America.

Second, this is one of the first book-length studies to focus specifically
on the practice in America of Theravada Buddhism, one of the three main
branches of Buddhism, which has traditionally been practiced in the Southeast Asian countries of Thailand, Sri Lanka, Laos, Burma, and Cambodia.[18]
Paul David Numrich's valuable book *Old Wisdom in the New World: Americanization in Two Immigrant Theravada Buddhist Temples* was the first, and
only other, book to describe Theravada Buddhism in the United States.[19] I
build on his work by comparing immigrant and convert Theravada Buddhists
in America and by recording the continuing story of their experience in the
decade since the period of Numrich's research.

This book is divided into two sections. First, I present a comprehensive
history of Theravada Buddhism in America, from 1966, when the first permanent Theravada Buddhist organization was started in Washington, D.C. While
existing media attention and research have tended to focus on Mahayana and
Vajrayana (Tibetan) Buddhism, Theravada has grown quietly and steadily since
it arrived in the United States.[20] For this reason, American religious historian
Richard Seager argues, it is likely to have an immense influence in the long
term.[21] I show how Asian and American-born Buddhists contributed to the
development of Theravada Buddhism in the United States and the many forms
Theravada Buddhism has, and continues, to take. The majority of the book
then focuses on two specific Buddhist centers: Wat Mongkoltepmunee (or Wat
Phila), a first-generation Thai immigrant temple; and the Cambridge Insight
Meditation Center (CIMC), a first-generation convert Theravada Buddhist organization. While these two centers are by no means representative of the range
of ways Theravada Buddhist organizations in the United States are adapting
Buddhism to the American context, I opted for depth rather than breadth in
this project and conducted extensive ethnographic research at each center that
enabled me to get to know the people who are involved with them, what the
organizations teach, and what the organizations and Theravada Buddhism,
more generally, look like through the eyes of the people involved.

## Religious and Cultural Globalization

While Buddhism is a relatively new addition to the American landscape, questions about how ideas initially taught or presented in one geographic location

are introduced and take shape in a new place are hardly novel. Historically, *ideas* moved largely with people and material goods along trade and shipping routes.[22] *Objects*, like ideas, also traveled.[23] In addition to ideas and objects, *practices* like water purification and organic farming also spread geographically over local, national, and international boundaries.[24] Increased trade, printing, and communication networks over the past five hundred years have made the spread of ideas, objects, and practices even easier than in the past. Five hundred years ago, an idea that originated in China could not have reached someone in North America, let alone be communicated. Now an e-mail sent from Sri Lanka can arrive in Pennsylvania in less than one minute. Hailed by politicians, pundits, and researchers as globalization, the increased number of linkages and exchanges between people in different geographic locations leads material goods as well as cultural ideas and systems to move rapidly around the world.[25]

Recent empirical research about the cultural aspects of globalization examines the implications of these movements. In *Many Globalizations: Cultural Diversity in the Contemporary World*, Peter Berger and Samuel Huntington show how cultural globalization is happening in a number of countries through international business networks, academic and intellectual contacts, popular culture like movies and music, and through religious networks, particularly those developed by evangelical Protestant organizations.[26] While some cultures fully accept new cultural forms, leading to a kind of global culture that is largely American, others reject them or respond and adapt in creative ways. While most of the cases Berger and Huntington examine show aspects of culture moving from more to less developed countries, they note that some aspects of culture also move from less to more developed countries, as in the case of some forms of Buddhism and other Asian religions that have made their ways to the United States.

As one cultural aspect of globalization, scholars agree that religions, defined institutionally or culturally, have been transported around the globe by merchants, politicians, and missionaries on trade and other economic and political routes for thousands of years.[27] Sometimes linking people beyond national boundaries, religion is both a homogenizing force and, conversely, a way that individuals construct unique identities.[28] Scholars often mention Christianity, particularly evangelical Protestantism, and Islam as particularly effective globalizing religions because of their commitments to proselytizing and converting.[29] Buddhism, however, has been more accretive than other missionary religions and has continuously adapted and changed in new local and national contexts.[30] Since the Buddha delivered his first sermon in the Deer Park outside what is today the city of Benares in northern India, Buddhism has been crossing national borders. From India and later Sri Lanka, Buddhism spread to East and Southeast Asia, moving most recently to the United States and other countries in the West, where all three of the main branches of Buddhism are practiced, for the first time, in the same national contexts.[31]

Religions in America have long been influenced by the movement of religious traditions around the globe. With the exception of Native American religions, Mormonism, and a few other religions started in the United States, American religious history is a story about how religions started in one place are carried along global networks and constructed and reconstructed in new ways on American shores.[32] Since 1965, this story has taken on new dimensions as dramatic increases in immigration to the United States have added new layers particularly to the Christian, Muslim, Hindu, and Buddhist traditions in the United States. These new immigrants build institutionally and culturally on specific religious traditions, raising questions about how new people contribute to existing religious traditions and construct new organizations in the United States.

Existing research about the globalization, migration, and development of religions in the United States has focused largely on the movement of people, particularly immigrants, to the United States. In *The Uprooted* and *Protestant-Catholic-Jew: An Essay in American Religious Sociology*, Oscar Handlin and Will Herberg respectively argue for the importance of religion in the lives of immigrants to the United States.[33] Since the mid-1990s, researchers have been investigating the role of religion in the lives of post-1965 immigrants to the United States, particularly the ways religion helps immigrants assimilate and adapt.[34] Religion is often viewed functionally in these projects as something that facilitates contexts in which ethnic identity formation takes place and social networks are formed. This approach is particularly evident in research designs that compare first-generation Hindus, Catholics, Buddhists, and members of other religions in a given geographic area, which allows researchers to make arguments about the common ways that first-generation immigrants experience religion and construct organizations, leadership structures, and gender relations.[35] It does not, however, by design, provide space for asking about whether there is something shared by Mexican, Guatemalan, and Salvadoran Catholics in the same or different geographic locations or if there is something about being a Catholic, Hindu, or Buddhist that is shared by people in the first, fifth, and eighth generations. These earlier studies provide few opportunities for thinking seriously about how the content of particular religious traditions informs practitioners' lives.

In addition to the one-time migration of people, religions in America today are shaped by the continuous movement of people and ideas across national boundaries. Peggy Levitt calls the ideas, behaviors, identities, and social capital that flow back and forth between host and sending countries "social remittances."[36] In her book *The Transnational Villagers*, Levitt shows how normative structures and systems of practice are exchanged in relationships between Dominicans living in Miraflores, a town in the Dominican Republic, and Jamaica Plain, a section of Boston. Among other things, these social remittances influence how religion is practiced in both contexts as, for example, Dominicans in Boston send new religious ideas and practices from Jamaica Plain back to Miraflores.[37] In addition to these transnational migrants, reverse messengers, or people in the United States who go abroad and return with religious ideas and teachings, have been instrumental to the development of several religions in the States, specifically Japanese Buddhism and Hinduism.[38] Henry Finney, for example, writes about traveling to Japan with an American Zen master who is officially confirmed as a Zen priest and teacher in the Soto sect, a confirmation that then allows the teacher to return and teach in the United States and provides tangible evidence of the tradition's diffusion to the United States.[39]

Increasingly, religions in America are also influenced by ideas and social remittances that move across national boundaries apart from the migration of people. Books written by monks in Thailand are available in the United States, for example, to be read by people who have never left the United States and might not even know where Thailand is. At several meditation centers in the United States, people gather once a month on Saturday evenings at 10 to watch a live broadcast of a monk at Wat Dhammakāya, a temple in Thailand, teach a meditation session.[40] While people and monks from Wat Dhammakāya came to the States originally to help establish these centers, people now quite literally consider themselves a part of these ceremonies in Thailand although they are in the United States. Similarly, some Buddhist temples in America lead meditation classes with taped teachings made by monks in Thailand. While these monks have never set foot in the United States, their ideas are influencing how Buddhism is understood and practiced by groups of people here.

Analytically, this book builds on existing research about the globalization, migration, and development of religions in the United States and addresses a broader question about the specific ways that people in the United States are constructing and practicing this religious tradition in their daily lives in a new environment. Theravada Buddhism and other religious traditions leave their former locations under numerous "contexts of exit" and arrive in the

United States under particular "contexts of reception."[41] By examining the case of Theravada Buddhism, a tradition that arrived in the United States along a number of global routes simultaneously, I provide a specific empirical case of how globalization influences the development of a religious tradition in the United States, and I show how the American "context of reception" shapes Theravada Buddhism for two very different groups of people.

## Approach to the Study of Religion

Before 1966, Theravada Buddhism did not exist institutionally in the United States. Mahayana Buddhism, the branch practiced in China and Japan and other parts of East Asia, had arrived in the States at the end of the nineteenth century with Chinese and Japanese workers on the West Coast. Vajrayana Buddhism, the branch practiced in Tibet, arrived in the 1960s largely after the 1959 flight of the fourteenth Dalai Lama from Tibet.[42] Theravada Buddhism, the third main branch of Buddhism, arrived in the United States between 1966 and the present in two main ways. First, immigrants born in Thailand, Sri Lanka, Laos, Burma, and Cambodia came to the United States in record numbers, bringing various forms of Theravada Buddhism along with them. Simultaneously, a first generation of primarily white native-born converts began to practice forms of it in the United States after two American Peace Corps volunteers in Thailand, Jack Kornfield and Joseph Goldstein, and other reverse messengers brought these forms of Buddhism back to the States and began to teach.

To examine how Theravada Buddhism arrived in the United States along global networks and was adapted, constructed, and acted on by people in local contexts requires a particular conceptual approach to the study of religion. Historically, religions are often conceived of as coherent systems of teachings, beliefs, and practices. Rather than viewing Theravada Buddhism as a coherent system, I imagine it and all religions as collections of teachings, institutions, people, and practices that are gathered in various combinations by people who want to understand or practice the tradition.[43] This approach to religion resembles Ann Swidler's understanding of culture not as monolithic but as repertoires or "tool kits" of "habits, skills, and styles from which people construct 'strategies of action.'" Or Robert Wuthnow's "ragbag" approach to culture, in which people pull together teachings, beliefs, and practices from different sources in the way that people make new items from scraps found in ragbags or drawers.[44] Similarly, the ways that people gather together various aspects of cultures, in this case religions, can be described metaphorically as individuals constructing their own tool kits, bags, or baskets from components of their religious traditions and their experiences in the world.

Many different elements are also normally gathered into descriptions and definitions of Theravada Buddhism at the macro or national level. People wanting to conceptualize and understand it in Thailand today, for example, would mention "suttas," the texts that are the closest approximation we have to what the Buddha actually taught. Ideas about merit that developed as the tradition moved through Asia would be included, as would the institutional history of Theravada Buddhism in Thailand and details of the relationship between Buddhist institutions and the state. The description of Theravada Buddhism would likely include mention of objects like stupas, Buddha statues, amulets, candles, and incense. Monks and lay people would be part of the description, as would particular practices like bowing three times to Buddha images, ritual exchanges between monks and lay people, meditation practices, chants, holy water ceremonies, and ceremonies for births and deaths.

Typically, everything included in the description of Theravada Buddhism in Thailand at the national level is called religion, and scholars study the collection of elements that make up this definition of religion from different vantage points. [45] Religious historians often study texts and discuss translations, particular words, doctrines in the texts, the history of the texts, and how different parts of the texts fit together. Anthropologists and anthropologically oriented historians focus on particular villages, ceremonies, or actions and interpret the significance of those actions sometimes for the people involved and sometimes for the history of Theravada Buddhism in Thailand generally. [46] Instead of looking primarily at one group of things (texts, institutions, objects, leaders, etc.) that are included in the national definition of Theravada Buddhism in the United States, I focus on the tradition holistically at the national level in the United States and on two particular organizations and on the lives of people involved with those groups.

In addition to definitions and conceptualizations at the national level, all religious traditions are conceptualized and understood in many ways by individual practitioners. Clifford Geertz and Peter Berger distinguish between religions as aspects of national cultures or societies broadly and religions as central components of the worldviews and reality structures that individuals construct personally. [47] Individual practitioners sometimes gather elements from the national definition of Theravada Buddhism into their own worldviews and approaches to the tradition and sometimes gather ideas, practices, and objects from other religious traditions or experiences in their lives. Theravada

Buddhist practitioners in Thailand today, for example, likely included items from the national definition that are important or meaningful to them in their own understandings of the tradition, ignoring elements that they do not know about or care about. If a person is not interested in the institutional history of Buddhism in Thailand, then that does not directly inform his or her own way of understanding the tradition. Some people are not interested in the names of texts, all of the precepts, or details about the lineages of monks. Many are interested in the teachings of the Buddha, but naturally only the stories they have heard or remembered are included in the collection of elements that make up their ways of understanding the tradition. People's personal conceptualizations of Theravada Buddhism in Thailand also include things particular to their own personal histories, such as stories of the Buddha passed down from grandparents, memories of offering food to the monks on a particular morning, or a particular amulet they bought at a Bangkok market. I talk here about the ways people gather together teachings, institutions, people, and practices into their personal ways of seeing Theravada Buddhism. As with all religions, this occurs through a process of selective appropriation, often unintentionally from day to day, as individuals learn about and live their religions.

Thus, following David Hall, Robert Orsi, and others, I privilege the voices and stories of ordinary religious practitioners in this book and strive to understand how they live and understand the Theravada Buddhist tradition inside and outside their religious organizations in what Peter Berger would call their everyday realities.[48] As Robert Orsi suggests, I "embed the religious person and community in history," and see that history and culture not as "something that religious persons are 'in' but as the media through which they fundamentally are." This approach, according to Orsi, further "understands the power of cultural structures and inherited idioms—what Pierre Bourdieu has named the 'habitus'—both to shape and discipline thought . . . as well to give rise to religious creativity and improvisation."[49] I describe individual people as "practitioners" throughout this study, in part, to show the active, often innovative and creative, roles they play in constructing their own approaches to Theravada Buddhism, the organizations they are a part of, and in turn the national history of Theravada Buddhism in America at the beginning of the twenty-first century.

I also distinguish analytically between national and personal or individual conceptualizations of Theravada Buddhism as a way to distinguish between all of the ideas and material objects that relate to a religious tradition generally in a culture and the specific ideas, teachings, and practices that matter to individual practitioners in that culture. This distinction further allows me to distinguish between all of the items that are part of Theravada Buddhism in Thailand and those items from Thailand that made it to the United States along one of several global routes. The selection of particular items is significant and part of what I explain throughout the book.

## The Study

This conceptual approach to religion leads me to approach Theravada Buddhism in America historically as well as from the perspective of particular organizations and people.[50] I first trace the development of Theravada Buddhism in America generally to show how the tradition came to the United States and has been practiced here. The majority of people involved are Asians who brought the teaching from Southeast Asia to the United States and white American-born people who learned about it through one of several reverse messengers. I then examine Wat Mongkoltepmunee (Wat Phila), an organization founded by first-generation immigrant Buddhists, and the Cambridge Insight Meditation Center (CIMC), an organization founded by first-generation convert Buddhists, as a way to understand how people understand and practice the Theravada Buddhist tradition and how their understandings and practices compare.

Immigrant practitioners who brought Buddhism to the United States are primarily divided by their countries of origin into Thai, Sri Lankan, Laotian, Cambodian, and Burmese temples, each of which is connected to its home country through its leadership, language, and culture. The extent of communication between these five groups is described in chapter 2. I studied the immigrant group at Wat Mongkoltepmunee for theoretical and practical reasons. Thais, like Sri Lankans, were one of the first groups of Theravada Buddhists to arrive in the United States and start temples. Many of the early white Theravada Buddhist teachers spent time in Thailand, making a Thai temple an appropriate organization to compare to the groups being formed by whites in the United States. Unlike people from Laos and Cambodia who arrived in the United States largely as refugees, many first-generation immigrants from Thailand were professionals and had the resources and time to start religious organizations shortly after they arrived. Educationally and in terms of their financial resources, many Thai Buddhists resemble white Buddhist practitioners. Practically, I had an opportunity to study Thai language at a nearby university and had access to a Thai temple through advisors and friends who had been involved with the temple.[51]

I also studied the convert group at the Cambridge Insight Meditation Center (CIMC) in Cambridge, Massachusetts. It is through the early teachers like Jack Kornfield and Joseph Goldstein and the early groups, most especially the Insight Meditation Society, that many current convert practitioners learned about Theravada Buddhism. While Asian practitioners have created their approaches to Theravada Buddhism through time spent in Asia and the United States, many converts have constructed their approach to the tradition through their exposure to the ideas and practices that were carried from Southeast Asia to the United States by these early teachers. Convert Buddhists gather in loosely constituted and connected groups across the United States. Some groups identify with particular teachings and lineages and others do not. I studied CIMC specifically because it places itself in the Theravada Buddhist tradition. Some groups in the Theravada Buddhist tradition, like CIMC, refer to themselves as insight or vipassana meditation centers to emphasize the type of meditation practice that is at the center of their approach to the tradition. CIMC teachers allowed me to conduct research there and the practitioners welcomed me in their midst.[52]

Despite the many differences between Wat Phila and CIMC, structurally they are quite similar. Both are nonresidential centers (for lay people) where people go for a few hours each week for classes, talks, and practice. Wat Phila and CIMC were founded by ordinary lay people in the mid-1980s and have existed in the locations where they were founded since that time. The leaders who founded the organizations were still leading them at the time this research was completed and the core group of people involved with both centers was roughly the same size.[53] About two-thirds of the people involved with both centers were women and the average age of the practitioners was around forty-five. The majority of practitioners at both centers were professionals who did not live in ethnic or religious enclaves, and who lived at some distance from their families of origin. Almost everyone at Wat Phila was fluent in English. Neither organization has an automatic second generation; the children of the practitioners at Wat Phila generally do not come to the temple and few of the practitioners at CIMC have children who are also interested in CIMC or Buddhism generally. This lack of a second generation raises the question, in both cases, of how these centers and Theravada Buddhism more generally will continue in the United States beyond the first generation.

At Wat Phila and CIMC, I conducted participant observation and in-depth interviews with the practitioners and leaders for one year. At Wat Phila I attended Sunday services, festivals, Thursday morning cooking gatherings, and a range of other activities. I attended Thai language class on Sunday mornings and taught English to the monks for several months. At CIMC I attended classes, meditation sessions, Wednesday night talks, and a range of social activities. I also examined historical documents at both centers and interviewed approximately twenty monks and teachers outside Wat Phila and CIMC to learn about the history of Theravada Buddhism in America and to situate both centers in the broader Theravada Buddhist spectrum. A complete description of my methodology is provided in appendix A.

Throughout this study, I view Theravada Buddhism as a complex historic tradition, and I ask what pieces of this tradition the first generation of immigrants and converts have brought to the United States and are institutionalizing in Wat Phila and CIMC. Based on the pieces of the tradition brought to the United States, I compare the social processes by which immigrant and convert Buddhists have constructed their centers, their communities, and their individual identities. I find that Mai, Becky, and other immigrant and convert Buddhists share a few Buddhist beliefs and practices amid many differences. Some of the ways people at Wat Phila and CIMC are constructing their organizations, communities, and personal identities based on the Buddha's teachings, I argue, are common to individuals and groups in other religious traditions that begin to practice in the United States. Other ways these two centers are adapting suggest shared and uniquely Buddhist responses to the dilemmas of adaptation and change faced by all new religions when they arrive and are constructed in America.

꙳   ꙳   ꙳

Chapter 2 describes the category of Theravada Buddhism and its history in the United States from 1966 to the present. Readers more interested in my ethnographic research may wish to skip directly to chapter 3, where I describe how Wat Phila and CIMC were formed as organizations in light of existing institutional, social, and cultural *environments* in the United States. Certain kinds of structural spaces are available for religious groups in the United States and this chapter explains how each group approached these spaces and fit within them from their beginnings in 1985 to the present. This chapter also introduces the teachers and practitioners at each center and outlines how and why people get involved with each center. Chapter 4 examines how the Buddha's teachings at Wat Phila and CIMC are presented *ideologically* and interpreted and lived by the practitioners. I conceive of the organizations as containers and explain what is inside each container and how practitioners gather these ideas into their personal understandings, practices, and ways of seeing the world. By exploring the contents of the organizational containers and practitioners' individual understandings, I argue that Mai, Becky, and other people at Wat Phila and CIMC share some common understandings of the Buddha's teachings, amid their many differences.

Chapter 5 investigates how practitioners at Wat Phila and CIMC structure themselves inside each organization into *communities* or groups and relate to those groups. I find that people at both centers rely on the centers for religious or spiritual and social support, though the forms that support takes are quite different. Based on how practitioners at Wat Phila and CIMC constructed their organizations, the Buddha's teachings, and their communities, chapter 6 explores how practitioners construct *personal identities* in light of the Buddha's teachings and their involvement in Wat Phila or CIMC. I find similarities between the groups in the extent to which people describe themselves using the ideas of ascribed versus achieved identities, though at neither center is identity a central personal or organizational concern. Two-thirds of the people at Wat Phila and CIMC are women, and chapter 7 describes how *gender* cuts across the environmental, ideological, community, and identity themes addressed in previous chapters. The book concludes in chapter 8 by comparing the ways that immigrants and converts are adapting Buddhism in the United States to the ways that practitioners of other religious traditions have adapted those religious traditions since 1965. I point to the commonalities in adaptive strategies as well as to the distinctly Buddhist ways of adapting evident in these two organizations. The chapter concludes by considering the future of Theravada Buddhism in America.

※　※　※

On a hot summer day near the conclusion of this research, I drove to High View, West Virginia, to meet with Bhante Henepola Gunaratana, a Sri Lankan born monk who came to the States in 1968 to help lead the Washington Buddhist Vihara. Bhante Gunaratana went on to start the Bhavana Society, a monastery and meditation center in West Virginia supported by both Asian and white American Buddhist practitioners. Bhante Gunaratana is one of the few people in the States who has taught and spent time with immigrants like Mai and converts like Becky over many years. When I spoke with Bhante Gunaratana at the Bhavana Society, I asked him one of the questions that is at the center of this study: how are immigrants and converts both a part of the history of Theravada Buddhism in America?

Bhante Gunaratana thought for a moment and responded by telling me the Heartwood Sutta, a teaching of the Buddha.[54] "Somebody wanted to find a core, heart of a tree, heartwood," Bhante told me from memory. "He would go and bring back the leaves and twigs and say, 'I've got the heart.' Somebody would say 'this poor man doesn't even know what the heartwood is. He grabs all these leaves and twigs.' So another would go out and bring the outer bark of the tree and say he has the heartwood. A third would go and bring inner bark and then the fourth would go and bring the soft part, the softwood between the inner and outer bark. And the last one, the fifth person, would go and find the heart. The core, the very solid heartwood of the tree. So each of them is happy thinking that they got something. But only those that got the heartwood actually got the heartwood. It has to have a softwood, inner bark, outer bark, leaves, twigs, roots, everything. This all supports the tree. When all of this combines together, we call it a tree. Similarly all of these are important for the survival of Buddhism."

Bhante went on in our conversation to say that he sees Mai, and Asian or traditional Buddhists more generally, as like the first four people in this sutta who find the leaves, twigs, bark, and softwood. It is Becky and other white Americans, Bhante Gunaratana claims, who tend to find the heartwood, or core, of Theravada Buddhist teachings. Other teachers and monastics I spoke with during this research argue just the opposite, that it is immigrants and other Asians who have the heartwood, and the white Americans who are missing the core. My goal here is not to make an argument about who does and does not have the heartwood, but to describe and compare how the heartwood, and the many other branches of this Theravada Buddhist tree, look to the immigrant and convert practitioners who are its first generation in America.

*Chapter 2*

# THE HISTORY OF THERAVADA
# BUDDHISM IN AMERICA

To me, one way of looking at it . . . is that the Theravadin tradition is
simply the latest group of immigrants to come to the United States.
LARRY ROSENBERG

Thirty to fifty Thai and Lao people meet on Sundays at their temple—two
mobile homes and a multipurpose building—in Alabama under the guidance
of a Lao monk. Sri Lankans, Burmese, and Americans gather at the Washington Buddhist Vihara in Washington, D.C., for puja ceremonies on Sundays,
meditation classes during the week, and Buddhist festivals some weekends.[1]
American born, largely white Buddhist practitioners meet in small and large
meditation centers on weekends and weekday evenings across the United States
to sit in silence and practice sitting and walking vipassana meditation. Every year, Asian and American-born monks across the country spend the three
months of the rain retreats, often called Buddhist Lent, close to their temples
studying, meditating, and teaching. A group of lay, largely white, American-
born practitioners spends three months every year in silent meditation at the
Insight Meditation Society in Barre, Massachusetts.[2]

Theravada Buddhism is taking many forms in the United States. Some
groups meet in multimillion-dollar buildings, like the Thai temples in Los
Angeles and Washington, D.C., while others meet in rented apartments and
people's living rooms.[3] Some groups are led by monks, others by lay teachers, and still others by loosely assembled boards of directors or more informal
groups. Some groups include people all born in the same country while others
are much more mixed. Ceremonies and teachings take place at these centers
in Thai, Sinhala, Lao, Khmer, Burmese, and English languages, sometimes
simultaneously.

Buddhism has been in the United States since the nineteenth century, but
the branch called Theravada was not introduced institutionally and perma-
nently established until 1966 with the founding of the Washington Buddhist
Vihara. Changes in immigration laws in 1965 and the increased interest of
native-born Americans led to particularly dramatic growth in the number of

TABLE 2.1. Admissions to the United States from countries where Theravada Buddhism has traditionally been practiced

| Years | Burma | Cambodia | Laos | Sri Lanka | Thailand |
|---|---|---|---|---|---|
| 1969–1972 | — | — | — | — | 10,093 |
| 1973–1976 | — | — | — | — | 21,039 |
| 1977–1980 | 5,034 | 8,036 | 22,141 | 1,596 | 14,828 |
| 1981–1984 | 3,345 | 56,163 | 88,274 | 2,084 | 21,127 |
| 1985–1988 | 3,597 | 49,153 | 34,470 | 2,037 | 33,044 |
| 1989–1992 | 4,052 | 17,079 | 41,616 | 4,191 | 32,733 |
| 1993–1996 | 4,340 | 6,103 | 19,157 | 4,335 | 21,589 |
| 1997–2000 | 4,861 | 6,619 | 5,781 | 4,239 | 12,362 |
| Totals | 25,229 | 143,153 | 211,439 | 18,482 | 135,683 (1977–2000) |
| | | | | | 166,815 (1969–2000) |

*Sources:* 1969 to 1975 Annual Reports of the Immigration and Naturalization Service. 1976 to 2000 Immigration and Naturalization Service Statistical Yearbooks.

Theravada Buddhist practitioners in the United States.[4] Between 1977 and 2000 more than 500,000 immigrants arrived in the United States from countries where Theravada Buddhism was traditionally practiced (table 2.1). Immigrants from Thailand and Sri Lanka came primarily for economic reasons, while many from Burma, Laos, and Cambodia came as refugees fleeing oppressive governments in their home countries.[5] In the 2000 U.S. Census, 595,845 people identified themselves as Burmese, Cambodian, Laotian, Sri Lankan, or Thai, either alone or in combination with another race or ethnicity (table 2.2). While not everyone who was born in or identifies ethnically with one of these countries is Buddhist, many are.[6]

Not surprisingly, many of these immigrants began Buddhist organizations, and by the year 2000 people from these five countries had started approximately ninety-six Laotian temples, eighty-nine Cambodian temples, eighty-seven Thai temples, twenty-four Burmese temples, and twenty-one Sri Lankan temples across the United States.[7]

Hundreds of Theravada Buddhist meditation centers attended by Asian and native-born white Americans also exist across the country. Between 1987 and 1997, Don Morreale reported in *Buddhism in America*, the number of Theravada Buddhist meditation centers increased from 72 to 152.[8] As figure 1 shows, the number of meditation groups publicized in *Inquiring Mind*, a newsletter for English-speaking people interested in a Theravada Buddhist form of med-

TABLE 2.2. U.S. Residents Born in Theravada Buddhist Countries or Identifying Racially or Ethnically in Terms of One.

| Country | 1980 | 1990 | 2000 |
|---------|------|------|------|
| Burma | — | — | 16,720 |
| Cambodia | 16,044 | 149,047 | 206,052 |
| Laos | 47,683 | 147,375 | 198,203 |
| Sri Lanka | — | — | 24,587 |
| Thailand | 45,279 | 91,360 | 150,283 |
| Total | | | 595,845 |

*Note:* Census data from 1980 identifies only those people who were born in one of these five countries. Census data from 1990 and 2000 also include people born in the United States who identify racially or ethnically with one of these countries. Detailed data about race, ethnicity, or ancestry were not collected about people from these five countries in the 1980 census.

*Sources:* U.S. Bureau of the Census, *1980 Census of Population,* vol. 2, *Subject reports,* PC80-2-1E, *Asian and Pacific Islander Population in the United States,* issued January 1988. U.S. Bureau of the Census, *1990 Census of Population, Asian and Pacific Islanders in the United States,* issued August 1993, table 1: General characteristics of selected Asian and Pacific Islander groups by nativity, citizenship, and year of entry, 1990. U.S. Bureau of the Census, *2000 Census of Population and Housing,* Summary File 2, *Advanced National*; these data represent people who listed an Asian group alone or in any combination. It is not possible to determine the number of people from these five countries in the United States prior to 1980. The 1970 census shows that 1,581 people reported Burmese as their mother tongue and 14,416 people reported Thai, Siamese, or Lao as their mother tongue (U.S. Bureau of the Census, *1970 U.S. Census,* Subject Reports, *National Origin and Language,* table 19). In the 1960 census, 377 people reported Burmese as their mother tongue and 1,666 people listed Thai, Siamese, or Lao (U.S. Bureau of the Census, *1960 U.S. Census, Mother Tongue of the Foreign Born,* table 2).

itation called vipassana meditation, increased from 16 in 1984 to 232 in 2000. The number of people attending programs at Theravada Buddhist retreat centers also increased in the last twenty years. The number of people attending retreats at the Insight Meditation Society, the first Theravada Buddhist oriented retreat center founded by white American-born practitioners, for example, increased in the past ten years as evident in figure 2.[9]

Conservative estimates suggest that between 500,000 and one million people in the United States, the majority of them born in Asia or to Asian families in the United States, could be called Theravada Buddhists.[10] Hundreds of thousands more have been influenced indirectly by the teachings through their families, stress-relief programs, and popular writings.[11]

This chapter traces the history and development of Theravada Buddhism

FIGURE 1. Meditation groups listed in *Inquiring Mind* newsletter (1984–2000)

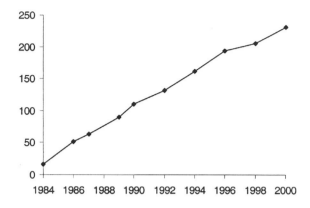

FIGURE 2. Number of practioners at the Insight Meditation Society (1990–2000)

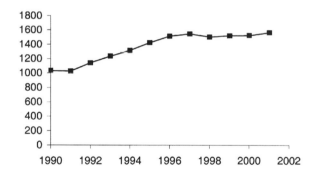

in America from 1966 to the present.[12] The combination of immigration and conversion that led Buddhism in general to grow so dramatically in the twentieth century has led many researchers to assert that there is not one but two Buddhisms in America, the Buddhism of immigrants and the Buddhism of converts.[13] These two Buddhisms have developed separately from one another, proponents argue, and have no history, organizations, teachers, teachings, or practices in common. Casual observation suggests this may be the case, but more detailed consideration of the history of Theravada Buddhism shows that the picture is considerably more complex. In his 1990 study of a Thai temple in Chicago and a Sri Lankan temple in Los Angeles, for example, Paul Numrich found groups of Asians and groups of white people meeting at these temples at different times for different practices but under the guidance of the same monks.[14] Several Thai people I interviewed in the course of this research excitedly described to me their visits to the Insight Meditation Society and Barre Center for Buddhist Studies, two lay-led, largely white Theravada meditation centers. And a meditation center in the tradition of S. N. Goenka in Shelburne Falls, Massachusetts, currently offers ten-day meditation retreats in English, Khmer, and Hindi languages. Two temples led by white monastics in California are attended by both Asian and white American-born Buddhist practitioners, and several Thais I interviewed told me about reading books in English by white meditation teacher Jack Kornfield. While the "two Buddhisms" model describes two impulses that led to the creation of Theravada Buddhist centers in America, it does not fully or accurately describe its history or the current configuration of Theravada Buddhist America.

## "Theravada" Buddhism

After the Buddha's death in approximately 483 BCE, groups of his followers formed many small schools and moved throughout India practicing and teaching.[15] The branch of Buddhism that has become known as Theravada or "Way of the Elders" spread from India to Sri Lanka in the third century BCE and to the countries that are now Thailand, Laos, Burma, and Cambodia in the early centuries CE. In the middle of the third century BCE, some groups settled in southern India, adopted Pali as their canonical language, claimed that their teaching was strict orthodoxy, and took the name Theravadins.[16] Around the same time, King Asoka in India sent Buddhist missionaries to Sri Lanka, and this form of Buddhism began to be practiced there. During the fifth century, a number of commentators in Sri Lanka, including Buddhaghosa, Buddhadatta, Mahanama, Upasena, Dhammapala I, and Dhammapala II, established the classical doctrinal form of the Theravada, and the basic structure and form of the Pali canon was established, which has remained central to the teachings and practice of Theravada Buddhism. This form of Buddhism later spread to Burma, Thailand, Cambodia, and Laos. The proximity of these countries to each other enabled Theravada Buddhism to flourish as individual countries received support from leaders in other parts of the region over the next several hundred years.[17]

For the purposes of this chapter, I define Theravada Buddhist groups as those that trace their lineage or history to Buddhism as traditionally practiced in Thailand, Sri Lanka, Laos, Burma, and Cambodia. The development of Theravada Buddhism in America is directly related to its history in each of these countries generally, and to the ways that it was shaped in Asia by Western and Christian influences in the nineteenth and twentieth centuries.[18] The majority of Asian temples described in this chapter clearly identify as coming from one of these five countries. Some white meditation centers clearly align themselves with Theravada Buddhist teachers or lineages, whereas others identify more generally or as nonsectarian—what Don Morreale calls "Buddhayana" in his book *The Complete Guide to Buddhist America*.[19] I will exclude groups who trace their lineage to a general or nonsectarian Buddhism or to Theravada in combination with another branch of Buddhism.

The majority of white meditation groups that I place in the Theravada lineage, like CIMC, teach "insight meditation," or vipassana meditation, which teaches practitioners to be aware of things as they are. Somewhat surprisingly, many practitioners are unaware of vipassana's origins or how it relates to other teachings of the Buddha and Theravada Buddhism more generally.[20] At a conference at the Barre Center for Buddhist Studies in 1995, Sharon Salzberg, one of the founding teachers of the Insight Meditation Society, the first Theravada Buddhist organization founded and attended largely by white Buddhist practitioners, explained, "There have been many instances when I have heard people say 'I am part of the vipassana tradition.' And I say, 'What is the vipassana tradition?' Vipassana is a technique or way of practice that is found in most and perhaps all of the Buddha's teachings. . . . I think what has happened is that vipassana as a mind training has been separated from its base in a tradition . . . and transmitted to the West as a thing in itself, as though it had a separate existence apart from these roots, which I actually don't think is true."[21] I also place meditation centers in the tradition of S. N. Goenka on the Theravada Buddhist spectrum, because they developed out of Buddhism as taught in Burma and carried to India and then to the United States.[22] These centers do not identify as Buddhist, let alone Theravada Buddhist, but I discuss them because they developed directly out of Buddhism as practiced in Burma in the early twentieth century.

## Theravada Buddhism in America

The origin of Theravada Buddhism in America can be traced to a speech made by Anagarika Dharmapala at the World Parliament of Religions meeting in 1893. Born in 1864 in Sri Lanka (then Ceylon), Don David Hewavitharne became a celibate layman and adopted the title Anagarika Dharmapala, meaning "homeless one," "guardian of the Dharma."[23] Heavily influenced by Henry Steel Olcott (1832–1907) and Helena Petrovna Blavatsky (1831–1891), Theosophists who first visited India and Ceylon from America in 1878 and 1880, Dharmapala spent his life spreading Buddhism around the world. At the Parliament, Dharmapala spoke about how Buddhism, Christianity, and scientific approaches to the world overlap, saying that the "Buddha inculcated the necessity of self-reliance and independent thought," and "accepted the doctrine of evolution as the only true one."[24] Theosophists and others in the United States were influenced by elements of Theravada Buddhism in the late nineteenth and early twentieth centuries.[25] Groups of Burmese and Sri Lankan monks visited the United States before the first Theravada Buddhist organization was formed in Washington, D.C., in 1966.[26]

The Washington Buddhist Vihara and the Buddhist Study Center in New York, the first two Theravada Buddhist organizations in the United States, were both founded and supported jointly by Asian and American-born people. The Washington Buddhist Vihara began in Washington, D.C., in 1966 following the 1964 visit of Sri Lankan monk Most Venerable Madihe Pannasiha Mahanayaka Thera.[27] Sent by the Asia Foundation on a tour, he happened to be in Washington on Vesak, the Buddhist holiday that commemorates the birth, death, and enlightenment of the Buddha. He celebrated in a park with a few people from the Sri Lankan Embassy and, after conversations with an officer from the embassy, decided to begin a temple in the United States.[28] Most Venerable Madihe Pannasiha Mahanayaka Thera returned to Sri Lanka and collected funds for the temple from the Sasana Sevaka Society, an organization of Sinhalese lay Buddhists, and from Sri Lankans and Americans living in the United States.[29] Another Sri Lankan monk, Ven. Bope Vinitha, had recently returned to Sri Lanka after two years of study at Harvard University and was asked to return to the States to direct the temple in Washington. He arrived carrying a Buddha statue and relic of the Buddha, and in December 1966 the Vihara held its first meeting at the All Souls Unitarian Church on 16th Street NW.[30] In 1967 the Vihara purchased a building at 5017 16th Street NW from the government of Thailand for a reduced price, where people continue to meet today.[31] The Washington Buddhist Vihara has been an international temple from the beginning, where services are held in English and Buddhists and friends of Buddhism from Sri Lanka, Thailand, Bangladesh, Burma, and America are included among the temple's regular members.[32] Sri Lankans and other Asians tend to come for devotional services and ceremonies, while white Americans come for meditation sessions and sutta study classes.[33] Monks from many countries have lived or stayed at the Vihara over the years. In January 2001 the Vihara housed four monks, two from Sri Lanka, one from Nepal, and one white American ordained in San Francisco according to the Burmese

FIGURE 3. Washington Buddhist Vihara, Washington, D.C. Founded 1966

tradition. Also in the late 1960s, Thai and American Buddhists founded the Buddhist Study Center in New York, which led many years later to the founding of Wat Vajiradhammapadip, a Thai Buddhist temple in New York.[34]

## 1970S: THE BEGINNINGS

In the early 1970s, Sri Lankan and Thai lay people and monastics began to organize temples, first in California. The group of white people who would form the first vipassana meditation retreat center in the United States met, and the Insight Meditation Society (IMS) was born. In 1972, Ven. Ananda Mangala Thera, a Sri Lankan monk who had been living in Singapore, visited Los Angeles and was asked by a handful of Sri Lankan families to start a Buddhist society.[35] In 1973 this group of Sri Lankan immigrants began an informal committee and consulted again with two visiting Sri Lankan monks. They incorporated as the Sri Lankan—America Buddha Dhamma Society in 1975 and a few years later began to collect funds to support a temple.[36] Ven. Walpola Piyananda, who would become the head monk at this temple, arrived in the United States on July 4, 1976, and was brought from the airport to the bicentennial parade in San Francisco, where he rode in an open-topped car with another monk and a Buddha statue.[37] He went from there to Northwestern University and then returned to California, at the request of the Sri Lankan community, to be the head monk of the still developing temple. He was joined by another Sri Lankan monk, Ven. Pannila Ananda Nayake Maha Thera, and together they lived in a house purchased by the Sri Lankan—America Buddha Dhamma Society in Hollywood, California, that became the Los Angeles Buddhist Vihara. Like many early Sri Lankan and Thai temples, this temple was attended not just by Sri Lankans but by Laotians and Cambodians as well. A conflict developed in the late 1970s over who was in control of the temple, and Ven. Piyananda was expelled from the temple. He and his supporters started a new temple in 1980, Dharma Vijaya Buddhist Vihara, a name that means "victory of truth."[38]

Between 1970 and 1974 Thai immigrants also began to organize temples in Los Angeles and Washington, D.C. In 1970 a Thai monk Ven. Phrakhru Vajirathammasophon of Wat Vajirathamsathit in Thailand was invited to Los Angeles to teach and perform Buddhist ceremonies. The Thai community formed the Thai-American Buddhist Association that year, and three additional monks visited the United States to plan the founding of a temple. In June 1971 a mission of Thai monks led by Ven. Phra Dhammakosacharn arrived in Los Angeles, and lay people began to raise funds to purchase land.[39] In 1972, land was donated and construction began on a main hall, a two-story Thai-style building, that was completed and dedicated in 1979.[40] Buddha images for the shrine hall and two sets of scriptures were carried to the United States by monks and lay people from Thailand, and in 1979 His Majesty the King and Her Majesty the Queen of Thailand presided over the casting of the principal Buddha image for the temple at Wat Po (officially called Wat Phra Chētuphon, or the Monastery of the Reclining Buddha) in Thailand.[41] Wat Thai L.A. has grown dramatically since 1971 and is currently the largest Thai temple in the United States, serving thousands of people per year. As in Los Angeles, a group of Thai lay people in Washington, D.C., began to raise funds for a temple of their own, and two Thai monks took up residence there in 1974.[42] Vajiradhammapadip Temple in New York, Wat Buddhawararam in Denver, and Wat Dhammaram in Chicago were also started before 1979. These temples were attended largely by Thai people and also Lao people in the early years. The Council of Thai Bhikkhus, an umbrella organization designed to oversee all of the Thai temples in the United States, was started in 1977.[43]

The Insight Meditation Society (IMS), the first Theravada Buddhist organization founded completely by non-Asians, also started in the mid-1970s.[44]

FIGURE 4. Wat Thai Washington, D.C. Founded 1974. Photo courtesy of Taan Supichaya Esawanish.

At the end of the 1960s and beginning of the 1970s, largely white native-born Americans who would start this organization were returning from their travels in Asia. Jack Kornfield returned to the States as a monk in 1972 after spending several years in the Peace Corps and in various temples and monasteries in Asia.[45] Joseph Goldstein returned as a lay person in the 1970s, also after spending time in the Peace Corps in Thailand and in monasteries and meditation centers throughout Southeast Asia.[46] Sharon Salzberg, the third founding teacher of IMS, returned after studying Buddhism with teachers in India, Nepal, Bhutan, Tibet, and Burma. In 1973, Jack Kornfield met Tibetan teacher Chogyam Trungpa at a party in Cambridge, Massachusetts, and Trungpa invited him to come to Boulder, Colorado, in the summer of 1974 to teach at a new school he was starting, the Naropa Institute. It was at the Naropa Institute in the summer of 1974 that Jack Kornfield met Joseph Goldstein and the two formed a relationship that shaped much of the way Theravada Buddhism was taught to white people in the United States for the next decade.[47]

While the Thais and Sri Lankans forming temples were looking to import Theravada Buddhism as it was practiced in their home countries, Kornfield, Goldstein, Salzberg, and other early teachers were not interested in Theravada as practiced popularly in Thailand or Burma. Rather they were interested in vipassana, or insight, meditation. First popularized for lay people in Burma, this form of meditation emphasizes being aware and present with physical and mental experiences as they are happening so as to see things clearly as they are. Believing that most Asian Buddhists do not actually practice Buddhism, Kornfield explained that the early teachers "had to learn to simplify the practices we learned in an attempt to offer a clear straight forward form of Buddhist practice in the West. We left much of the Eastern culture, ritual, and ceremony also behind in Asia . . . we felt that for Americans it was an unnecessary barrier. It seemed to us that for our culture the simplicity and straightforwardness of mindful practice itself would speak best to the heart of those seeking practice."[48] Leaving behind what they often called the "cultural baggage," the first white teachers sought to find the "original teachings" of the Buddha, which they believed were centered in vipassana meditation, and to pass them on through "a container provided by the west."[49] Psychedelics and other drugs brought many early practitioners to the meditation practice.[50]

After meeting at the Naropa Institute in 1974, Jack Kornfield and Joseph Goldstein began to teach meditation retreats around the country, and with Sharon Salzberg and Jacqueline Schwartz they started a meditation center for teacher and self-led meditation retreats. Called the Insight Meditation Society (IMS), the center was incorporated on May 19, 1975, and aimed to "provide a secluded retreat environment for the practice of meditation in the Theravada Buddhism tradition."[51] A letter was sent to possible contributors in November describing the purpose of the center and requesting donations toward the purchase of a building. In January 1976, IMS purchased a building on seventy-five acres of rural farmland in Barre, Massachusetts, about two and a half hours outside Boston.[52] The building, a mansion called the Father of the Blessed Sacrament, was sold by the Catholic novitiate and had single rooms plus dormitory space, a large chapel, and kitchen and dining facilities.[53] Shortly after the building was purchased, someone climbed to the top of a twenty-foot extension ladder and rearranged the letters over the main entrance to read "Metta," a Pali word meaning loving-kindness.[54]

When they started IMS, the teachers made a conscious decision to keep the center grounded in the Theravada Buddhist tradition, and that grounding, Joseph Goldstein argues now in retrospect, has been a source of institutional focus and strength. "It was a conscious choice to have it not become a center where even very enlightened teachers from a range of traditions would come," Goldstein remembers. "We felt that it would really dilute the vision."[55] Several months after the building was purchased, the center offered teacher-led courses and self-retreats, primarily in the style of Burmese meditation masters Mahasi Sayadaw and U Ba Khin and in the Thai forest tradition of monk Ajahn Chah.[56] Retreats typically ran for ten days during which participants maintained complete silence.[57] A three-month retreat, modeled after the three-month rain retreat taken by monastics in Southeast Asia, also took place every fall from September through December. Jack Kornfield, Joseph Goldstein, Ruth Denison (a German-born woman who studied in India and Burma, par-

FIGURE 5. Insight Meditation Society, Barre, Massachusetts. Founded 1976. Photo courtesy of the Insight Meditation Society.

ticularly under Burmese lay teacher U Ba Khin), and others taught many of the early courses. Most had little teaching experience and tried to transplant what they had learned in Asia to the United States with an emphasis on preserving the "dhamma," or teachings of the Buddha. The questions the teachers concerned themselves with in the early years, Sharon Salzberg remembers, were about what it meant to take the Buddhist tradition, steeped in the imagery and metaphor of Asia, to try to find its unchanging essence, and then to express that essence in the imagery of a new time and place: "We are discovering new metaphors," Salzberg has written, "that connect us to a reality and a teaching that is timeless and universal."[58] Connections between the teachers at IMS and their teachers in Asia were strong and lasting. Thai forest monk Ajahn Chah, Burmese monks Ven. Mahasi Sayadaw, Ven. U Pandita, Ven. U Silananda, Indian lay teachers Anagarika Munindra and Dipa Ma, and the Tibetan leader the Dalai Lama visited IMS in the late 1970s and 1980s, and the teachers at IMS returned to Asia to study with their teachers there.[59]

While the first Theravada Buddhist organizations founded largely by Asians and white Americans had little contact with one another, they occasionally shared teachers and influenced each other in unexpected ways. Between 1979 and 1982, for example, famed Burmese meditation teacher Mahasi Sayadaw traveled around the United States and Europe spreading the Buddha's teachings.[60] Another Burmese monk, the Most Venerable Taungpulu Kaba-Aye Sayadaw, also came to the United States in 1978 at the invitation of Rina Sircar, a woman born to Indian parents in Burma who had come to the States to pursue graduate study. In 1979 Mahasi Sayadaw came to the United States with U Silananda and U Kelatha, in part in response to an invitation from the Insight Meditation Society to lead a retreat there. During their time in the States, among other things, the three Burmese monks visited a Burmese community in the San Francisco Bay area. At the request of that Burmese community, Mahasi Sayadaw agreed to leave U Silananda and U Kelatha behind when he returned to Burma, and shortly thereafter (between October 1979 and February 1980), one of the early Burmese Buddhist organizations in the United States, the Theravada Buddhist Society of America, was formed.[61] A lay association, the Theravada Buddhist Society of America, then started a temple, Dhammananda Vihara. This temple joined a Burmese temple that already existed in Los Angeles. Shortly after the founding of these temples, additional Burmese temples were started in Washington, D.C., and other cities across the United States.[62]

Quite apart from white Theravada Buddhist practitioners, groups that eventually founded the first Laotian and Cambodian temples in the United States were also started between 1978 and 1980 in the Washington, D.C., area. Migration from Laos and Cambodia peaked in the early 1980s and these early groups slightly predated those peaks.[63] The temple called Wat Buddhikarana that currently serves Cambodian Buddhists in the Washington, D.C., area was first organized in 1978 when people began worshiping together in converted houses.[64] Before 1978, Cambodians in Washington, D.C., had attended the Washington Buddhist Vihara.[65] In the late 1970s, the Khmer Rouge regime systematically killed Buddhist monks throughout their reign of terror in Cambodia, and a few of the surviving monks arrived in the United States and were involved in the construction of early temples. Before 1980, Lao people in the Washington, D.C., area attended Wat Thai D.C. or other centers. In 1979 they began to organize among themselves, and in 1980 Lao monks formed a small community in a rental property. The Lao Buddhist Association purchased a house and one-acre lot in 1980 where services were held, but problems with zoning regulations led the temple to relocate several years later.[66]

Buddhist tradition states that the Buddha's teachings have truly arrived in a new country when sons and daughters of good families in the country join the monastic order.[67] By this logic, Buddhism is fully established in a new geographic area only when native-born people join the sangha, or order of monks. While numerous white American-born men had become monks in Southeast Asia in the 1960s and 1970s, the first Theravada Buddhist higher ordination took place on United States soil in 1979 at Wat Thai Los Angeles. Scott Joseph DuPrez, a native Californian, had received his *samanera,* or first level of ordination into the monkhood, in Sri Lanka in 1975, taking the name Yogavacara Rahula. In May 1979 he received higher ordination at the Thai temple in Los Angeles. Sri Lankan monks Ven. Jinaratana (preceptor), Ven. Dhammaratana (teacher), Ven. Ananda, and Ven. Piyananda, who were living in the United States, presided at the ceremony.[68]

By the end of the 1970s, Theravada Buddhist centers had been established or initiated by Sri Lankans, Thais, Burmese, Cambodians, Laotians, and native-born Americans in the United States, and a native-born American had received higher Buddhist ordination on American soil. While the temples started by each of the five Asian groups had their own connections to their home countries, IMS was not so formally linked and traced its lineage to the teachings of Mahasi Sayadaw in Burma and the Thai forest tradition in Thailand. While the Asian temples were formally led by Asian monks, lay people were integral to their founding and maintenance. IMS was founded and led by lay white people, though monastic and lay teachers from Asia visited and led retreats. In their day-to-day lives, lay Asians typically attended the temple of their home country, and if there was no temple, they attended other Asian temples despite the fact that they may not have understood some of the service. Much of the chanting and ritual at Asian temples is conducted in Pali, the scriptural language of Theravada Buddhism. While most lay people do not understand Pali, the language sounds familiar enough to many that if they attend a temple where they do not speak the vernacular language, the chanting and ceremony still often sound familiar. Monks also occasionally visited or stayed at temples led by monks from Asian countries. White people generally attended IMS. While white people attended the Washington Buddhist Vihara, there is little evidence that they attended other Theravada Buddhist organizations led by Asians or by monks in the 1970s.

## 1980S: CONTINUED GROWTH

Immigration from Theravada Buddhist countries continued in the 1980s, particularly from Cambodia and Laos, and the number of temples in each of the five Asian groups continued to increase. Whereas there were five Thai temples in the United States in 1980 for example, there were more than forty at the end of the decade (fig. 6).[69] These included temples associated with the Mahanikaya or Council of Thai Bhikkhus and the Dhammayut Order.[70] Like immigrants from Thailand, temples started by Thai-born people were initially concentrated on the East and West Coasts, with the majority in California.[71]

Most Thai temples followed similar patterns in their development. A group of lay people in a given city who were interested in building a temple first formed a committee to consider the issues involved. They often sought advice from the monks at Wat Thai L.A. or Wat Thai Washington, D.C., or from monks that they knew in Thailand. Often a monk came to the area to visit and meet with people, and then the committee started to collect donations from Thai people in the area. An apartment or single-family house would be rented or purchased and monks would take up residence, normally from Thailand rather than from another temple in the United States.[72] Many temples remain in these original buildings now, while others, particularly those that continued to accumulate financial resources, purchased new buildings or land and often began to build Thai-style buildings. Many took loans from banks to continue this construction and many remain in debt today. Some temples, like Wat Phrasriratanaram Buddhist Temple of St. Louis, moved into existing buildings, in this case a former Assemblies of God church. In many cases, the traditional rules regarding the construction of temples were amended slightly, for example, when portions of temples normally housed in separate buildings in Thailand were combined for reasons of cost or practicality. The distinctions between commercial and residential zoning were particularly challenging for many Thai and other Asian temples, and many had to relocate to areas zoned for religious gatherings.[73]

The number of Cambodian temples on American soil particularly increased during the 1980s as the number of Cambodians in the United States increased from 16,044 in the 1980 U.S. Census to 147,411 in the 1990 census. The Cambodian monk Ven. Maha Ghosananda, a disciple of the former head of the Cambodian Buddhist Sangha, the late Samdech Phra Sangha Raja Chuon Noth, was living in Thailand when refugees from Cambodia began to flood into Thailand in the 1970s. In 1978 he began to establish Buddhist temples in refugee camps and in 1981 came to the United States to head the Cambodian Buddhist community in Rhode Island, which became the center for establishing Buddhist temples in the Cambodian refugee community around the world.[74] Between 1983 and 1986, more than eighty monks came to Providence from Cambodia and were sent to the forty-one temples that had opened in the United States and Canada.[75] Some of these monks came through centers that

FIGURE 6. Number of Thai temples in the United States, 1970–2000

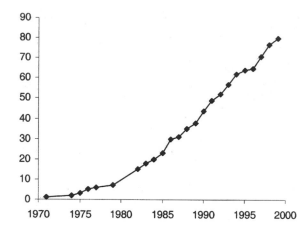

had been established in Thailand; in fact, many of the monks that currently lead Cambodian temples were born in Thailand and grew up speaking Khmer, but spoke Thai at school. Not surprisingly, many have strong friendships with monks serving Thai temples.[76]

The number of Theravada meditation centers founded and attended largely by white people also increased during the 1980s, and the number of people attending existing centers rose. The number of sitting groups listed in *Inquiring Mind*, a newspaper-like journal started by Wes Nisker and Barbara Gates in California in 1983, for example, increased from sixteen in 1984 to ninety in 1989, as evident in figure 1.[77] The reach of Theravada Buddhist meditation groups also widened in the 1980s. In 1984 these sixteen groups met in eight states, while in 1989 the ninety groups listed met in thirty-two states. New groups also began in the 1980s; Vipassana Hawaii, for example, currently led by white lay teachers Steven Smith and Michele McDonald-Smith, began with meditation retreats of varying durations.[78] The numbers of retreats offered and practitioners sitting retreats at IMS increased throughout the 1980s, and IMS experienced some growing pains as tensions developed around how the center should institutionalize and plan for the future, financially and otherwise. In 1986, responsibility for administrative, policy, and fiscal matters related to IMS was placed in the hands of nine board members selected from the community.[79] By the end of the decade, IMS was advertising for an executive director and associate director, in part to lead the organization through a master development plan in the 1990s. The leadership saw a master plan and new leadership going hand in hand and described IMS as an "adolescent approaching adulthood." [80] The future direction of IMS was also influenced in the 1980s by founding teacher Jack Kornfield's decision to leave IMS for California in the fall of 1984.

Vipassana retreats had been taking place in California since the early 1970s, and they began to take a new direction in the 1980s when Jack Kornfield arrived and began to teach at Insight Meditation West, formerly the Dharma Foundation. The first board meeting of Insight Meditation West was held in 1984, and after 408 acres in Marin County, north of San Francisco, were purchased in 1987, a fundraising committee was formed to raise the money for construction. By the end of the decade, funds were being raised, programs were being held elsewhere around San Francisco, and the number of small meditation groups that had grown out of existing programs had skyrocketed. [81]

Programs at Insight Meditation West tended to be more experimental than those at IMS and often drew on ideas and techniques outside of Theravada Buddhism and vipassana meditation. The line between vipassana meditation and psychotherapy has been blurry at some insight meditation centers, and the teachers at Insight Meditation West more openly incorporated ideas from psychotherapy into their teachings than did teachers at IMS. After returning from Asia and before helping to start IMS, Jack Kornfield completed a PhD in clinical psychology. His approach to teaching at Insight Meditation West combined insights from vipassana meditation, psychotherapy, and other spiritual and therapeutic practices.

Meditation centers in the tradition of S. N. Goenka, a layman born to Indian parents in Burma, also began to develop in the United States in the 1980s. Although people involved with these centers do not place themselves on the Theravada Buddhism spectrum, centers in this lineage are treated in this chapter because they developed directly from the teachings of Burmese lay teacher U Ba Khin. Goenka studied with U Ba Khin for fourteen years in Burma before moving to India in 1969 to teach vipassana meditation to Indians and later to travelers from America interested in his ten-day structured silent retreats. [82] Joseph Goldstein, Sharon Salzberg, and other teachers involved with IMS spent time at Goenka centers in India in the 1970s. Goenka traces his teachings to the Buddha and describes vipassana meditation as "pure science," saying that the "teacher . . . gives a path. . . . [E]ach individual has to walk on the path." [83] In the more than thirty years since he started teaching, Goenka has strictly avoided the words "Buddhism" and "religion." "For me, Buddha never established a religion, Buddha never taught Buddhism. Buddha never made a single person a Buddhist." The day "Buddhism" happened, "it devalued the teachings of the Buddha. It was a universal teaching and that made it sectarian," Goenka has said.[84] Since 1976, Goenka has been based in India, and in 1982 he began to appoint assistant teachers who were born and raised in the West.

While some people who studied in the Goenka tradition mixed the teachings with ideas from other traditions, others like Goenka himself wanted to keep the teachings pure and free from other influences. Unlike the teachers at IMS, who aimed to find the essence of the Buddha's teachings and express that essence through "a container provided by the west," practitioners in the lineage of Goenka believe that the teachings do not need to change or be adapted to the West. The Buddha was an enlightened person, Goenka and his followers argue, so nothing from him needs to be changed. In 1980, people who had attended retreats at the Goenka center in India began to rent sites for ten-day retreats in the United States and in 1982 they incorporated and established the Dhamma Dhara Vipassana Meditation center in Shelburne Falls, Massachusetts, the first center in the Goenka lineage outside India.[85] Eight students came to the first course, which, like all courses at Goenka centers around the world, was taught using videotapes of Goenka himself teaching. All of the ten-day courses taught around the world, therefore, have been identical. Assistant teachers are present at each course to guide students in their practice, but Goenka himself remains the teacher, and no other methods, techniques, or teachings are supported on retreats. "In this tradition we take a very conservative approach," Luke Matthews, the current manager of the Dhamma Dhara Vipassana Meditation center explained, "feeling that what was already given was so good and has worked in so many cultures for so many centuries. Does everything really have to be adapted for the American culture? I would say let's adapt the culture and keep this as we had it."[86] In addition to the center in Shelburne Falls, the California center called Dhamma Mahavana was started by students of Goenka in 1983. Both of these centers were initially attended largely by white people with an interest in vipassana meditation.

In addition to the growth of Asian temples and largely white meditation centers in the 1980s, the Bhavana Society, a monastery founded and attended both by Asian and by white American-born people, was started by Sri Lankan monk Bhante Henepola Gunaratana and lay white American meditator Matthew Flickstein in 1983. Bhante Gunaratana came to the United States from Sri Lanka in 1968 to help lead the Washington Buddhist Vihara in Washington, D.C.[87] In 1976 he met Flickstein at the Vihara when Flickstein came for meditation instructions. After several years, they began to speak about Bhante Gunaratana's dream of beginning a meditation center. In May

1983 they formed the Bhavana Society and began to look for land where they could build their center. After one failed attempt at raising money, they purchased thirteen acres in West Virginia in May 1984, and a few months later chanted suttas on the land, made speeches, and expressed appreciation to the people whose donations enabled them to purchase the property. One year later they began to build, but ran into numerous practical problems. In May 1987, Ven. Rahula, the American-born monk who had received higher ordination at Wat Thai L.A. in 1979, contacted Bhante Gunaratana and came to stay for a few weeks on the land that the Bhavana Society had purchased. Bhante Gunaratana asked him to stay on, and in August 1987 Bhante Gunaratana led the first meditation course on the land, attended by seventeen people.[88] Bhante Gunaratana was the head monk at the Washington Buddhist Vihara when he established the Bhavana Society, and in 1988 he left the Vihara to become the society's president. Reflecting on the importance of a place like the Bhavana Society in an interview in *Tricycle*, a Buddhist magazine, Bhante Gunaratana said, "If you do not preserve the form of Theravada Buddhism, the original form, eventually people won't even know what it is."[89] Sri Lankans and Americans sit on the board of directors, and Asians and American-born people both support the center financially.[90] American-born people generally attend the meditation retreats at the center, and Asians tend to come to make offerings to the monks and nuns.

When Asians and Americans are both at the Bhavana Society, a certain diplomacy is required to negotiate their activities. "We have dispensed with much cultural trappings and most of our daily visitors and retreatants are American," Bhante Gunaratana explained. "However, because there are monks here, we do occasionally experience cultural flavor. People from Buddhist countries will come on full moon days or to offer lunch to dedicate the merit to someone who has died, and so forth. During silent retreats some visitors may show up who want to follow some particular custom from their home country. Occasionally during a silent retreat the dining hall is filled with completely silent American meditators who are eating slowly and mindfully while in the adjoining hall several families of people from an Asian country sit boisterously chatting with their children running around."[91] Asians and American youth mix most at youth retreats at the Bhavana Society that have taken place in the summer for many years.[92]

While a higher Theravada ordination took place on American soil at Wat Thai L.A. in 1979, one of the early *samanera* ordinations occurred at the Bhavana Society in 1989.[93] This ordination included the largest ever gathering of monastics from Theravada Buddhist countries in the United States, twenty-

FIGURE 7. Bhavana Society, High View, West Virginia. Founded 1983.

eight monks and nuns. In July, monks and nuns from Cambodia, Sri Lanka, Thailand, Burma, Vietnam, and Laos who were living in the United States gathered at the Bhavana Society with the three men and one woman who would be ordained.[94] Sri Lankan–born monk Ven. Havanpola Ratanasara of the Buddhist Sangha Council of Southern California officiated. The ceremony began with the establishment of a *sima*, a physical area, in this case in the woods, where monks could meet without the laity and an ordination could take place. Tom West, Matthew Flickstein, Shibaya, and Misha Cowman were ordained. Tom West, a Canadian, had been a permanent resident at the center for some time, and Matthew Flickstein had helped to start the center. Shibaya, a Japanese man, had previously ordained in the Mahayana school of Buddhism. He had been living at a Sri Lankan temple in Los Angeles and in this ceremony switched his vows to Theravada. Full Theravada ordination for women in Sri Lanka, Thailand, Laos, Burma, and Cambodia ended in the eleventh century. Misha Cowman was ordained not by monks from one of these five countries but in the lineage of Ven. Dhammadeepa, a fully ordained nun from Vietnam.[95] The ceremony lasted for two and a half hours, and these were the first of twelve or thirteen people that Bhante Gunaratana has ordained over the last twelve years in the United States.[96]

By the end of the 1980s, the number of Asian temples in the United States had increased, as had interest in meditation centers founded and attended largely by white Theravada Buddhist practitioners. Insight Meditation West and the Goenka center in Shelburne Falls, Massachusetts, were open, and Asians and Americans were both involved with the Bhavana Society in West Virginia. Some white American-born people had probably started to attend meditation classes at Asian temples across the country, although this is difficult to demonstrate empirically. With the ordination at the Bhavana Society, Theravada Buddhism was becoming even more established in the United States. Its largely Asian and largely white segments worked together to some extent in the 1980s, through Buddhist councils like the Buddhist Sangha Council of Southern California (1980), American Buddhist Congress (1987), and Buddhist Council of the Midwest (1987).[97] Asian and American college-aged practitioners also sometimes worked together through Buddhist organizations on college campuses. Bhante Gunaratana was appointed as the Buddhist chaplain at American University in 1974 and Bhante Uparatana in 1989. The Sri Lankan-born monk, Ven. Piyananda, was appointed the first chaplain of the newly formed Buddhadharma Fellowship at the University of California-Los Angeles in 1988 that serves Asian and American Buddhists.

## 1990S: GROWTH AND MIXING DEMOGRAPHICS

The 1990s showed continued growth in Buddhist organizations founded and attended largely by Asian and by white practitioners, but also showed new growth in the number of organizations led and attended both by Asian and by white practitioners. Some of the mixing between Asians and Americans occurred in temples started by Sri Lankan, Thai, and Burmese immigrants to the United States, as opposed to those started by Lao and Cambodian refugees. This likely occurred because the monks and first-generation immigrants involved with Thai, Sri Lanka, and Burmese temples had a better command of English and were more assimilated to U.S. society than the monks and lay practitioners at Lao and Cambodian temples.

The mixing of Asian and native-born American Theravada Buddhist practitioners was first pointed out by Paul Numrich in his study of Wat Dhammaram, a temple started by Thais in Chicago, and Dharma Vijaya Buddhist Vihara, a temple started by Sri Lankans in Los Angeles.[98] Numrich found that groups of white people were involved with each of these temples in addition to the Thai and Sri Lankans. While white people have often attended

Asian temples, particularly Thai temples, as the spouses and family members of Asians, the white people involved in these two temples were involved without a familial connection.[99] At Wat Dhammaram, for example, Thai people came to participate in ceremonies on weekends, while white people came to meditation classes and retreats often on weekday evenings. The two groups rarely interacted, though they met in the same spaces under the guidance of the same monks at different times during the week. A similar pattern was evident at Dharma Vijaya. Interestingly, the majority of non-Asians who attended these two parallel congregations were men, in comparison to IMS, where the majority of practitioners have been women.[100] Many more Thais and Sri Lankans were involved in these two temples than white Americans, and there was little evidence that the white Americans had much say in the leadership of the temple.[101] While researchers do not know when these parallel congregations began or how numerous they are across the country, Numrich's research showed that in the 1990s the demographics of Theravada Buddhism in America were not simply a matter of groups of Asians and white Americans practicing at geographic, cultural, and social distances from one another.

Apart from these parallel congregations, several Theravada Buddhist centers led and attended by Asian and white people began in the 1990s. The late Ajahn Suwat Suvaco, a Thai monastic, started Metta Forest Monastery (also called Wat Metta), a temple in a sixty-acre avocado grove outside San Diego, California, in 1990. At the time, he had been a monk for more than fifty years, forty of which he had spent training in the forests of Thailand under some of the most respected Thai teachers. He had been in the United States for ten years before he started the center, largely through a donation from an American Buddhist practitioner. Thanissaro Bhikkhu, a white American monk born as Geoffrey DeGraff, graduated from Oberlin College before going to Thailand in the 1970s, where he was ordained and practiced meditation for fourteen years, primarily under the guidance of Ajahn Fuang Jotiko, a teacher in the Thai forest tradition.[102] Several years after his teacher's death, Thanissaro Bhikkhu returned to the United States. In 1991 he began to help with the leadership of Metta Forest Monastery, and in 1993 he became the abbot or head monk of the temple.[103] Financial and practical support from Thais, Laotians, and Americans has been central to the development of the temple. Preserving the monastic form, or monkhood, as at Wat Metta, is central to preserving the dhamma, Thanissaro Bhikkhu argues. He has described dhamma in the United States as something like the game of telephone: "Things get passed from one generation to the next until they are garbled beyond recognition."[104] In part to combat this tendency, he has translated many of the talks and teachings given by monks in the Thai forest tradition into English and distributed them for free across the country.

Ajahn Amaro, a British monastic, helped to start Abhayagiri Monastery in California, a monastery founded and led by white monastics and increasingly attended by both Americans and Asians. Ajahn Amaro was born as Jeremy Horner and after graduating from university went to Thailand, where he began to study at Wat Pah Nanachat, a forest monastery for Western students started by Thai forest teacher Ajahn Chah. Ajahn Amaro was ordained as a monk in 1979 and later returned to England, where he lived at temples in the Ajahn Chah lineage there.[105] Between 1990 and 1995, Ajahn Amaro visited the United States several times to teach at various Buddhist organizations. A group of lay supporters in California organized themselves into the Sanghapala Foundation, and in 1995 Ajahn Amaro and three other monks spent the three-month rain retreats in tents at Bell Springs Hermitage north of San Francisco. Ajahn Sumedho, the most senior monk in the Ajahn Chah lineage in the West, had become friends with the Chinese Mahayana monk Ven. Hsuan Hua, the abbot of the City of Ten Thousand Buddhas in California. Just before Ven. Hsuan Hua passed away, he gifted the sangha of Ajahn Sumedho with 120 acres of wooded land near the City of Ten Thousand Buddhas. The new monastery was named Abhayagiri, meaning "fearless mountain" after the ancient monastery in Anuradhapura, Sri Lanka, where Theravada and Mahayana monks once lived together. The monastery opened in June 1996 with Ajahn Amaro and Ajahn Pasanno, a Canadian, as the co-abbots. Funds to support the monastery came from Americans as well as from people in Thailand. Maha Prasert, the Thai abbot of Wat Buddhanusorn in Freemont, California, has been a friend to the monastery. For the first few years, the temple was attended mainly by white people, and then later by Thai, Lao, and Cambodians. Word of the temple spread in an organic way, Ajahn Amaro says, and now there is "a lot of ease between the two groups [Asian and American]. It's not like friction. They seem to delight in each other's company." The first full bhikkhu ordination at Abhayagiri took place on Vesak in 1998 with the ordination of Karunadhammo, a white man born in North Carolina.[106]

Ajahn Amaro describes the Theravadin tradition as "very workable" and he works both with Asians and Americans in the United States. The monastic form is important, he thinks: "People have to understand that renunciation and celibacy are not some kind of weird quirks left over from a spiritual authoritarian. . . . Why was the Buddha a monk? Why did he live in the forest? And the answer, I feel, is that the simplicity of living is the most delightful way to be."[107] By virtue of their unique experiences in Thailand and the United

States, Ajahn Amaro and the first generation of other white monks are in many ways ideally suited for talking with the Thai second generation and helping first-generation parents understand their children's experiences. A Thai college student born in the United States, for example, approached Ajahn Amaro to talk about whether or not to live with her boyfriend, an issue she said she could never bring up with her first-generation parents. Ajahn Amaro and other monks from Abhayagiri monastery have worked more formally in summer camps for Thai students at MIT and with Thai associations at the University of Washington and other universities. "There is an ease of communication between white monks and Thai kids," Ajahn Amaro observes. [108]

At temples led by white monastics, Asian and white monastics together, and Asian monastics alone across the country, boys and men of all ages were ordained for varying periods of time throughout the 1990s. In Thailand and some other Asian countries, young men are temporarily ordained for a few weeks or months as a rite of passage on their way to adulthood. This is a way young men thank their families, particularly their mothers, for raising them and show that they are prepared for marriage. [109] Temporary ordinations took place at the Washington Buddhist Vihara and Thai temples in the United States from the time the temples started, and this continued through the 1990s. [110] In addition to Karunadhammo, there have been eight men ordained as *samaneras* (initial order) and five as *bhikkhus* (higher ordination) at Abhayagiri Monastery. [111] Thanissaro Bhikkhu ordained two Americans in the 1990s, and Bhante Gunaratana continued to ordain people in the 1990s. [112] Also, in June 2002, Maha Prasert, the Thai-born founder and abbot of Wat Buddhanusorn, in Freemont, California, ordained a Thai immigrant and an American-born white man, Michael Lightfoot, who had grown up in a neighborhood not far from the temple. [113]

Apart from the growth of organizations led and attended by Asian and American Buddhist practitioners, Asian temples and largely white meditation centers also continued to grow into the decade. The number of Thai temples in the United States, for example, increased from just over forty in 1989 to more than seventy-five by the end of 1999. The number of meditation groups across the country grew during the 1990s, as evident in the number of sitting groups listed in *Inquiring Mind*, the number of people attending retreats at IMS, and Don Morreale's "unscientific study" of Buddhist America. [114] At IMS, an executive director was appointed in 1990, and the center became more professionally organized and operated. The Barre Center for Buddhist Studies, founded to try to "find a meaningful bridge between study and practice, between the communities of scholars and meditators, between the ancient orthodox tradition and the modern spirit of critical inquiry," opened one mile down the road from IMS in 1989 and held its first conference in March 1990. While IMS is based around practice, Sharon Salzberg described the Barre Center for Buddhist Studies as helping people understand their connections to Asia. "When we started IMS," she explains, "it was basically something we did [i.e., meditation practice]. We had no sense of history. We had very little sense of a connection to a tradition in Asia although we had all learned and benefited a tremendous amount from our time in Asia. And there was very much a sense of, well, we're here today and may not be here tomorrow. . . . And things went on like that for many years. The times have changed a lot since then and our relationship to the teachings and the traditions have changed a lot. I think now as we start this place we have a greater sense of history and of planting seeds with this center that will be long enduring and have a very great impact on the transmission of those teachings to this country."[115] With the initial encouragement of the Barre Center for Buddhist Studies, John Bullitt started *Access to Insight* in the early 1990s, a Web site that houses more than seven hundred suttas and several hundred articles and books about Theravada Buddhism.[116] This Web site complemented the Dharma Seed Archive, a collection of taped Theravada teachings given in the United States, started in the early 1980s.[117]

Insight Meditation West, which changed its name to Spirit Rock Meditation Center in 1993, also became firmly established in California during the 1990s. They put the first trailers on the land in 1991, constructed their first building, and hired an executive director. Fundraising and building continued through the decade, and the first residential retreat took place on the land in 1998.[118] The Kalyana Mitta program (which means "spiritual friends") was started in the 1990s as a series of small study groups run by a pair of facilitators, and the Community Dharma Leaders program was started in 1997 by James Baraz, a teacher affiliated with Spirit Rock. "It became clear that there were a lot of Dharma students out there looking for guidance and there weren't enough teachers to go around," Baraz explained. "There were also a lot of very experienced practitioners who had touched some real wisdom and who were dedicated to serving the Dharma. It seemed like a good fit to train some of those people to help serve their communities."[119] Spirit Rock held retreats and programs for gay men and lesbians, people of color, families, and youth throughout the 1990s. At the end of the decade, Ajahn Sumedho, the highest-ranking monk in the lineage of Ajahn Chah in the West, brought some of Ajahn Chah's ashes to Spirit Rock as a blessing for the center.

FIGURE 8. Spirit Rock Meditation Center, Woodacre, California. Founded 1993. Photo courtesy of Spirit Rock Meditation Center.

## An Aerial View

The history of Theravada Buddhist America, like the current map or schema, is complex with many branches, crossed lines, and points of overlap and divergence. The history provides an overview of events that led to the current map but says little about how to interpret it. The overall schema and the connections between the various groups and branches within it look different at present depending largely on what question is prioritized when the schema is examined. While it is the clear that Theravada Buddhism is more than groups of Asians and Americans practicing in organizations that are completely distinct from one another, it is not clear what model or approach best describes the current landscape. I suggest three ways to understand the history and current configuration of Theravada Buddhist America.

First, if I focus on the question of where the founders of the centers were born, an overall schema with three main branches emerges. The first branch includes approximately ninety-six temples started by Laotians across the United States, eighty-nine temples started by Cambodians, eighty-seven temples started by Thais, twenty-four by Burmese people, and twenty-one started by Sri Lankans. The people who started these temples were first-generation immigrants to the United States, and most of the monastics who lead them were born and trained in Asia.[120] These five sets of temples are linked to temples in their home countries in a range of ways. The second branch includes IMS, Spirit Rock, the centers in the tradition of S. N. Goenka, and hundreds of medium-sized and smaller meditation and retreat centers started by the first generation of convert white American practitioners in the United States. Smaller groups, like sitting groups in California, are loosely linked to Spirit Rock, IMS, or a Goenka center as mother ships, but there is little formal relation. These groups are led by largely white lay meditation teachers who studied in Asia and teach in the United States. The third branch includes organizations started by Asians and Americans together, like the Washington Buddhist Vihara, the Bhavana Society, Metta Forest Monastery, and Abhayagiri Monastery in California. Each of these groups is led by Asian or white monastics trained in Asia. Described this way, these three main branches seem quite distinct, though there is some overlap between them, in which the third branch provides a kind of middle ground.

Second, Theravada Buddhist America can be described according to where the people who attend the centers were born. Four broad branches emerge in answer to this question. First are centers that are attended only by people who were *born in the same country in Asia.* A few Asian temples are attended exclusively by people born in Cambodia, Laos, or Sri Lanka (and perhaps their children who were born in the United States). Second are centers that are attended only by people who were *born in Asia* and their children born in Asia or the United States. Most Thai temples, for example, include at least a few people born in Laos or Cambodia, and many Sri Lankan temples also include other Asians. In interviews with the monks of sixty Thai temples in the United States, only a very few reported that only Thai people come to their temples.[121] Third are centers attended both by people *born in Asia and by people born to non-Asian parents in the United States.* The Washington Buddhist Vihara, Bhavana Society, Metta Forest Monastery, and Abhayagiri Monastery fall into this group, as do parallel congregations of Asians and white native-born Americans across the country like those described by Numrich. Interviews with the monks at sixty temples founded by Thai people in the United States reveal that more than one-third of the temples have some kind of parallel congregation in their midst.[122] At Wat Promkunaram in Arizona, for example, three-day meditation retreats are attended by white and Asian-born practitioners; at Wat Buddhajakramongkolratanaram in California the monk leads white practitioners in meditation on Fridays. A monk from Wat Thai D.C. currently travels to Penn-

sylvania to teach meditation classes in a yoga studio.[123] Evidence also suggests
that close to one-third of Sri Lankan temples in the United States have parallel
congregations, as do some Burmese temples. Some white meditation centers
also fall into this category. While the majority of practitioners at IMS and those
attending events at the Barre Center for Buddhist Studies are white, a few
Asians do attend. A few Asians are also involved in sitting groups around the
country. The fourth branch of centers that emerge from the question of where
practitioners were born are centers attended only by *people born in the United
States*. These centers include primarily white Americans.

Third, Theravada Buddhist America can be described according to the lineage of its organizations, or how they trace their teachings. While the leaders of
all of these groups trace their teachings to the Buddha and to the tradition of
Theravada Buddhism, the organizations name many teachers in their lineages.
While the lineages of Thai, Sri Lankan, Lao, Cambodian, and Burmese temples differ from each other, there are also differences within each group, like
the Mahanikaya and Dhammayut orders in the Thai branch, or the Mahasi
Sayadaw and other two components of the Burmese branch. Largely white
groups like IMS and Spirit Rock trace their lineages to Mahasi Sayadaw, the
Thai forest tradition, and other places to varying degrees. Tracing the lineage
of organizations rather than the homelands of their founders or their attendees
shows contours on the Theravada Buddhist map that were not otherwise obvious. Groups that trace their history to Ajahn Chah or the Thai forest tradition
in the United States, for example, include Ajahn Amaro and the Abhayagiri
sangha, Thanissaro Bhikkhu and Metta Forest Monastery, Jack Kornfield and
Spirit Rock, Jack Kornfield and IMS, the largely Thai-attended temple Wat
Dhammabucha in San Antonio, and others.

Finally, the schema of Theravada Buddhist America might be rejected altogether because the category of Theravada is too porous and fluid. Thai and
Sri Lankan temples, a critic might argue, are no more similar to each other
than are Thai and Chinese temples. Seeing them on the same schema or map
is not analytically or descriptively useful. Similarly, IMS and Spirit Rock might
be seen as influenced by many different Buddhist lineages in a way that makes
singling out the Theravada Buddhist influence artificial and not reflective of
each center's complete history. While these arguments may find empirical support in the future, I reject them at the current time and hang on to the value
of a schema of Theravada Buddhist America for three main reasons. First, the
organizations described in this chapter share a history and one of several lineages of Buddhism as traditionally practiced in one of five largely Theravada
countries in Southeast Asia. Second, the first generation of immigrant and

convert Buddhist practitioners explicitly drew on their Theravada history, in varying degrees, but in ways that demonstrated that it was meaningful to them at the time. Third, Buddhist history in America can be outlined through many analytical lenses, and the Theravada lens provides a nuanced view of the historical and current Buddhist landscape that current lenses, particularly those that describe Buddhism dichotomously as either immigrant or convert, Asian or American, ethnic or new, necessarily overlook.

Regardless of which of these four questions is prioritized in schematizing and understanding Theravada Buddhist America, it is important to recognize that Theravada Buddhist organizations are only loosely bound to each other in the United States. While the Asian temples are overseen by organizations like the Council of Thai Bhikkhus, the Dhammayut Order, the Sri Lanka Sangha Council, and the Laotian Bhikkhus Council, the extent to which these groups influence activities in individual temples is an open question.[124] The teachers at IMS and Spirit Rock began holding meetings in the 1980s together with teachers at Gaia House, a Buddhist organization in England, but these meetings have been more for discussion than to produce any binding policies, rules, or guidelines that will influence how they teach or run their centers. In particular geographic locations, like the Midwest, some groups are linked informally through Buddhist councils, though it appears that this leads to minimal communication between groups.

Since the Washington Buddhist Vihara was formed in 1966, much has changed in Theravada Buddhist America. The number of temples in the United States has grown from one to more than two hundred. IMS has grown from an organization with a small volunteer staff and little formal organization to a significantly larger and more structured organization with an operating budget of just over one million dollars in 2001.[125] Buddhism and meditation have both become slightly less foreign and more socially accepted in certain sectors of U.S. society. In 1974, Joseph Goldstein remembers people driving past IMS: "As people would drive by, just local people, and see people walking mindfully, they thought it was a drug rehabilitation center. 'What are those weird people doing?' Now . . . it's just in the culture. . . . I think a lot of that has come through the stress reduction programs. I think the Dalai Lama has had a great influence."[126] In 2001 and 2002, Spirit Rock Meditation Center offered programs for adults, children, teens, people of color, and gay men and lesbians.

Building on this historical overview, the remainder of this book focuses on how Theravada Buddhism is understood, practiced, and lived in two very different organizations in the United States. While understanding the history of

Theravada Buddhism in America only as a history of immigrant and convert practitioners developing separately from one another is overly simplistic and omits a great deal, I focus on one immigrant and one convert Buddhist organization precisely because of the rich empirical and theoretical insights such a comparison allows. Coupled with this history, my studies of Wat Mongkoltepmunee, the Cambridge Insight Meditation Center, and the teachers, monks and practitioners at each provides a thorough picture of how Theravada Buddhism arrived in the United States along global routes and continues to be adapted here.

*Chapter 3*

# NEW ORGANIZATIONS: WAT MONGKOLTEPMUNEE AND THE CAMBRIDGE INSIGHT MEDITATION CENTER

When the Buddha's teachings arrived in the United States, they encountered new institutional and cultural environments in which they could take root. This first generation of immigrant and convert Theravada Buddhist practitioners knew something about Buddhist temples in Thailand and other parts of Southeast Asia and varying amounts about religious organizations in the United States. Taan Čhaokuhn Rattanamēthē, the founding monk of Wat Mongkoltepmunee (Wat Phila), came to the United States at the request of Thai lay people in the Philadelphia area to start a Buddhist temple. Larry Rosenberg, the founding teacher of the Cambridge Insight Meditation Center (CIMC), taught for many years in Cambridge before finally deciding to start an organization. Neither Taan Čhaokuhn Rattanamēthē nor Larry Rosenberg had explicit models of the kinds of organizations they would create in the United States through which they would convey the Buddha's teachings.

Although many Theravada Buddhist temples and organizations existed in the United States in 1984 and 1985 when Wat Phila and CIMC were started, neither the leaders nor early practitioners paid a great deal of attention to these organizations as they constructed their own. Unlike many new Christian, particularly Catholic, religious organizations, which are often created and adapt in the United States through their interactions with existing organizational hierarchies and structures, neither Wat Phila nor CIMC were formally a part of such institutional structures.[1] Although neither organization was consciously modeled after another specific organization, both adapted, consciously and unconsciously, to existing models of religious organization in Southeast Asia, particularly Thailand, and the United States.

## Wat Mongkoltepmunee: Preservation and Innovation

Wat Phila occupies thirteen and a half acres in a mostly white middle-class suburb of Philadelphia, Pennsylvania. It is thirty minutes from the center of Philadelphia by car and five minutes from I-95, the primary north-south interstate highway that runs between Maine and Florida. It is across the street from local government buildings, next to a picnic facility that is rented out for large parties, and just on the border of a residential neighborhood. From the main road, it is difficult to see the temple buildings themselves because they are behind a fence and down a driveway about two hundred feet from the road. Once visitors go through the front gates, though, many say they feel like they are in Thailand. Rose bushes and flowering plants line the driveway and Thai, American, and Buddhist flags fly in front of the temple on festival days. The main building, a Thai-style temple with a red roof and brick sides, is the largest structure and was completed in 1994 after ten years of planning. A four-bedroom structure called a *kuti*, or monastic residence, is across from the temple and was also completed in 1994. Behind this residence is a smaller three-bedroom house that was on the land when the property was purchased and served as both the temple and the living quarters for the monks between 1986 and 1994. It is now used for occasional meditation retreats and to house visitors to the temple. A long clearing under a canopy of trees running behind the temple is where festivals take place in the spring and summer. The entire temple complex is filled with trees, rose bushes, and gardens planted and cared for by the five resident monks and lay practitioners.

Following Thai custom, visitors leave their shoes on a rack by the door before going inside the main temple building. Pungent smells of cooked rice and Thai food often drift outside from the large, well-equipped kitchen just inside the door. As in many homes, the kitchen is almost always a hub of activity where women warm and prepare food they serve to the monks for breakfast and lunch every day. The *ubōsot* hall where religious activities take place and the *sālā* where social activities occur occupy most of the first floor of the main temple building. While the *ubōsot* and *sālā* are often separate buildings at temples in central Thailand, they are integrated into one building at Wat Phila and are separated by a red carpet and large marking stone.

The *ubōsot* where religious gatherings and ceremonies take place features a floor-to-ceiling altar that holds a ten-foot-tall gold Buddha image, several smaller Buddha images, statues of Luāngphō Sot (an important monk around whose teachings this temple was partially founded), candles, flowers, and incense. Many of the images on the altar were brought from Thailand and do-

FIGURE 9. Wat Mongkoltempunee, Bensalem, Pennsylvania

nated to the temple by families who regularly attend. Paintings of scenes from the Buddha's life cover the walls around the main altar and Kuan-yin, a *bod-hisatta* of compassion, sits near the floor on the left side of the altar.[2] Paintings and carvings of Luāngphō Sot hang on the walls on both sides of the altar. A second, smaller altar, sits to the right of the main altar and holds smaller Buddha statues and small American and Thai flags. A piece of string called a *sāi sin* connects the largest gold Buddha, an image of Luāngphō Sot, and a smaller gold Buddha to a ball of string that is unwound and held by the monks during special chanting ceremonies. A raised platform runs along the right-hand side of the room where the five resident monks sit on cushions dur-ing ritual occasions. The *ubōsot* was marked as sacred space when the building was constructed by placing *sima*, or round marking stones, underneath the ground around the perimeter of the building and at the center. Behind the *ubōsot* is the *sālā*, a linoleum-tiled area where people eat and socialize after the ceremonies on Sunday mornings. Beneath the first floor of the building, on the basement level, is a classroom and a second large hall where people gather during festivals that are not held outside.

While Wat Phila currently occupies thirteen acres and several buildings, the buildings themselves are less than twenty years old. The idea for Wat Phila was

FIGURE 10. Wat Mongkoltempunee, Main Hall. Photo courtesy of Sompoppol Jampathom.

first discussed in the mid-1980s by a group of Thai people in the Philadelphia area who had been going to Thai Buddhist temples in New York and Washington, D.C., for festivals and holidays.[3] At that time, there were no Theravada Buddhist temples in the Philadelphia area. These Thai lay people had a series of conversations, and twenty of them decided to contribute one thousand dollars each to a fund to support a new temple. Ven. Somdej Phra Maha Racha Mangkalajarn, the abbot of a temple called Wat Pāknām in Thailand, had visited the Philadelphia area before these conversations started, and when the lay people decided they wanted to start a temple, a doctor on the developing lay committee in Philadelphia contacted him. He agreed to send two monks to the United States to begin a new temple and contributed money to support the monks when they first arrived. The lay committee incorporated as a nonprofit organization in June 1984 with a mission statement that said they would "promote the teaching, practice, and understanding of Buddhism . . . Thai culture, ceremonies and language . . . and meditation."[4]

The new nonprofit organization was named Mongkoltepmunee Buddhist Temple or Wat Mongkoltepmunee, after a monk in Thailand known as Luāng-phō Wat Pāknām. Wat Pāknām is an ancient temple located in the Thonburī province in Thailand that is one of about 150 temples in Thailand designated as royal monasteries. Wat Pāknām was made famous by an abbot or head monk, the late Phra Mongkhon Thepmuni, often referred to as Luāngphō Sot or Luāngphō Wat Pāknām.[5] The story is told that in 1916 Luāngphō Sot rediscovered the kind of meditation the Buddha had been doing when he attained enlightenment. Unlike the forms of Theravada Buddhist meditation called vipassana or insight meditation, which lead meditators to observe the thoughts and sensations moving through their bodies, this method, called dhammakaya, leads the meditator to enlightenment through a combination of concentration (*samadhi*) and insight (*samadhi-vipassana*) meditation techniques.[6] Luāngphō Sot taught this form of meditation, and many people were attracted to Wat Pāknām after he became the abbot there and began to teach.[7] He died in 1959 and his followers have continued to teach and practice dhammakaya meditation, one of the forms of meditation that has been a part of several Buddhism movements in modern Thailand.[8] Wat Phila was started as a branch of Wat Pāknām, and their abbots have been in regular communication since the founding.[9] Wat Phila is the only Thai temple in the United States that is related to Wat Pāknām in this way.

After Ven. Somdej offered to send two monks to begin a temple, the lay people in Philadelphia began to look for an apartment where the monks could stay while suitable land for a temple was located and purchased. None of the apartment buildings they visited would rent to people interested in having Buddhist ceremonies, and two days before the monks were to arrive the lay committee did not have a place for them to stay. Vajiradhammapadip Temple, a Thai Buddhist temple in Long Island, New York, agreed to host the two monks, and when Taan Rattanamēthē and Taan Sommanathamasmāthān arrived at John F. Kennedy airport in June 1984, a layman picked them up and took them directly to that temple.[10] For the next eighteen months, Taan Rattanamēthē, generally called Taan Ajahn, which translates as "venerable teacher," lived at Vajiradhammapadip Temple and searched with the lay committee in Philadelphia for a suitable location for the temple in the area. (Taan Sommanathamasmāthān returned to Thailand after six months.) Early on, they found a piece of land in Chester County, but at the county hearing required to change the zoning of the land from residential to commercial, a group of angry residents protested, and the Thais withdrew their application.[11] "The neighbors didn't want the temple. Everyone was against it," one of the founding lay members remembers.

In October 1985, Taan Ajahn and the lay committee found a second piece of land with a single-story three-bedroom house on it in Bensalem, another suburb of Philadelphia, and the committee again approached the local zoning board. There were no protests this time and in March 1986 the zoning was changed to accommodate a religious center and the lay committee purchased the land and small house for $135,000. The deposit was collected from do- nations from people in the United States and Thailand and a loan was also made to several lay people from a bank in the United States. The abbot of Wat Pāknām in Thailand also made a donation to help with the purchase. Two laywomen spent a weekend scrubbing the small house, and the lay committee and other Thai people in the area donated Buddha images and other religious materials they had brought with them from Thailand for the altars. Shortly af- ter the house and land were purchased, Taan Ajahn moved to Bensalem from New York and two other Thai monks, one who had been living in Los Angeles and another who had been living in Thailand, came to live at the new temple. In October 1986, the temple celebrated its grand opening, and people began to meet regularly on Sunday mornings. The purpose of the temple, as stated in the founding documents, was to teach about Buddhism via Sunday gather- ings, tapes, and books; to organize religious and nonreligious ceremonies (Thai holidays); and to serve as a center of information and information exchange between Thai, Lao, Cambodian, and American people. [12]

From 1986 through 1994, services nearly identical to the ones held now oc- curred regularly at Wat Phila in the small house. Money was collected from lay people in the United States and Thailand to build a larger Thai-style temple. A Thai architect living in the United States was hired to design the building, but the lay committee helping to coordinate the construction ran into many problems obtaining permits and legal documents from the township. "They [the city] didn't understand Buddhism," one person told me. Permits were eventually granted, construction started in 1993, and the Thai temple and a *kuti* were completed in June 1994. The main building cost $1.9 million and the monks' residence $200,000. The temple also purchased an adjacent piece of land in 1994 so they would have a wooded piece of property where they could hold outdoor festivals. [13] The buildings were dedicated in 1996 and the mayor of the city attended. Since January 2001, temple members have been collecting donations for a new building to be constructed on the property.

The group of lay people with the initiative and the financial resources were necessary prerequisites to the founding of Wat Phila; their ability to locate Thai monks to assist them and then to negotiate with local and state agencies around zoning, building permits, and tax issues allowed the group to obtain nonprofit status, purchase land, and build a physical structure. Throughout this devel- opment, Taan Ajahn's leadership in the States and the lay people's continued support for him was critical and was directly related to his knowledge about Theravada Buddhism as practiced in Thailand and his ability to convey the

Buddha's teachings to the lay people in ways that they were familiar with. As they created Wat Phila, Taan Ajahn and the lay practitioners moved back and forth between models of religious organization in Thailand and the United States to design and construct the physical buildings as well as to craft the leadership structure, organizational structures, and ways lay people would be involve.

## LEADERSHIP

Like most temples in Thailand and many Thai Buddhist temples in the United States, Wat Phila was, and continues to be, organized hierarchically. After a conflict about donations in the early years, the temple bylaws were written so that the monks, rather than the lay people, were formally in charge. The abbot was named the president of the temple and the other monks were arranged below him. As in Thailand, each monk's place in the hierarchy was determined by how many years he had been a monk. Taan Ajahn, the founding monk of Wat Phila, was the president of the temple from its inception until his death in March 2002. He was born in 1938 in Suphanburī province outside of Bangkok, became a novice at Wat Nopphutthā*ng*kūn in Suphanburī at age fourteen, and at the age of twenty went to live at Wat Pāknām. He was in the top of his class in Buddhist studies at Wat Pāknām and between 1976 and 1979 studied political science and sociology at Poona University in India. He started to direct ceremonies at Wat Pāknām in 1960 and achieved the seventh level of *parīan*, a level of academic distinction for monks. Before coming to Philadelphia, Taan Ajahn was on several committees responsible for educating new monks in Thailand and he was trained as a teacher of both samathi and vipassana meditation. He was appointed an assistant to the abbot of Wat Pāknām in 1994 and was awarded the title Čhaokuhn, a title of distinction among monks in Thailand. Taan Ajahn's vision and leadership were central to the founding of Wat Phila, and until just before his death he organized and led all of the gatherings and events at the temple. He taught meditation and gave dhamma talks on Sundays as well as during the week and was always available for conversation with individual practitioners and families.

Taan Ajahn was assisted over the years at Wat Phila by a number of monks born and trained in Thailand. In 2000 and 2001, four monks helped Taan Ajahn to perform ceremonies and lead the temple. Called missionary monks, these monks were selected by Taan Ajahn and came to the United States initially for a period of two years, after many years of training in monasteries in Thailand.[14] Maha Nom Kalasang, the most senior monk apart from Taan

FIGURE II. Monks at Wat Mongkoltempunee when this research was conducted. Standing, left to right: Taan Nom Kalasang, Taan Supichaya Esawanish, Taan Charin Waisurasingha, Taan Laothong Puenpa. Seated: Taan Ĉhaokuhn Rattanamēthē (Taan Ajahn).

Ajahn, came to Wat Phila in July 2000 to teach dhamma and help run the temple while Taan Ajahn was battling the cancer that eventually led to his death. Maha Nom was a novice for ten years and then a monk for ten years at Wat Pāknām, and he studied public administration at Mahāchulālo*ng*kōn Buddhist University in Bangkok before coming to Wat Phila. Maha Charin Waisurasingha was born in Bangkok in 1961. He graduated from high school and lived at Wat Pāknām before coming to the United States in 1995. Maha Supichaya Esawanish was born in 1951 in the south of Thailand and has been a monk for fourteen years. After graduating from high school he worked as a travel agent, among other things, before becoming a monk in his mid-thirties. He planned to become a monk just for a few weeks, but after experiencing what he calls the peacefulness of life as a monk he decided to stay in robes. He is the only monk at Wat Phila fluent and comfortable speaking English and therefore does most of the translation and public relations work for the temple.[15] Maha Laothong Puenpa was born in 1970 on the border between Thailand and Laos and came to the United States with Maha Nom in July 2000.

Despite the temple's hierarchical leadership, lay people are generally more involved in decisions made within that hierarchy than they are in Thailand.[16] The temple does not have formal committees, like at some other Thai temples in the United States, but numerous informal committees and individuals provide the information necessary for Taan Ajahn to make key decisions about the temple. All of the negotiation around contracts and other public matters at Wat Phila, for example, are conducted by lay people because they speak English fluently, whereas most of the monks do not. Having lived and negotiated life in the United States, lay people are also more familiar with American customs and norms. For example, when the temple needed a new fence several years ago, Kop, a lay leader, and his wife Som obtained estimates and spoke with contractors and then gave all of that information to Taan Ajahn so he could make a decision. Taan Ajahn made the decision and then Kop negotiated the transaction, made the arrangements with the contractors, and oversaw much of the construction.

## ORGANIZATIONAL STRUCTURE

The leadership at Wat Phila closely resembles the leadership of temples in Thailand, but the structural or operational form the organization takes is quite different. Like many first-generation immigrants across the United States, practitioners at Wat Phila adopted a congregational form in which people come to the temple on Sunday mornings for meditation, chanting, and rituals that are largely the same from week to week.[17] While some temples in Thailand do have these regular gatherings, they normally take place on *wan phra* days, days based on the phase of the moon, which fall on different days of the week. The monks at Wat Phila distribute a calendar to the lay people every January that has the *wan phra* days, among other days, marked on it, but because of their work schedules, very few people come to the temple on these days and rarely are large gatherings or activities held at Wat Phila on days other than Sundays.[18] Meeting regularly on Sunday mornings is one of the primary ways that monks and practitioners at Wat Phila structurally adapted Buddhism to the U.S. norm.

Most Sunday mornings people begin to gather at Wat Phila around nine. Taan Ajahn leads a class from nine until ten-fifteen that is taught with an audiotape of the late Luāngphō Sot teaching meditation in Thailand. Between five and eight children attend a Thai language class taught by Taan Supichaya, held from nine until ten-thirty.[19] By 10:30 between fifty and sixty people are generally at the temple. While monks in Thailand traditionally make alms rounds every morning to collect their food for the day, on Sundays at Wat Phila they enact the alms rounds by gathering cooked rice and other food items from lay people who line up along the linoleum floor inside the temple. After this *tak bāt* ceremony, the lay people serve food they brought from home to the monks for lunch. As the monks eat, the lay people participate in a chanting and meditation service that is the same every week. It includes thirty minutes of chanting in Pali, the scriptural language of Buddhism, followed by a short period of meditation. One of the monks then gives a dhamma talk or teaching before the morning concludes with a potluck lunch for the lay people. Lunch normally begins around one and people leave the temple between two and four.

In addition to these regular Sunday gatherings, Wat Phila has festivals on Sundays about eight times per year.[20] These festivals mark important dates in the Buddhist year such as the Buddha teaching 1,250 *arahants (Mākhabūchā)*, or the birth, death, and enlightenment of the Buddha (*Wisākhābūchā*) or important dates in the Thai calendar such as Thai New Year (*Songkrān*) and the king's birthday. On festival days, between two hundred and four hundred people normally come to the temple. Festivals start at nine or nine-thirty with chanting and meditation and then the monks make alms rounds, often outside if the weather is warm, by walking past a long row of people and accepting cooked rice, eggs, fruit, soap, and even toothpaste into their begging bowls. The lay people then serve lunch to the monks before themselves eating the large quantities of food they have prepared. One of the monks gives a dhamma talk or teaching in the afternoon and, depending on the holiday, the lay people participate in other rituals that often include chanting and circumambulating (walking around the outside of the temple). Lay people also make financial donations to the temple throughout the day. Festivals are based on the month and phase of the moon and normally take place on the Sunday closest to the actual festival day.[21]

In addition to festivals, people sometimes celebrate birthdays or other special events at the temple on Sundays, usually in the midst of regular morning services. Sometimes one or a group of people dresses in white and comes to the temple on a Sunday to spend the day. They take the Eight Precepts, and spend the day chanting, meditating, and learning about dhamma. On a Sunday close to his twenty-ninth birthday, for example, a practitioner named Sang came to the temple wearing white sweatpants, a white sweatshirt, and white socks. He took the Eight Precepts by chanting them responsively with the monks, and a place was set for him to eat at the back of the main meditation hall.[22] He ate at the same time as the monks (before noon) and planned to spend the rest of the day at the temple and at home meditating and studying dhamma. He did this, he told me, to "remember that life is suffering." People also celebrate anniversaries of births and deaths as well as marriage ceremonies at the temple in the midst of weekly Sunday services. Occasionally lay people do meditation retreats which involve staying overnight in the small house behind the main temple building.

ROLE OF LAY PEOPLE

Taan Ajahn and the lay founders of Wat Phila again moved between models of religious organization in the United States and Thailand in creating ways for lay people to be involved in almost all aspects of temple life.[23] Lay people initiated the formation of the temple, gathered the funds needed to bring the first monks, found a physical location and constructed a new building, provide the monks with their daily food and other support, physically and financially support the upkeep of the temple buildings and grounds, organize all of the activities at the temple, and maintain the financial records, among other things. Lay people at Wat Phila are generally more involved in all aspects of the temple's organization than they are in Thailand for several reasons. First, many of the monks at Wat Phila do not speak much English and have less experience with American customs and norms than do lay people, as mentioned earlier.

Second, and more important, the monks at Wat Phila, like all Theravada Buddhist monks, live according to the *vinaya*, guidelines for conduct outlined by the Buddha.[24] These rules govern every aspect of a monk's life and outline punishments when rules are violated. Most notably, monks do not trade or use money, drive, prepare their own meals or store food, eat solid food after noon or before dawn, or marry or have relations with women.[25] Monks wear robes and carry themselves in ways that render them worthy of respect and reverence. Many lay people hold the monks to high standards around the *vinaya*.[26] Attempting to live by the *vinaya* in the United States leads the monks at Wat Phila to rely on lay people more than they do in Thailand because of numerous practical challenges. Monks in many parts of Thailand, for example, can walk or ride the bus if they need to travel, but there is little public transportation around Wat Phila and the monks do not drive. Some day-to-day tasks, like going to the post office, however, require a car, so the monks rely on the lay people for transportation.[27]

The monks at Wat Phila also rely on the lay people for their food, the preparation and distribution of which requires much more effort in the United States than it does in Thailand. In Thailand, many lay people prepare and offer food to the monks. The monks typically go on alms rounds in the morning, moving from house to house to collect this food, which is all of their food for the day. Since there is no lay Buddhist community close to Wat Phila, the monks at Wat Phila have relied, since the temple was started, on the lay people to bring them breakfast and lunch daily. Rather than walking from house to house, the monks walk from their *kuti* to the main building where the lay people prepare or deliver their food. Every day, the monks rise and do chanting from five-thirty until seven, and are then served breakfast by one person or group. Dr. Malin, for example, a Thai laywoman, brings breakfast for the monks every Tuesday morning on her way to work as an administrator at a nearby university. "I serve the breakfast, they give the blessing, and I pack and go to work," she explained to me. A second individual or group serves a midday meal to the monks at eleven. Sometimes this food is served quickly, in the way that Dr. Malin serves breakfast, and other times it is part of a longer ceremony. Every other Thursday, for example, a group of women who call themselves the New Jersey group meet at the temple to serve lunch to the monks. After they prepare and serve the food, they hold a service of chanting and meditation while the monks eat, and then often one of the monks gives a dhamma talk. People who go to Wat Phila and offer food to the monks are considerably more involved with the center than are lay people in Thailand, who typically go just outside of their houses, rather than to the temple, to offer food to the monks on morning alms rounds.

The lay people who support the monks at Wat Phila fall into two broad groups: a more peripheral group and a group of people at the core. When Wat Phila first opened, it was primarily supported by a core group of twenty lay families and a group of Thai students who regularly attended. Several of the founding families are still involved, but many other individuals and families now participate. Wat Phila, like all Thai temples and most other Asian Theravada groups in the United States, does not have members in a formal sense in the way that churches or synagogues do. People do not join the temple as members and there is no membership list. Rather there is a core group of fifty to one hundred supporters who come to the temple on a weekly or biweekly basis, and a larger periphery group of two hundred to four hundred people who come for festivals several times a year.[28] The majority of people who come to the temple once or twice a week live in Pennsylvania, New Jersey, and Delaware. Three or four families live within a five-minute drive of the temple, and the majority travel about forty-five minutes from their homes to the temple.

The majority of lay people at Wat Phila are first-generation immigrants born in Thailand, though there is a significant minority of other Asians and Asian Americans who attend. The majority of Thai immigrants who attend the temple arrived in the United States in the 1970s and are now between the ages of forty and sixty. Socioeconomically they are divided among doctors, nurses, and academic PhDs, people who own their own restaurants and small businesses, and people who work in blue collar jobs such as waitressing and janitorial positions. All of the teaching at Wat Phila is conducted in Thai and very few members of the second generation regularly attend the temple.[29] The majority of Thai people who attend the temple are Buddhists, although a few identify as Christian. The other Asians include people from Laos, China, and Indonesia. Several non-Asians attend, almost exclusively African American or white men who are the spouses of Thai women. This pattern is not unusual, as evident in census data showing that more than half of foreign-born Thai women living in the United States are married to non-Thai men.[30] Many of these couples met when the American-born men spent time in Thailand while serving in the military during the Vietnam War. Some American-born husbands never come to Wat Phila; others come and wait in the car or at the back of the temple,; and still others sit with their wives and participate in the chanting and meditation services. About two-thirds of the people who are regularly involved with Wat Phila are women.

The lay people who started and are involved with Wat Phila are proud of their temple and the care with which it is organized and led. Many have devoted considerable amounts of time and money to the temple since it was started and have done everything from building construction and food preparation to caring for the abbot when he was sick and teaching new monks about how things are done at this temple. Wat Phila is called both a "Buddhist" organization and a "religious" organization by the monks and lay practitioners alike, and there is little ambivalence overall about its organization and goals. While some Thai temples in America are a bit looser in their organization and maintenance, I overheard one practitioner tell several visitors who came to the temple during my research that this temple has "real monks" and "real Buddhists." It is a "real" Buddhist temple, he was saying.

## CIMC: A Place of "Practice"

CIMC is located in a large three-story house on Broadway halfway between Harvard and Central Squares in Cambridge, Massachusetts. From the sidewalk, the only indication that it is not a house or apartment building is the small black sign with gold letters next to the mailbox that reads, "CIMC." Cambridge Health Associates is next door, and a convenience store, gas station, Korean restaurant, and big steeple church are also on this block of Broadway. The area behind the building is entirely residential. CIMC is sheltered from the sidewalk and street by a tall wooden fence built for seclusion.[31] A garden that includes a Buddha statue surrounds the house on three sides. Visitors open one of two wooden gates to enter the garden and walk up several steps to enter the front door.

Off-white walls and light-colored carpets welcome visitors into the stillness of CIMC. Shoes are placed on a rack underneath the stairs inside the door and coats are quietly hung in the closet. Inside the main door to the right is the room known as the reclining Buddha room, which has a statue of a reclining Buddha against one wall and a few cushions and chairs where people may sit and converse. To the left is the dining room, furnished with folding tables and chairs and several pieces of Buddhist art. The kitchen, with a brand-new range and fridge, is behind the dining room. Bulletin boards hold announcements of upcoming events at CIMC and in the area, dhamma retreats across the country, and community news and requests. A red dhamma wheel is quilted onto a tapestry that hangs in the main hallway. Downstairs, on a floor that is mostly underground, is a large meditation hall, a small room where teachers meet with students, and a small residence for one of the two caretakers. The second floor holds the main office, library, another room where teachers meet with students, and the second small residence. Photographs of Buddha images and the images themselves sit throughout the center, and a shelf in the library holds photos of teachers, including Vimala Thakar, Ajahn Chah, Krishnamurti, Ajahn Buddhadasa, Seung Sahn, Ajahn Maha Boowa, the Dalai Lama, and Dipa Ma. A few images of the Chinese *bodhisatta* of compassion, Kuan-yin, also hang throughout the center.

Most activities at CIMC take place in the large hall that is on the third, and top, floor of the building. The meditation hall comprises the whole floor and is centered on a deep mahogany altar that is about four feet tall and three feet wide. Carved by a Korean monk, the altar has the figures of Manjushri, a *bodhisatta* who cuts through ignorance and illusion, and the more feminine figure of Kuan-yin. Kuan-yin holds a lotus flower, and clouds carved into the altar behind the two figures symbolize impermanence. A small dhamma wheel is also carved into the altar.[32] A two-foot-tall gold Buddha sits in lotus position on a cushion on top of the altar next to two vases of flowers and a Japanese bell. A green cushion for a teacher sits in front of the altar and faces a sea of forty flat cushions with small round cushions on top arranged in semicircles around the altar on the hardwood floor. Chairs line the back wall for people uncomfortable sitting on the floor, and sunlight and air stream through a skylight and windows on three sides of the meditation hall. When the building was renovated in 2000, an architect studied the style of temples in Thailand and consciously tried to incorporate aspects of Thai architecture into this design.[33] While some people, especially since the renovations, refer to CIMC as

FIGURE 12. Cambridge Insight Mediatation Center, Cambridge, Massachusetts. Photo courtesy of Pash Voynow.

the "upper middle way," the building and community have been evolving from more humble beginnings since the center opened in 1985.

Before CIMC was started, its founding teacher Larry Rosenberg lived in Somerville, Massachusetts, in a friend's apartment. He was trained as a social psychologist at the University of Chicago and held positions there, at Harvard Medical School, and at Brandeis University before leaving the academy to study with spiritual teachers in the United States and throughout Asia. When he returned to Cambridge in the mid-1970s, he began to give classes at the spiritual center Interface, a spiritual bookstore called Seven Stars, the Cambridge

FIGURE 13. Cambridge Insight Meditation Center, Main Hall

Center for Adult Education, and in a friend's acupuncture office after hours in Harvard Square.[34] In those days, thirty people or more would gather in one of these places and Larry would give meditation instructions and a dhamma talk. An envelope was passed around after each session and Larry supported himself on whatever *dana,* or donations, practitioners gave. At certain times during the week, he answered questions about meditation practice while eating at a natural foods restaurant, Lata Karta. "He supported himself on next to nothing," one longtime practitioner told me.[35]

In 1983, a student offered Larry funds to purchase a space where he could teach and the group of practitioners gathering around him could meet regularly. Larry kept the money for a few days and then gave it back, feeling that it was not the right time. In 1985 an anonymous donor who had been working with Larry as a student offered money, and Larry felt the time was right to start an organization. As at Wat Phila, there was a small group of people interested in starting a center who had the financial resources and time necessary to do so. Larry remembers there was "a core of people who I didn't have to convince. From their own experiences they had tasted the real benefits that come out of sincere meditation . . . I felt the best way to do this [have a center] is to have a core of people who sit every day or who sit very often, and to have no advertisements. Just the power of people's practice would start to attract people."[36] A student of Larry's who was a realtor began to look for a suitable place and found a dilapidated house at 331 Broadway.[37] The building was purchased and volunteers began to renovate.[38] Some people climbed on the roof to remove a broken chimney; others helped the contractors; and a group of volunteers from the Cambridge Zen Center helped to dig hundreds of pounds of sand out of the basement. People brought lamps, silverware, and other items to furnish the inside of the building. The center was first incorporated as an educational nonprofit, and a few years later changed to a religious nonprofit.[39] It officially opened on July 21, 1985.

Before Larry started CIMC, he consulted monks and Buddhist teachers, who mostly advised him about the ideas he should keep at the core of the center. The Dalai Lama advised Larry to keep the Four Noble Truths central because they are ideas about which all Buddhists agree.[40] When Larry was in Thailand he spoke with Ajahn Buddhadasa, an influential and somewhat radical Thai monk, who told him that to start a center in the West he had to be both very conservative and very radical. "To be radical in not being afraid to change cultural things, things that developed as Buddhism moved from country to country," Larry explained, "but very conservative in not losing what is at the core of the tradition."[41] Larry defined meditation as that core, particularly the form of meditation taught in the Anapanasati Sutta, a teaching of the Buddha, and he continued to teach it at CIMC as he had been doing throughout Cambridge before the center opened. He designed the center to build momentum around that practice by providing a place where people could be protected from physical distractions as they learned to meditate.[42] In naming the center the Cambridge Insight Meditation Center, Larry and the first board consciously emphasized the practice: "I wanted to make it clear that you're coming here to learn how to meditate. . . . It's not a temple, it's a place of practice."[43] It was called "insight" rather than "vipassana" meditation because Larry and others thought "insight" would be more immediately recognizable to people.[44] Before starting CIMC, Larry had been teaching at the Insight Meditation Society in Barre, Massachusetts, and his decision to start CIMC developed in part from his experiences there. While IMS provides an ideal setting for ten-day retreats and longer practice, Larry noticed in his teaching that many practitioners at IMS were not prepared to return to their daily lives and needed support with their practice. Identified by Joseph Goldstein, one of the founders of IMS, as the Sir Galahad of lay people, Larry developed CIMC in explicit relationship to IMS as a place that would support people who have both a sincere interest in practice and a commitment to living in the world.[45]

In the first few classes at CIMC, Larry outlined this vision for the center. While it was clear to Taan Ajahn and the lay people from the beginning that Wat Phila would be a temple built around aspects of Buddhism as practiced in Thailand, the purpose of CIMC had to be developed and clearly presented. Although he had learned about several Eastern religions during his travels in South, Southeast, and East Asia, Larry was clear in beginning this center that its roots were in Buddhism, Theravada Buddhism, and the Thai forest tradition. The cushions in the first meditation hall at CIMC were green, to symbolize the nourishment of the forest in Thailand.[46] While the current teachers have studied in the Zen and Tibetan traditions as well as the Theravada tradition, Narayan Liebenson Grady, one of the teachers, explained to me the importance they place in their teaching on being clearly connected to one lineage: "We find it valuable to ground the teaching within one lineage while being open to other lineages as well. This clarity is necessary because people can be so easily confused."[47] Despite its Theravada Buddhist focus, Larry has always emphasized that everyone was welcome.[48] While Larry emphasized the Anapanasati Sutta in his teachings, Narayan Liebenson Grady, and later Michael Liebenson Grady, when he began to teach, emphasized the Satipatthana Sutta, another teaching of the Buddha, in their teachings.

In constructing CIMC, Larry Rosenberg and his early students molded it in response to existing models of religious organizations in Asia and the United States. First, they rejected monastic leadership and the monastic form evident at Wat Phila to begin a center led and operated by lay people. Organizationally, they also rejected the traditional congregational model of religious practice adopted at Wat Phila. As Larry clearly stated, the center was not a "temple" but a place centered around "practice," practice that took place primarily in a series of small groups. While Wat Phila and CIMC have different approaches to leadership and organization, they have similar approaches to the extent to which lay people should be and are involved with the organization.

## LEADERSHIP

Larry Rosenberg and the early founders of CIMC rejected the monastic form and monastic leadership evident at Wat Phila and throughout the Theravada Buddhist world of Southeast Asia, in favor of an organization led by lay teachers and a board of directors. This form of organization is less hierarchical, though the teachers, like the monks, continue to have a very large influence in decisions made at the center and are fully dependent on the lay practitioners for their financial support.

The leadership and form of organization at CIMC have been evolving since the center started. When Larry first started the center, he was the teacher, and a group of his students formed the first board of directors. Until a lawyer pointed it out to him, Larry did not realize that when he initially drafted the rules and bylaws of the organization he gave all the power to his students. The rules and bylaws were then revised so that the teachers sat on the board and had a say in most decisions, particularly those about classes and teaching plans.[49] In the early years, decisions about CIMC were largely made by Larry in consultation with the board of directors. The board, including Larry, now makes the decisions, functioning much like boards in other nonprofit organizations in its focus on current problems and future concerns, with an eye toward the financial stability of the organization.[50] Many of the original board members served for many years, turning over the reins only in the last few years to a group of new board members who are currently very active in the community.

Since the teachers at CIMC are not monastics, like the monks at Wat Phila, they do not live by the *vinaya*. They are, however, dependent on the lay people for their financial support, which leads to a similar kind of mutual dependency between the teachers and lay practitioners. In the early years of the center, Larry and Narayan lived in an apartment at CIMC and the board guaranteed each of them a small stipend. Later they each moved to apartments owned by the center and they are supported exclusively by *dana*, or donations from practitioners. The yearly amount of support provided to the teachers at CIMC is decided by the board and paid to the teachers as a stipend, and the teachers also receive health insurance through CIMC.

At the present time, Narayan Liebenson Grady, one of the teachers, is the president of the board; Larry Rosenberg the vice president; and Michael Liebenson Grady, another teacher, the secretary. Larry was born in a Russian Jewish immigrant community in Brooklyn in 1932. His father was a taxi driver and Larry studied at the City University of New York, Brooklyn College, and Cornell University before completing a PhD in social psychology at the University of Chicago, where he worked with Anselm Strauss and Everett Hughes.[51] After completing the PhD, he was an assistant professor in the psychiatry department at Harvard Medical School. A witticism among the more experienced professors there was, "The secret of success is to think Yiddish but dress British." So Larry bought a tweed coat and new identity, but learned quickly that putting his hopes in something external was not going to work for him. "I realized at a certain point," he explained, "I really know a lot about how everyone lives, and their minds, but I don't know much about my own mind . . . I'd been looking in the wrong place . . . I had underestimated the importance of finding out who the researcher is . . . it was someone who didn't want to learn about himself."[52] Rosenberg's movement away from the academy began in 1968 when he was teaching at Brandeis University and spent ten days with Krishnamurti, who was visiting from India. Krishnamurti advised him to go on teaching while looking at how he actually lived moment by moment. After doing so, Larry concluded that "the gap between my resume and how my inner life was being experienced was like a grand canyon."[53] Though Krishnamurti teaches a pathless path, Larry felt he needed a practice, and in the years that followed his departure from the academy, he studied in the United States and Asia with Vimala Thakar, Vedanta master swami Chinmayanda, Korean Zen master Seung Sahn, Japanese master Katagiri Roshi, Tibetan lama Tara Tulku, and Thich Nhat Hanh.[54] Bhikkhu Vimalo, a German-born monk who studied for twenty years mostly in southern Thailand, first told Larry about the Anapanasati Sutta, a Buddhist text that outlines a form of breathing meditation, which now forms the basis of his teaching.[55] Larry writes that his conversion to the Anapanasati Sutta came during an intense two-hour meeting with Ajahn Buddhadasa, in his eighties at the time, who went through the sutta step by step. Larry was also strongly influenced by the teachings of Ajahn Chah, Ajahn Maha Boowa, and the Thai forest masters. Larry felt a particular affinity with Ajahn Chah because his teachings were "more simple . . . less technique oriented . . . more spontaneous."[56]

Larry describes his own approach to Buddhist teachings, which is reflected in CIMC as an organization, as having a classic bent: "From the first day I wanted to know the teachings of the Buddha; I didn't want to know diluted or watered down versions of it. . . . I've mainly been interested in meditation. I'm not a scholar; what I like is meditating. . . . I like to read the sermons of the Buddha. I don't read the commentaries so much."[57] He sees the Buddha as teaching self-education and was attracted to Buddhism from the beginning by its path of responsibility. As he explained in a 1996 article, "You have to walk the path. That is what attracted me to Buddhism from day one: it's a path of responsibility. I see myself as a gatekeeper, a doorman. A person says, 'I'm trapped in this room. I'm very unhappy.' I point to the door. The door is in their own mind. I tell people that the exit from their suffering is as close as their breath. It's in the same places as the suffering. . . . In some cases, I know I've done my job well when a person doesn't show up anymore."[58] Larry has been married for the past ten years, and while he says he benefited enormously

FIGURE 14. Teachers at CIMC, left to right, Larry Rosenberg, Narayan Liebenson Grady, Michael Liebenson Grady. Photo courtesy of Pash Voynow.

from short-term monastic practice, he has never been attracted to a long-term monastic life.[59]

Narayan Liebenson Grady, also a teacher at CIMC, met Larry in the 1970s when she literally bumped into him in a health food store. She was trying to leave a Sikh group she was involved with at the time and the conversation she had with Larry about Krishnamurti, whom she had read at the age of sixteen, made a strong impression on her.[60] She was raised in suburban East Haven, Connecticut, and at the age of eleven remembers checking out some books from the library and trying to focus on yogi postures and the flame of a candle. In her own words, as a young adult she was a "very devoted eccentric Catholic and then a Sikh."[61] After her encounter with Larry in her early twenties, Narayan learned about vipassana. "When I discovered this path, I felt I was home. There was a great sigh of relief." She explains, "I felt I had found a path that resonated with my spiritual aspirations. It seemed to me that there was nothing extra added such as extensive rituals or reliance on ideological beliefs; the whole idea is to be aware of the way things are."[62] Narayan was "delighted to see people going away for three months to IMS without having to be monks or nuns," and had the sense of finding something that "truly resonated on all levels." [63] She began to sit at IMS in 1978 and studied at Ajahn Maha Boowa's monastery in 1987 for two months. Narayan considers her main teachers to be Ajahn Maha Boowa, Ven. U Pandita, and a Ch'an master named Master Sheng-yen. [64]

Narayan was centrally involved with the founding of CIMC in 1985 and began to teach there when it opened. At the time she says she was "passionate about practice," and had been supporting herself with service jobs such as taking care of older people. When she learned that she could go to IMS for free with unlimited days to sit if she was a teacher trainee, she signed up, with Larry's encouragement. [65] Narayan gave her first dharma talk, on fear, at CIMC in November 1986. In the late 1980s, she began to teach in creative ways at CIMC around themes that seemed to bring more people into the center. She also began to teach metta or loving-kindness meditation, which she and Larry found "made vipassana practice more accessible and led to more warmth between the yogis [practitioners]. It was a doorway for many people and functioned both as a community builder as well as a way to access the practice of insight meditation." [66]

Michael Liebenson Grady, the newest teacher at CIMC, began to teach there in 1994. He was raised in an Irish Catholic family and started his own spiritual searching in the 1970s via yoga and Krishnamurti. He found Buddhist meditation and began to practice vipassana meditation in 1973. He sat with a Tibetan group in Cambridge and went to the Naropa Institute in 1974, the year it opened, where he took classes with Tibetan, Zen, and vipassana teachers. After the summer at Naropa—the summer that Joseph Goldstein and Jack Kornfield met—he began to travel around the country doing retreats and sat a three-month retreat in Bucksport, Maine, a year before IMS was founded. From there, Michael moved to the Cambridge Zen Center, where he met Larry Rosenberg, another resident, and they began a long friendship. After a few years he studied with several teachers before going back to serve on the staff at the Insight Meditation Society. Michael was on the staff at IMS intermittently from 1978 to 1983. In 1984 he left what he calls the "dharma scene" and after receiving a bachelor's degree at Amherst College began graduate school in sociology at Brandeis University. While in graduate school he returned to more intensive practice at Maha Boowa's monastery, with Narayan. Narayan and Michael were married in 1991. Michael has seen himself as a vipassana student since he began to practice in 1974. [67] "It was the simplicity and approach of the practice. Vipassana is direct, rational, practical." [68] Even when he lived at the Zen Center, Michael was doing vipassana meditation, influenced by the kind of mental noting taught by the Mahasi Sayadaw school. Teaching at CIMC came quite naturally to Michael, and he prepared by sitting in on interviews during the three-month retreat with Joseph Goldstein and Steven Smith at IMS.[69]

Narayan describes herself, Michael, and Larry as very good friends. They have known each other and worked together for a long time, and share a common vision of the center. "We are not particularly interested in becoming well known or in getting much bigger, "Narayan explained. "If that happens, it's fine, but it is not our intent. . . . We value simplicity in our personal lives as well as in how we try to present the dharma teachings. This has helped to keep us clear at times when we have needed to be clear. As teachers we share the same values."[70] All three teach at IMS as well as CIMC and are committed to their own long retreats, often two months or more per year.[71] While some white monks and vipassana meditation teachers have joined the lecture circuit, giving talks in centers around the country, Larry, Narayan, and Michael have generally chosen not to travel extensively and instead to teach locally, allowing for a greater continuity with practitioners at CIMC. The teachers at CIMC have also not been involved with any of the sex scandals that have troubled other meditation centers across the country.[72]

While the board members and three teachers make the decisions about how the center will be run, most of the day-to-day work of the center is completed by three staff members and numerous volunteers. While the monks at Wat Phila, with the help of volunteers, do the administrative work of the temple, the administration of CIMC is done by three staff members with the help of volunteers. Maddy Klyne is the administrative director, Pash Voynow is the assistant administrative director, and Jef Weisel is office staff.[73] Maddy, Pash, and Jef are each long-term practitioners who have been involved with CIMC for many years apart from their positions on the staff.

### ORGANIZATIONAL STRUCTURE

Unlike at Wat Phila, which functions much like a traditional congregation in the United States with meetings on Sundays, the teachers and early practitioners at CIMC rejected both traditional congregational forms in the United States and looser forms of temple organization in Southeast Asia in favor of a structured series of classes and smaller gatherings that take place throughout the week. When CIMC started its first set of classes and weekly dharma talks in the fall of 1985, ninety-minute meditation sittings were held every day in the morning, at noon, and in the evening, and longer meditation sessions were held on some Sunday afternoons. Every Wednesday night a dharma talk followed the evening sitting on topics such as right-mindfulness, parenting as practice, working with grief, meditation and psychotherapy, meditation and the path of peace, and music and meditation. Later in the center's development, Narayan started a drop-in practice group on Thursdays. A Pali language course was occasionally taught at the center, and a Pali chanting group began. The number of social and community activities at CIMC also increased in the 1990s via community potlucks, a holiday party, and gatherings to take the refuges and precepts (words that signify commitment to Buddhist teachings and an ethical life). Wednesday night dharma talks continued over the years, and the range of people actually giving the talks expanded.

In 2001, a class or meditation session was held at CIMC almost every day. Every morning, while practitioners at Wat Phila served breakfast to the monks, practitioners at CIMC gathered for a meditation session. Daily sittings were also held in the evening, and longer sessions were held some Sunday afternoons. In addition to these quiet times to sit, the teachers held classes that met one evening a week for a number of weeks with titles such as Living in the Present, Anapanasati and Choiceless Awareness, The Third Foundation of Mindfulness, and Mindfulness in Relationships. Beginners could enroll in a class called The Way of Awareness: An Introduction to Vipassana Meditation, or attend a drop-in class on Tuesday evening or a day-long workshop on one of several Saturdays. Workshops and retreats, led by one of the three teachers or a visiting teacher, were often held on weekends and covered topics like Working with Fear, Metta, Compassion, and Wise Speech. An Old Yogis group of experienced practitioners also met regularly on Tuesday evenings. CIMC loosely follows an academic calendar, with several sessions of classes, and limited classes and talks in January and August. Community events included regular center housecleaning as well as gardening days, a community potluck, spring and fall cleaning days, a gratitude gathering on Thanksgiving, a storytelling gathering, and a bereavement ceremony. Opportunities to take the refuges and precepts continued. More than eighty people attended a holiday dinner in December, and people meditated into the new year on New Year's Eve. In the aftermath of the September 11 events, about 175 practitioners gathered to hear a talk by Joseph Goldstein. In addition to these activities, practitioners also came to the center regularly for interviews with one of the three teachers. Scheduled in advance, these interviews were an opportunity for practitioners to speak individually about questions and concerns encountered in meditation practice.[74]

### ROLE OF "LAY" PEOPLE

Like Wat Phila, CIMC was started only when there was a committed group of lay people with the time and financial resources to devote to a center, and it thrived over the years because of the continued support of many of these people. Lay people helped to locate the building for the current center and renovate and furnish it. They continue to support the center financially and through their volunteer work in a number of ways.

Financially, lay people provide most of the resources needed to support the center. Practitioners are invited to join the center for a membership fee and are charged for classes. Work exchanges, scholarships, and other forms of financial aid are available, and no one is turned away from the center for financial reasons. Many practitioners also give money to the center yearly, or more regularly, or donate items that the center needs.[75] Practitioners are also involved with the center as volunteers in many ways. Twenty-five people at CIMC volunteer to lead meditation sessions as "practice leaders"; several people clean the center each week; and others cook for retreats, help with mailings, and do other tasks. While the administrative staff does some of this work, it is only the support of many volunteers that makes the activities and programs offered at CIMC possible. Although CIMC is led by lay people rather than monks, the extent to which the lay people support the teachers and are involved in almost all aspects of the center is quite similar to that at Wat Phila.

As at Wat Phila, and many other religious and secular organizations in the United States, practitioners at CIMC include those both on the periphery and in the core of the organization. The core group includes fifty to sixty people who regularly take classes and attend events at the center. The periphery group is much larger and includes people who occasionally come to sittings or talks at the center or who have taken one class and sometimes come by for an event. In 2001, between three and ten people normally attended the daily morning and evening meditation sittings and between sixty and 120 would gather on Wednesday evenings for the weekly dharma talk. Weekly classes had between fifteen and forty-five students. Formally, CIMC had 406 members.[76]

The majority of people involved with CIMC live in the Boston area and come to CIMC by car. About half were born outside Massachusetts and moved to Boston either as students or young adults. Like the practitioners at Wat Phila, many practitioners at CIMC live at some distance from their birth families. The majority of people at the center are baby boomers now in their forties and fifties. The majority of people who attend are white, though there are a few African Americans, and are generally middle class and well educated.[77] All of the teachings at CIMC are given in English.[78] About two thirds of the people involved with the center are women.[79] There are few programs for children, and very few of the people at CIMC have children who are also involved with the center.[80] Close to two-thirds of the people I interviewed in the course of this research were single; many of these have been divorced. A sizable number of gay men and lesbians are involved with the center. Close to one-third of the people I interviewed were born in the Jewish tradition, one-third were born in the Christian tradition, and the remaining third were born secular, atheist, or in other religions. The people I interviewed have been involved with the practice from one to twenty years and have been involved with CIMC for an average of eight years.[81]

Although the teachers clearly see CIMC as a Buddhist organization, and Buddha images sit throughout the center, practitioners themselves fall along a long continuum in response to questions about whether CIMC can be considered a "Buddhist" or a "religious" organization. It often takes practitioners a few visits before they recognize the Buddhist tradition that underlies the center. Although most eventually tend to agree that the center can be considered Buddhist, that designation says nothing specific about the religious or spiritual identities of the people who attend. Practitioners are more divided over whether it is appropriate to consider CIMC a "religious" organization. Many prefer to substitute "spiritual" for "religious" or would rather that the center be seen instead only in terms of the meditation practice it teaches.

## Motivations: Why Do People Get Involved?

Since Wat Phila and CIMC were started, practitioners have come to the centers through a wide range of channels and articulated their reasons for being there in many different ways.[82] In the midst of this research, at a *Kathin* celebration (a festival that marks the end of the monastic rain retreats), individuals at Wat Phila told me they were there to make merit, eat Thai food, see friends, and talk with the head monk about learning meditation. When I asked people in interviews at CIMC why they were involved there, one woman said she came to learn how to meditate, a second was in search of a spiritual community, and a third wanted a place to meditate as well as a way to advertise her services as a yoga teacher and therapist. Conversations with practitioners throughout this research showed that individuals often have several reasons for coming to Wat Phila or CIMC on a given day or becoming involved over several months, and that the motivations among the groups of people who attend these centers are equally varied.[83]

When the practitioners at Wat Phila and CIMC are divided into the core group of people who come to the center weekly or biweekly, often volunteer around the center, or regularly support the center, and people who are more on the periphery, clear differences in the motivations they articulate for having contact with the centers emerge. People more peripherally involved in Wat Phila come to the temple primarily for festivals. Many view the temple largely as a cultural center where they can spend time with Thai people and make merit for themselves and their families by participating in religious ceremonies. People on the periphery of CIMC, on the other hand, typically take one meditation class or retreat and may drop into a morning or evening meditation sitting now and then. Many of these people are only superficially interested in Buddhism and come to the center primarily to learn meditation as a technique for stress reduction or as a technique to deal with other physical or emotional issues. Although people on the periphery of both centers sometimes become more regularly involved, people attracted by Wat Phila's regular festival schedule can and do remain on the periphery for years. In contrast, people on the periphery of CIMC tend either to move into the core group of regular practitioners or fall away from any involvement with the center.

Practitioners who are centrally involved in Wat Phila and CIMC give many reasons for their involvement. Phim, a Thai woman in her fifties, comes to Wat Phila every other Thursday with a group of friends to prepare lunch for the monks as a form of *dana*. Involvement in the temple for her is a way to continue the Buddhist tradition in her family: "Buddhism is mostly passed down through my family. I learned from my mother and then I pass it along." Mong, an immigrant from Malaysia, first came to the temple in 1995 when he was opening a Chinese restaurant: "When I first opened my restaurant, I asked the head monk to come and give some blessings and things. He came and did some chanting. Some people think it brings luck. And it might help more people come to the restaurant." And Sang, a student from Indonesia, started to come regularly to the temple and lived there for a few weeks as a monk because he wanted to learn more about Buddhism than he already had on the Internet and because he wanted to be part of a practicing Buddhist community. He explains, "When I first came, I didn't know anything. The first day I was here I didn't understand anything that the abbot said because I don't speak Thai . . . I was lost. But I could feel that the people were so hospitable. It was a good atmosphere. It felt right. And the people here are so nice to me. They have taken me in as family."

At CIMC, people's reasons for being involved in the core group are equally varied. Kevin, a practitioner in his early forties, first came to CIMC in search of meditation instruction: "It came time when I just got this sense that I needed to be silent. . . . So I got the yellow pages and I saw this place. I came here and it was a form that fit." After reading about Buddhism, Bob, who became a member of the board of directors, was interested in the ideas and attracted by the experiential component of practice and came to CIMC to learn about both. David, a practitioner for more than twelve years, had been going through a difficult time in his personal life when he picked up a few spiritual books at a Cambridge bookstore and tried meditating on his own. He took a weekend workshop with Larry and gradually came to CIMC: "I went over to CIMC just very gradually. I have to admit I was a little leery at first. I was cautious about getting involved in any groups because of things I'd heard about cults and weird eastern religions. I was a little skeptical. When I started going to CIMC it felt like a really genuine, friendly, welcoming place and there was no pressure to sign up or keep coming. It was very laid back, which was just right for me."

Listening to people's stories of how and why they got involved in Wat Phila and CIMC points to three general factors that, in different proportions, motivate everyone who is involved in the core group at Wat Phila or CIMC. First, they want to learn about or practice Buddhism, broadly defined. Second, they are seeking some social or communal interaction with like-minded people. And third, the factor that often catapults people to both centers, is a difficult personal situation like a divorce, the death of a loved one, or a move to a new city. The Buddha might see these reasons for getting involved in Wat Phila and CIMC as part of a common human desire to get rid of suffering.

First, people come to Wat Phila and CIMC because they want to learn about or practice Buddhism, broadly defined. Dr. Malin comes to Wat Phila to get teaching from the monks, Sam, a practitioner in his forties, told me that he comes to learn about meditation, and Plā, a layman, comes to "cleanse his soul." Phæm, a laywoman, comes because she "wants to do good deeds, like when we take food or go to offering." At CIMC, Art, a long-term practitioner, says some people come "because of the teaching" and others come to do meditation. While some people who initially come to CIMC are more interested in meditation as a technique than in Buddhism as a set of ideas, most who remain involved and become a part of the core group are also interested in the teachings that frame the technique.

Second, the majority of people at both centers have some interest in gathering with like-minded people or those with whom they share something in common. In addition to coming to the temple to do "good deeds," Phæm explains, "I lived in the United States for twenty-seven years. I really didn't know any Thai people . . . but when I went to the temple [five years ago] I met some

nice people and I learned a lot." Kanyā, a regular temple attendee, explains that
for Thai people the temple is a social and cultural place: "Thai people, you have
to understand, when we are homesick, even when we go to a different country,
the first thing we look for is a Thai temple. To see a statue of the Buddha it
makes a feeling of home." People at CIMC are also looking for community
with like-minded people, though they are primarily looking for support for
their meditation practice through silent sittings and later conversations and
secondarily for people to spend time with socially. Gary, a relative newcomer
to CIMC, became involved with the center in search of "a little bit of support
for big blocks of meditation" and because he wanted to "meet other people who
are involved with the practice just to try and get some sense of whether this has
really helped them." After learning how to meditate at CIMC and reading many
books about the history and development of Buddhism, Katie, a practitioner
for more than ten years, describes her motivations for involvement with the
language of "relying" on the community: "It's best for me to use it [CIMC] as a
help in my regular sitting practice. To use the community, to go on Wednesday
nights, to go on Thursday mornings, Sunday afternoons, whatever. And try to
build that onto my life as a reinforcer." Carol, another long-term practitioner,
explained, "I decided I needed to be around people who also practiced, at least
once in awhile. My personal friends were not participants and didn't study
Buddhism so if I was going to have a group of people who did, I should at
least hear their experiences." She arranged her work schedule so she could go
to CIMC for long sittings on Thursday mornings that are followed by a group
lunch so she could practice and spend time speaking with other meditators.

The third factor that sends people to Wat Phila or CIMC is a difficulty in life
such as a move, a divorce, a health problem, or the death of a spouse. Plā first
came to Wat Phila ten years ago "with a broken heart" and also because he was
having a series of sinus problems. Mai went to the temple "not very often and
then in 1997, right after my husband died, I woke up one morning and said
I'm going to the temple." Dr. Nūang, an academic, also started coming after
her husband passed away: "The temple became a spiritual place for me in the
grieving process. Without the spiritual support from the monks here it would
be difficult." Sam lived in the United States for five years, but it was not until
he "got involved in something that I'm not supposed to" that he first visited the
temple. Dr. Malin, Tam, and several others came to the temple after moving
to the area from other parts of the United States. Mike began meditating while
going through a drug detox program and came to CIMC a few years later when
struggling with depression. Michelle, a practitioner in her thirties, got involved
with meditation to stop smoking, and after her father died of lung cancer a few

months later, she came to live at CIMC. And Jon began meditating at CIMC in the midst of coming out as a gay man. Several others described first coming to CIMC in the midst of a divorce or job change, or after moving to the area.

Suffering is seen as the underlying reason for people's involvements in both Wat Phila and CIMC by leaders in both groups. Michael, one of the teachers at CIMC, told me, "I would say most people come because they are facing some difficulty in their life." Kop, a lay leader and longtime supporter of Wat Phila, describes Theravada Buddhist temples as analogous to roads or highways to the ultimate freedom, freedom from suffering. His description also applies to meditation centers. People enter and exit the highway to ultimate freedom from suffering, in his metaphor, at many points. "Some of these people might be coming to the temple to become rich and famous, increase their capabilities and power to obtain material things. Some of them come to the temple because they have family, relationship, health, or business problems. It is safe to say that most of them come to the temple because they are experiencing some form of suffering." He observes that people who are doing well financially tend not to come to the temple. It is not until something goes wrong in peoples' lives, "like business went south, their children are taking drugs, or their health is threatened," that people regularly seek help at the temple. Larry Rosenberg made a similar observation in a beginning meditation class. He observed that some people come to CIMC only when things are going very well or very poorly: "Someone will come and say they are getting over the breakup of a relationship. And then they won't come for awhile. When they come back again, I'll say, oh, a new relationship ended? And they'll say, how do you know?" Kop believes the different distances between where people enter the highway and the destination are based on individuals' different levels of merit or wisdom. Larry and other white teachers tend to understand people's entry to the "highway" and their progress along it in terms of their faith in the practice and their individual experiences. "Faith I think inescapably is very important. But if people don't at a certain point start to flower . . . and start experiencing the actual truth firsthand, personal discovery of the value of vipassana practice . . . dharma practice, for the most part isn't strong enough to keep them," Larry told me.[84]

There has been little change in the composition of people involved with Wat Phila and greater change in the backgrounds of people involved with CIMC since the centers opened. This change in people's backgrounds and experiences has taken place in Buddhism as practiced by white people generally as well as at CIMC specifically, Larry Rosenberg has observed. The people who were involved in the early years, Larry told me, were largely misfits, eccentrics, hippies, ex-psychedelics, ex-political radicals. Most had a very romantic idea about the wisdom of the East and many went east. "And then when people came back," Larry explains, "the vocabulary of motives that people might give might have to do with wanting to find out my true nature, wanting to come to God, the truth, enlightenment, and all of that." He continues, "But the truth is I think that what brought us to it all along was just suffering." The first generation's romanticism about Asia is mostly gone now and the people who come to CIMC are a broader cross-section of the population, though still largely skewed to the middle and upper classes. What has changed dramatically, Larry believes, and my observations support, is that people who are getting involved with Buddhism and meditation at CIMC now lead more "normal" lives. "They have jobs, children, or want one or both of those things," Larry explains. "And they come because they are stressed out, that's the vocabulary now. But what is stress really? It's another word for dukkha or suffering to me."[85] People's motivations for getting involved with CIMC are similar now to what they were in the beginning: dukkha or suffering. What has changed is how they are articulated, and perhaps some of their causes.

Whether they articulate them using the language of dukkha, stress, or something else, people describe their reasons for being involved with Wat Phila and CIMC in many ways. People who are on the periphery of Wat Phila and CIMC are there for very different reasons while people at the core of each center share a number of similar motivations. Researchers often describe the religious centers of first-generation immigrants as ethnic centers where people gather to maintain their language and cultural traditions related to food and national holidays, and indeed that is true of Wat Phila, although the core group also wishes to learn about and practice the Buddha's teaching. Similarly, insight meditation centers have tended to be portrayed, in the media and elsewhere, as little more than educational centers where people in the core group go to learn about Buddhism and meditation but not to find like-minded people or build relationships. While people come to CIMC to learn about Buddhism and to meditate, many are also interested in building relationships with other practitioners through involvement in a community.

## Conclusions

Wat Phila and CIMC are two of many Theravada Buddhist organizations through which the Buddha's teachings have been institutionalized and are being taught in the West. The monks, teachers, and practitioners who began each organization built their organizations from the ground up working within the institutional and structural spaces available in the United States for new secular and religious nonprofit organizations. While Theravada Buddhist teachings were central to the founding of both Wat Phila and CIMC, neither group was started within another religious organization or formal institutional structure, with the result that the teachers and practitioners at both centers had considerably flexibility in crafting these new organizations.

Lay people with links to Theravada Buddhist teachers, financial resources, time, and the ability to negotiate with the state enabled both of these organizations to be started in the early 1980s. The monks, teachers, and early lay practitioners successfully incorporated as nonprofit organizations, purchased buildings, dealt with issues around zoning and building codes, and filed financial forms with federal, state, and local officials. While both groups acted like other nonprofit organizations in incorporating and purchasing property, they acted as religious organizations in their interactions, particularly with state and federal officials, around questions related to tax status and the payment and support of the monks and teachers.

Both Wat Phila and CIMC were successful, by which I mean they continue to exist in the locations where they were started and have continued to attract new practitioners over the years, for a number of reasons common to successful new religious and secular nonprofit organizations. Both groups had clear purposes from the start, for example, and strong leaders. The leaders and lay practitioners of both groups were generally in agreement about the goals of the organizations, and power struggles did not ensue. Both groups also had or created access to lay people, in addition to those who were centrally involved in starting the group, to draw on for practical and financial support as the centers began and continued to grow. The leaders of Wat Phila and CIMC and the organizations themselves had loose ties to monks and teachers at other similar organizations in the States and abroad who have provided occasional advice over the years.

The history and organizational structure of Wat Phila and CIMC and the reasons why people say they are involved point to a number of broader factors to consider when asking how organizations in religious traditions new to the United States are constructed.[86] Society's overall openness to the religious tradition, whether it will be a majority or minority religious tradition, and the laws that currently govern the founding of new secular and religious nonprofit organizations are key factors to consider. The presence or absence of other religious organizations in that tradition in the new location is also an important factor. The form and structural organization of the religious tradition in its home country must be considered in addition to the ways in which the tradition travels and the continuity of its links to the home country. Social, demographic, and economic characteristics of the leaders, teachers, and lay people who are starting the new organizations and their broader reasons for being in the United States and their goals in this country also have an important influence on the kinds of organizations that are started. In addition to these environmental, historical, and organizational issues, the teachings around which new religious organizations are formed are critically important to understanding how they adapt in the United States. The teachings presented by the monks and teachers at Wat Phila and CIMC and lived by the practitioners in their day-to-day lives are the subject of the next chapter.

## Chapter 4

# LIVED BUDDHISM:
# THE CONSTRUCTION OF
# TEACHING AND PRACTICE
# AT WAT PHILA AND CIMC

I arrive at Wat Phila at ten-fifteen on a Sunday morning in September. The meditation class has just finished and thirty people are moving around the kitchen greeting one another, drinking coffee, and preparing food for the monks. I put the hot cooked rice I brought from home in a small bowl and join the twenty or so women and men who are forming a line around the perimeter of the main hall of the temple. When Taan Ajahn and the other four monks enter the hall, everyone in the line is silent and those still in the kitchen hurry to join. We kneel down, hold our bowls of rice above our heads, and repeat in Pali the words Taan Ajahn leads us to say. He and the other monks then hang their begging bowls from their shoulders and walk quietly along the line accepting spoonfuls of rice into their bowls. In a few minutes the monks and lay people have completed *tak bāt,* or alms rounds, inside the temple. Some people return to the kitchen to finish preparing food and I kneel with others on the red carpet at the front of the hall to request the refuges and precepts from Taan Ajahn. I later present lunch to the monks with the lay people, and while the monks eat we recite a series of chants in Pali that begin with praise of the Buddha, the dhamma, or his teachings, and the sangha, or order of monks who carried his teachings to the present.

After the monks finish eating and the lay chanting service ends, everyone who has come to Wat Phila today kneels or sits on the red carpet in front of the altar for a dhamma talk. The five monks sit on an elevated platform that runs along the right-hand side of the room, and Maha Nom, one of the monks, begins the talk. He tells us in Thai about the Buddha's teaching three months before his final passing away, the *parinibbana.* The Buddha said that anyone who wants to live a full life should follow the *Iddhipada,* which has four components. First, *chanda,* you should love what you do. Second, *viriya,* you should do what you love diligently. Third, *citta,* you should do what you love with a fully focused mind. And finally *vimangsa,* you should do whatever you do with wisdom.

Maha Nom then tells a story about when the Buddha was Mahosadha, a king in one of his previous lives who was focused on improving his wisdom. One day, a young woman was bathing her baby at a pond near Mahosadha's palace and put the baby on a blanket on the ground to dry. A female asura, or demonic entity, was passing by and wanted to have the baby for lunch. The asura transformed herself into a beautiful woman, began to play with the baby, and then, when the young woman was not looking, ran off with the baby. The woman caught up to the asura just outside Mahosadha's palace and the two women began to argue. Mahosadha heard the argument and came outside to settle the dispute. He drew a line on the ground and told the women to lay the baby down with half of the baby on each side of the line. He then instructed the asura to hold one of the baby's arms and the young woman to hold one of the baby's legs. He told them both to pull, saying that whoever pulled the baby to her side of the line would be the mother. The women began to pull, and the baby started to cry. The young mother, hearing her baby cry in pain, immediately let go of the child, allowing the asura to quickly pull the baby to her side. With this, the young woman began to cry thinking she had lost her baby forever. Mahosadha then turned to the crowd that had gathered and asked them which woman was the real mother. Everyone in the audience said the woman who let go of the baby was the real mother, and Mahosadha took the baby from the asura and gave him back to the young woman.

After this story, Maha Nom talks about Phra Indra, one of the Hindu Gods, and tells a story about the age of human beings. Maha Nom says that when Phra Indra created the earth he created human beings as well as buffalos, dogs, and monkeys. He created each creature to live for thirty years, but the buffalos, dogs, and monkeys all said they did not want to live for that many years. The human beings heard this and asked that the life years Phra Indra took away from these other creatures be given to humans, and they were. Maha Nom then said we humans should look now at how we live our lives. For the first thirty years, he said, we tend to live pretty freely—growing, getting an education, starting our families, and so on. From age thirty to fifty we work, like the buffalo working in the rice fields, to accumulate wealth, name, and fame. From fifty to seventy we protect our wealth, fame, and fortune—like a dog minding his properties. And from seventy to ninety we are like monkeys because we do not have much to do except make funny faces to get giggles from our grandchildren. Everyone gathered laughs as Maha Nom tells this story and at certain points he has to stop the telling because he is laughing too hard to continue. When Maha Nom finishes the dhamma talk, two laymen pass out small silver containers of water to each family and everyone participates in *trūat nām,* a short ritual in which the monks chant as we lay people pour water between two vessels to symbolize the merit we have made and to share it with our deceased relatives. The service ends, and I talk with a few people as we sit on the floor at the back of the hall together eating a potluck lunch.[1]

❧ ❧ ❧

On a Wednesday evening in April, I join about eighty people at CIMC for meditation and a dharma talk titled "Mindfulness in Relationships" by Narayan Liebenson Grady, one of the teachers. At 6:45, Narayan silently enters the main meditation hall and sits quietly at the front of the hall, facing me and the other practitioners who sit silently with eyes closed. About twenty minutes into the meditation sitting, Narayan slowly and quietly begins to speak: "Whenever you become aware that your attention has drifted away into thoughts about what has been or about what might be, bring the attention back to the here and now . . . relaxing your eyes, relaxing your face, relaxing your belly . . . experiencing this sitting breathing body . . . when you find yourself drawn away by a particular worry, plan, or fantasy, try to be aware that thinking is happening and gently let it go." After forty-five minutes, Narayan concludes the meditation session, saying, "May all beings have ease of mind, may all beings have compassion of heart, and may all beings be free." She strikes a bell three times with a mallet and as the sound of the bell fades away, people begin to move around and to stretch. A few leave the room and many more enter before Narayan begins the evening's talk.

When everyone is settled again on their zafu cushions and meditation benches, Narayan begins her talk with a story from the Tibetan Buddhist tradition about Milarepa, who went to collect firewood outside the cave where he was practicing. When he went back into the cave he saw seven demons with enormous bodies and eyes the size of cups. He was frightened and meditated on the Buddha. He thought they might be local deities of the place and realized he had been using the cave for many months and had not praised them or given them food. He sang a song of praise and a song of confidence and six of the demons vanished. Then, with friendliness and compassion, he placed himself in the mouth of the remaining demon and the demon vanished. I wanted to begin with this story, Narayan says, because our inner demons or torments of heart—greed, hatred, and delusion—are revealed as we practice and we need to learn how to recognize them, relate to them, and let them go.

When we see these demons in others, we tend to see others as obstacles. We may unconsciously relate to people as either problems or saviors instead of looking within at our own fears and desires.

She continues, speaking about the potential split between meditation practice on the cushion and practice in everyday life. An integrated life is possible, she says, when we are committed to being mindful in the formal practice of sitting on the cushion as well as the informal practice of trying to be present and attentive in our contact with people throughout the day. Being present in relationships with others means taking an interest in the person we are relating to in a given moment and being aware of the physical and mental reactions that may arise in this encounter. When we are more present in relationships we are more able to experience the joy of connection—instead of being preoccupied and disconnected inwardly. When we cultivate mindfulness in relationships, we begin to make the discovery that our usual habitual ways of relating to others are inherently unsatisfying and the source of much suffering. This insight into the nature of suffering and the path toward freedom from suffering arises as awareness matures in practice . . . each relationship becomes a mirror for deepening our understanding of the nature of suffering. What we see becomes material for inner liberation. Wisdom develops in relationships when we see for ourselves what actions are skillful and lead to happiness and what actions are unskillful and lead to unhappiness and confusion. The practice of being mindful in relationships helps us, Narayan summarizes, to see the difference between attachment and connection. When we have a personal agenda and are trying to exert control over another, disappointment and disconnection are the results of this attachment. By being willing to be more present, we gradually let go of the attachment to controlling others and the suffering that follows this way of relating, and, instead can cultivate connection and a willingness to be more open. Being more deeply connected allows us to be more available and receptive. What comes of this, she concludes, is a greater sense of inner freedom, expressing itself through the qualities of loving-kindness, compassion, joy, and equanimity. Narayan ends her talk with a quote from the poet Mary Oliver and answers a few questions from the people gathered. She then invites us to go downstairs for tea.[2]

༈ ༈ ༈

As these two snapshots suggest, the teachings and practices presented at Wat Phila and CIMC take several forms that overlap and diverge in many ways. Teachings from the Buddhist tradition begin each of the dhamma talks described, but Maha Nom ends with a story of a Hindu god and Narayan with a poem by Mary Oliver. Maha Nom's talk is part of a series of activities on Sunday mornings that include food donations to the sangha, chanting, and merit making, while meditation is the only formal activity at CIMC in addition to the dharma talk on Wednesday evenings. Building on the history and organization of Wat Phila and CIMC presented in chapter 3, this chapter describes the teachings and practices around which each center is based and the ways practitioners at each center understand and bring these teachings into their day-to-day lives.

For the purposes of this chapter, I imagine Wat Phila and CIMC as two organizational containers that hold the dhamma, or teachings of the Buddha, as well as a range of other ideas, practices, rituals, and ceremonies.[3] The dhamma is at the core of Wat Phila and CIMC and the first section of the chapter describes how the dhamma is understood and taught at both centers, with specific attention to the place of meditation, the practice at the heartwood of both centers, in that teaching. The dhamma is joined at both centers by a range of other ideas, practices, rituals, and ceremonies—what Bhante Gunaratana might describe as parts of the sapwood in his telling of the Heartwood Sutta—which I also describe to fully portray the contents of Wat Phila and CIMC as organizational containers and to explain how and why the contents of the centers differ.[4] Practitioners at Wat Phila view authentic or genuine Theravada Buddhism in the United States as including both the meditation at the heartwood and the sapwood. Practitioners at CIMC initially took a more reformist or traditionally Protestant approach, focusing on meditation alone, only later realizing that the some of the sapwood was needed to support the meditation practice. Practitioners at both centers describe their lives as changed in large and small ways, and both groups emphasize that the teachings and practices have influenced how they tell right from wrong in making ethical decisions. Practitioners at Wat Phila generally describe the criteria they use in making ethical decisions utilizing what sociologist Steven Tipton calls a regular or authoritative ethic, while practitioners at CIMC more often use a relativistic and largely expressive ethic that reflects their understandings of the Buddha's teachings.

## History of the Dhamma

Prince Siddhattha Gotama, who became the Buddha, was born into a life of luxury between 566 and 486 BCE on the present-day border between India and Nepal.[5] As he gained maturity, he realized that he, like all other beings, was subject to aging, illness, and death, and he renounced his life and left the palace where he lived to seek "unaging, unailing, deathless, sorrowless, unde-filed, unexcelled security from bondage, nibbana."[6] He became a wandering ascetic and studied with various teachers, fasted, and traveled for several years. Eventually, he sat in meditation under a sacred tree, where he had an experience that affected him profoundly. As he sat there, Buddhist legend says, Mara, a personification of death, delusion, and temptation, came to tempt him but withdrew in defeat. He passed through three stages of knowledge or awareness and came to know all his previous lives, the mechanism of kamma, and all the laws underlying kamma and conditioned experience. These insights led to his unconditional release, or simply put, to his enlightenment or nibbana.

Now called the Buddha or Awakened One, he thought about whether he should teach. The Buddha considered not teaching, but a Buddhist sutta says that Sahampati Brahma, one of the highest gods in popular religion at the time, appeared and spoke to him. After this appearance, the Buddha decided, out of compassion for all beings, to teach, and he wondered at first whom to revere or serve as his teacher. Finding no one superior to himself, he decided to revere the dhamma he discovered in his enlightenment.[7] He began to teach and gave his first sermon in the Deer Park at Sarnath near Benares, where he outlined the Four Noble Truths and the Eightfold Path. These truths state that in our lives there is dukkha, most commonly translated as "suffering," but also as "dissatisfaction" or "stress." The origin of this suffering is craving, which leads to further desire, but the cessation of suffering is possible. The way to end suffering is the Noble Eightfold Path, a path between the extremes of sensual indulgence and self-torture that consists of wisdom (right view and right resolve), virtue (right speech, right action, right livelihood), and concentration (right effort, right-mindedness, and right concentration). The Buddha said he became enlightened only when he truly understood each of these truths and had performed the tasks appropriate to each. This was the first of thousands of sermons the Buddha delivered to people of all backgrounds and experiences throughout his lifetime. In one of these talks, he told listeners he was not teaching them everything, but only those things that would lead to the end of suffering. For the next forty-five years, the Buddha traveled around the central Ganges River plain spreading his teachings, saying that when he was gone, the dhamma he taught and the *vinaya* he promulgated would be a guide. The Buddha's name for his teaching was Dhamma-Vinaya, the doctrine and the discipline.

The dhamma, or teachings of the Buddha, were memorized and passed down orally for several generations by Ananda, the Buddha's cousin and assistant, and other monks, nuns, and disciples. Shortly after the Buddha's death five hundred *arahants*, or enlightened people, took part in a communal recitation of his teachings. From this and later recitations, the Buddhist canon developed and was organized into three *Pitakas* (baskets, collections, or oral traditions) called the Suttas, *Vinaya*, and *Abhidhamma*. The *Sutta Pitaka* includes prose, dialogues, stories, and teachings delivered by the Buddha, and it is organized into sets of discourses.[8] The *Vinaya Pitaka* is divided into three sections that outline the code of discipline for the monastic community and how the monastic sangha should be governed.[9] The third collection, the *Abhidhamma*, or "higher dhamma," as the word is translated, consists of seven scholarly works. All three collections were brought orally from northern India to Sri Lanka in the third century CE and were subsequently written down in Pali, forming the Pali canon, the textual basis of the Theravada Buddhist tradition. By the fifth century BCE, the Pali canon existed in Sri Lanka in much the same form as it does today and it is the only canon of the Buddha's teachings to survive, seemingly completely, in an Indian language.

## Organizational Constructions

### WAT PHILA

At Wat Phila, Maha Nom described the dhamma as the Buddha's discovery of how nature works. The Buddha decided to teach only one subject, Maha Nom taught in a dhamma talk one Sunday, which was "how individuals can liberate themselves from the endless cycles of suffering, birth, old age, sickness, and death."[10] The dhamma is at the core of all of the teachings, ceremonies, and rituals that take place at Wat Phila, and it is formally taught to practitioners through daily and weekly dhamma talks the monks give on broad themes like wisdom, generosity, desire, and decision making and specific issues relevant to practitioners' lives like the challenges of marriage and caring for children and the importance of giving. Sometimes the telling of a sutta is the content of the dhamma talk, while other talks are based on the Buddha's teachings more generally. In teaching about the importance of good communication, for example, Maha Nom referred to the Buddha's teachings generally, but the talk was not focused around a particular sutta.[11] *Jataka* tales, or stories of the Buddha in his previous lives, are also particularly popular subjects of talks, as are stories about people and places in Thailand. Many dhamma talks, like the one described at the beginning of this chapter, include several of these elements in an attempt to appeal to the different interests of the people gathered.

In addition to dhamma talks, practitioners at Wat Phila learn the dhamma

FIGURE 15. Maha Nom leads chanting at a festival to celebrate *Wisākhābūchā*. Photo courtesy of Thira Thiramongkol.

through teachings about meditation that take place in Sunday morning classes and are based on the dhammakaya form of meditation originally taught by the late Luāngphō Sot at Wat Pāknām in Thailand. Meditation is taught by Taan Ajahn and also through audiotapes of Luāngphō Sot. Taan Ajahn teaches meditation by first guiding practitioners to focus their attention on a large crystal ball at the front of the main temple hall. He tells practitioners to imagine the crystal ball entering their bodies and coming to rest two inches above the navel. With experience, practitioners develop greater concentration and move through a series of stages in this meditation practice.[12] One Thursday Ōi, a laywoman in her fifties, led a guided meditation for a group of women gathered to prepare lunch for the monks. Slowly and deliberately she instructed people to "visualize the crystal ball entering your right nostril . . . you need to think about it moving slowly. Each time that it reaches a resting place you repeat, silently to yourself, 'sangham saranam gacchami.'[13] Visualize the ball moving to the back of your throat, down your windpipe, and then down your throat as you are swallowing. It moves slowly down into your stomach and then back up to rest near your navel. Concentrate there. You can see the ball multiplying into six and then you can see your body in the crystal ball and then two bodies.

It is a crystal ball so it is clear and you can see through it in your meditation and concentration."

The dhamma at Wat Phila is undergirded by practitioners' varying degrees of adherence to a traditional Buddhist cosmology or system of belief that includes teachings about nonhuman beings, merit, kamma, realms of existence, and Buddhist heavens and hells. This cosmology is central to how Buddhism has been understood in Thailand and other traditionally Buddhist countries, but individual monks and traditions have interpreted it in a number of different ways. Some Thai monks in Thailand and the United States draw on this cosmology to emphasize the supernatural components of the Buddhist tradition through healing, the supernatural powers of monks, meditation, and fortune-telling, for example.[14] The monks and most of the practitioners at Wat Phila do not emphasize these supernatural aspects of the tradition, but do emphasize other elements of the cosmology. Samsara, or the ongoing cycle of death and rebirth, underlies how the dhamma is taught at Wat Phila. Practitioners assume they will be reborn, and many of their practices are aimed at improving their chances and their relatives' chances of a favorable rebirth in the next life. Most lay people also believe in kamma, a kind of currency people accumulate through their present and former lives based on good and bad action. People see themselves accumulating good kamma by participating in merit-making ceremonies at the temple as well as through small acts of generosity in their daily lives. At Wat Phila, and in Thai Buddhism more generally, merit-making ceremonies are based around exchanges between the monks and lay people. Lay people accumulate merit and good kamma by providing food and other material goods to the monks, and the monks complete the exchange by acting as fields of merits and by providing the lay people with spiritual teachings.

Practitioners at Wat Phila vary in the extent to which they adhere to a Buddhist cosmology and the ways they interpret each of these ideas. Some people take all of these ideas strictly on faith, while others more closely follow Maha Nom's instructions to judge for themselves whether they are true.[15] Most practitioners have a sense of the boundaries of accepted practices at the temple, as evident in a story people occasionally tell about a layman who used to come to the temple wanting to tell people their fortunes. Taan Ajahn did not approve of this practice and asked the man to stop. When he refused, Taan Ajahn asked him not to come to the temple anymore. While some of the practitioners wanted to have their fortunes told (and occasionally now see him outside the temple), all learned that this kind of practice was not welcome at Wat Phila.

Rituals and ceremonies are another central component of Buddhism at

FIGURE 16. Lay people participate in chanting and meditation on a Sunday morning at Wat Phila.

Wat Phila as described by Maha Nom.[16] Rituals such as taking refuge, taking precepts, chanting, and making offerings to monks occur regularly, and ceremonies occur on important Buddhist holidays like *Āsālahabūchā*, *Kathin*, and *Mākhabūchā*. Many of these rituals and ceremonies developed as Buddhism spread through Southeast Asia and Thailand, and many are being adapted or amended in the United States. Every time practitioners come to Wat Phila for a service or ceremony, for example, they begin by taking the refuges and precepts responsively from one of the monks. Taking refuge is a way of showing commitment to the Buddha, the dhamma, and the sangha. Taking precepts is a way of promising to live according to certain ethical guidelines. (Both are outlined in appendix B.) At the end of each service, people do the *trūat nām* ceremony in which every individual or family takes a small silver pitcher filled with water and a small bowl. In the act of water pouring, people transfer the merit they have made during their time at the temple to all beings, most particularly to their families and deceased relatives. At the end of this ritual, the people move close to Taan Ajahn, who chants with the other monks while stirring a sacralized bowl of water with a wooden whisk. As the monks chant, Taan Ajahn sprinkles water onto everyone gathered so they will be protected and have good luck. Many ceremonies also take place around donations of money.

In addition to rituals and ceremonies, the veneration of monks is an important component of what takes place at Wat Phila and has a long history in Thai Buddhism and Buddhism more generally.[17] The late Luāngphō Sot, the monk who discovered the form of meditation taught at Wat Phila, is the most venerated monk there, and photos and images of him hang throughout the temple. For the New Year 2002, the monks distributed bright pink paper calendar pages attached to a laminated photograph of Luāngphō Sot. Some lay people were upset that the photo was attached to a calendar, feeling that the photo itself was too sacred or special to have something mundane, like a calendar, attached. As I left the temple with my calendar, I was stopped twice on the way to my car and instructed. One man told me to take the calendar off the photo as soon as I got home and to hang the photo in my Buddha room. The second person, a woman, stopped me and implied that I could keep the calendar attached to the photo but that at the end of the year I was not to throw the photo away but to frame it and hang it in a special place in my house.

In addition to displaying photos of Luāngphō Sot in their homes, people often wear pins with photos of Luāngphō or have small images of him in their cars or wallets. Much as Catholics pray to Saint Jude or the Virgin Mary, practitioners at Wat Phila bow and pray to images of Luāngphō Sot, often appealing to him for help.[18] Shortly after I began to prepare lunch for the monks on Thursdays at Wat Phila with a group of women, one of the women took me aside and told me, "You have done a good thing. Now when you need help, just pray to Luāngphō and he will help you." Another day, Tui, a Thai woman in her sixties, spoke with me about her husband who had recently recovered from a serious illness, saying, "It's because of Luāngphō." And Čhēt, a young Thai man, told me he was accepted to college and passed his driving test all because of Luāngphō. Several weeks later he told me about his new job at H&R Block. I said there must be a lot of work as the tax season approached, and he corrected me saying, "I got the job because of Luāngphō. I prayed to him and people like me because of him." As he spoke, he patted his chest where an amulet of Luāngphō hung under his shirt. While most people appeal to Luāngphō for help with the problems of daily life, not all believe that help comes in supernatural forms. When I asked Dr. Malin whether Luāngphō has the power to help people, she replied, "Power? I think knowledge. It's like when you look at an elephant. He saw the whole elephant and I see only one hair."

Practitioners at Wat Phila also wear amulets (*khrūang rāng*) or small images of the Buddha or important monks like Luāngphō Sot inside clear lockets

around their necks or on key chains for protection. These amulets can be purchased in markets or temples in Thailand or are given to lay people by monks
and are often passed down through families. For the New Year 2001, Maha
Nom distributed amulets with images of the Buddha and Luāngphō Sot to
people at the temple. Thip, a laywoman, took the three amulets I was given
and laid them on the kitchen counter to give me a lesson. The one with a color
image of Luāngphō Wat Pāknām's face she said I should wear around my neck
all the time on a silver or gold chain for good luck and protection. The gold one
shaped like a lotus leaf I should put in my car or give to someone else. And the
third one, shaped like a triangle with a carving of Luāngphō Sot on the front,
she told me was good for meditating and should be put in the place at home
where I meditate. Another day Mū, a fifty-year-old Thai man, explained to
me over lunch at the temple that amulets are "good luck charms that protect
you when you are out of the house." He tugged at a gold chain around his
neck and pulled out an amulet from under his shirt that he had gotten from
his grandfather. Several people told me it is important to respect whoever gave
you any amulets that you wear. Næn, a laywoman, told me that when her
daughter was getting teased in first grade, she gave her a Luāngphō amulet to
wear to school so she could be strong. In addition to protection and good luck,
some people, like Dthoo, an engineer in his late thirties, wear amulets more as
reminders of the Buddha's teachings. One Sunday when people were showing
each other their amulets over lunch and talking about where they got them,
he showed me his, saying, "I wear this to remind me at all times of what it is
about." Earlier he had been telling me that some people get so wrapped up in
the ceremonies and festivals at Buddhist temples that they start to forget the
Buddha's teachings at the core of the tradition.

By listening to dhamma talks, meditating, carrying amulets, and participating in rituals at Wat Phila, practitioners believe they will experience less
suffering and have better lives, whether through insights gained in meditation
or through protection granted by Luāngphō Sot. Most people do not believe,
however, that they will attain nibbana or enlightenment in this life. Many
believe it is possible for the monks to achieve nibbana but think that the best
lay people can do is be reborn in a better life and continue to accumulate
kamma. "To attain nibbana," Dr. Malin explained, "you have to come back to
earth. . . . You have a chance to be born as a human to do good and to build
up to nibbana." Later in our conversation she told me that making donations
to the monks or to charity is a good way to have a better future life. Some people believe they must be reborn as monks before nibbana or enlightenment
is possible, and others do not. Lay practitioners, therefore, are serious about

hearing the dhamma and practicing meditation but are equally serious about participating in rituals and ceremonies at the temple that not only generate kamma for them, but also support the monks in meditation practices that might help the monks attain nibbana. At the heartwood of the center, then, is the meditation that may enable them monks to attain nibbana and end the cycle of birth and rebirth, and also enable the lay people, through kamma and merit, to have favorable rebirths.

It is important to mention one largely unspoken assumption that is present within Wat Phila as a container and influential in how the teachings are presented—around money. All of the teachings at Wat Phila are offered without charge and people are free to come and go without paying membership fees or fees for classes or to attend ceremonies. This approach to finances follows the Buddhist traditions of *dana*, in which lay people make voluntary donations of food, money, and other goods to the monks to support them and the temple. There is informal pressure to donate, especially money, and this approach is an important component of Wat Phila. The monks give dhamma talks about the importance of generosity, people circulate during festivals collecting financial donations for the temple, and some lay people put indirect pressure on others they do not feel are donating appropriately or enough.

## CIMC

Like Wat Phila, CIMC as an organizational container includes formal dhamma teachings and meditation instruction and increasingly a number of what might be called rituals as well as several largely unspoken ideas about the teachings. The dhamma is at the center of what is taught at CIMC, and meditation instruction and practice by the teachers and the lay people are clearly at the heartwood. Unlike the lay practitioners at Wat Phila, who generally do not believe that they will attain nibbana in this lifetime and believe they must support the monks in the monks' attempts to do so, many practitioners at CIMC believe nibbana (more often phrased as freedom or liberation) is possible for them in this life through the meditation practice. By emphasizing the texts and meditation practice as the essence of the tradition and rejecting rituals, ceremonies, and other practices deemed excessive and unnecessary, the founders of CIMC and other white Buddhist organizations took a particularly Protestant or reformist approach to Buddhism as practiced in Asia.[19] In an interview in 1995, Jack Kornfield explained, "We wanted to offer the powerful practice of insight meditation . . . as simply as possible without the complications of rituals, robes, chanting, the whole religious tradition."[20]

The dhamma is taught by each of the three teachers at CIMC through talks and classes. Narayan Liebenson Grady defined the dhamma as truth, and said that taking refuge in the dhamma is taking refuge in truth, the teachings of the Buddha, and practitioners' abilities to be aware and mindful from moment to moment.[21] While the teachers at CIMC place the center in the Theravada tradition, they draw from teachings in several different Buddhist traditions. While the Buddha's teachings or Buddhist traditions underlie most of the dharma talks at CIMC, they are explicitly referred to in varying degrees. Like Maha Nom, some speakers tell a specific sutta and reflect upon it. Other speakers build their talks on a teaching from the Buddhist tradition, like the story of Milarepa from the Tibetan Buddhist tradition quoted at the beginning of this chapter. Still other teachers rarely mention specific texts or traditions, but refer to the Buddha's teachings in more general ways or occasionally not at all. Dharma talks on Wednesday nights at CIMC cover a wide range of topics and themes such as the Noble Truths, mindfulness, wise speech, and wise effort. In the last several years Narayan has given a series of talks on the *paramis*, or Ten Moral Perfections, and Larry has given a series of talks on death and dying, and self-knowing. Talks about relationships and about right livelihood or work are quite popular and are designed not necessarily to improve people's relationships or increase their incomes but to see in both of these realms opportunities for practice.[22]

The dhamma at CIMC is taught largely through meditation instruction. An interest in meditation is assumed when people walk through the front doors, and people who are interested in Buddhism but not in meditation rarely stay at CIMC. Outside of meditation classes, there is little opportunity for hearing the dhamma at the center. People new to CIMC normally come in through a beginner's drop-in class or an introductory class that has meditation at the core, and classes for more advanced students are also based around meditation instruction. This instruction includes not only guidelines for how to meditate but also teachings about the Four Noble Truths, Eightfold Path, and other aspects of the Buddhist tradition that the teachers view as intimately related to the meditation practice.[23]

Larry, Narayan, and Michael each teach a slightly different form of the Theravada Buddhist meditation methods called samathi and vipassana. These kinds of meditation are designed to quiet the mind and allow practitioners to focus their attention both on particular places or activities and on all activities without distracting thoughts. Larry teaches Anapanasati, or breathing meditation, based on the Anapanasati Sutta, a teaching on meditation given by the Buddha. Larry teaches by first leading practitioners to focus on the breath. He has found that the breath is an ideal way to teach Buddhism in the West be-cause it does not carry the "cultural baggage" other methods do.[24] The sutta is composed of sixteen contemplations divided into four sets. The first set focuses on awareness of the breathing as it manifests in the body. The second focuses on feelings, and the third on the mind and mental formations. The fourth set emphasizes wisdom and seeing the lawfulness that underlies all phenomena.[25] In the Way of Awareness class at CIMC in April 2001, Larry taught a con-densed method in four weeks that started with concentration on the breath, or *samathi*. After the first two weeks, Larry moved to pure vipassana, or an awareness of whatever comes into the mind. Larry generally teaches students to move back and forth in their meditation between *samathi* and vipassana. From the beginning he teaches students not just to meditate on the cushion, but to bring the meditation into their daily lives by doing only one thing at a time, paying full attention to what they are doing, bringing the mind back when it drifts away, and investigating their distractions as they go about their activities.[26]

Narayan teaches meditation based on the Anapanasati Sutta and also the Satipatthana Sutta, which emphasizes a focus on the body, feelings, mind, and mental states in all postures. Like Larry, Narayan emphasizes the importance of practice in daily life by encouraging people in her Old Yogis class, in partic-ular, to pick a verb like "reaching," "walking," or "climbing stairs" and bring their full attention to the action that verb describes when they do it during the day. She summarizes this approach in words and drawings in her book, *When Singing Just Sing: Life as Meditation*.[27] Narayan also began to teach metta or loving-kindness meditation at CIMC in the late 1980s.[28] To do metta medi-tation, practitioners are taught to repeat phrases such as "may I be free from danger," "may I have mental happiness," "may I have physical happiness," and "may I have ease of well-being." Practitioners first focus metta on themselves as they repeat these phrases and then on a friend, a person they feel neutral about, a difficult person, and then all sentient beings.[29] Michael tends to focus more on the Satipatthana Sutta and on relaxing the body than on Anapanasati or breathing meditation in his teaching at CIMC.[30]

The only time teachings are offered at CIMC apart from specific meditation instruction is on Wednesday evenings. As described at the beginning of this chapter, a meditation session is held for forty-five minutes and then additional people may join the group to hear the dharma talk, given by one of the three teachers or an invited guest.[31] All Wednesday night talks assume that listeners are interested in meditation or have a meditation practice. And regardless of the

FIGURE 17. Narayan leads a class at the CIMC. Photo courtesy of Pash Voynow.

topic, the questions that follow revolve around meditation practice or issues in daily life that develop for people out of their practice. After Narayan's talk about mindfulness in relationships, for example, a woman in the audience asked what she should do in her work as a therapist when she has clients who can not look at themselves without fear and distaste. This is a central question, Narayan responded, and suggested that the woman help clients develop a space either through meditation or in another way where they can turn internally when they are doing this kind of emotional work. Other people then raised questions about how to be aware and mindful when talking, when and how to separate thoughts and emotions in practice, and how to engage people in practice who run from problems. Even when talks are more philosophical or textual than Narayan's, practitioners' questions focus on the experiential and emotional components of talks as they try to apply the teachings directly to their lives.

While the dhamma as brought from Thailand to Wat Phila is undergirded by a traditional Buddhist cosmology, this cosmology is muted at CIMC. Supernatural ideas about the power of meditation or monks with special powers are completely absent from the teachings at CIMC. Samsara, or the continuous cycle of birth and death experienced by practitioners at Wat Phila through ideas about kamma, merit, and rebirth, is also muted at CIMC. Although the teachers say they believe in rebirth, they each articulate their beliefs differently and rebirth is not an obvious or central part of their teachings. Only a few practitioners at CIMC believe people have past and future lives, and none are concerned about accumulating kamma or merit to ensure a better rebirth in the next life. Kamma is occasionally mentioned by the teachers at CIMC, but most practitioners believe it exists only in this lifetime, often stating it more generally as "your actions have consequences." There is no discussion of merit at CIMC. Part of the reason practitioners at CIMC do not pay much attention to samsara and kamma is that most of them believe that freedom from suffering is available in this life. Although they rarely use the words "nibbana," "nirvana," or "enlightenment" to describe the goals or purposes of the practice, teachers and practitioners alike talk about "freedom," "ease of mind," "compassion of heart," and the possibilities found in that freedom as very real outcomes of their practice. While "freedom" at Wat Phila means freedom from the cycle of birth and rebirth in future lives, "freedom" at CIMC refers almost exclusively to the freedom from suffering that practitioners believe is possible in this life.[32]

The dhamma presented at CIMC does not include aspects of the traditional Buddhist cosmology, but is undergirded by a psychological cosmology or set of beliefs emphasizing meditation as a way for practitioners to look at themselves through the lens of the Buddha's teachings.[33] At the beginning of her drop-in-classes on Tuesdays, Narayan often says, "When the Buddha started teaching, he started by saying 'come and see.'" He was issuing an invitation, she explains, with open arms and an open heart. "Come and see" here means both "come and see what the Buddha taught" and "come to look at yourself and see what is inside." Larry began the second of his Way of Awareness classes in April 2001 saying, "I have nothing wise to say. . . . Many of you are looking very intently at me. You can't learn anything from me. I'm here to tell you to look at yourself." By interpreting the dhamma as largely about the mind and internal life, meditation at CIMC and vipassana meditation in the United States more generally maintain a close relationship with strands of psychology that emphasize the importance of self-examination.[34] When Theravada Buddhism was introduced to the United States in the 1970s, this emphasis on internal self-examination was developing, in part as a response to societal changes in the 1960s. An emphasis on the inner self as a way to relate to religious and spiritual teachings continued in the 1980s and 1990s as therapy and psychotherapy, developed through the influence of Freud, became an increasingly central component of contemporary American culture, particularly in the social circles in which Buddhism developed.[35] Larry Rosenberg asserts that modern psychotherapy, in particular, had to predate Buddhism as he teaches it at CIMC because psychotherapy itself legitimated the idea of internal self-examination. Without this legitimization, he argues, the meditative approach to self-examination taught at CIMC would not make any sense to practitioners.[36] Through their common focus on the mind, the nature of experience, and an attempt to end suffering, meditation and therapy, particularly psychotherapy, continue to exist in close relation with one another at CIMC and at other Theravada Buddhist centers started by white teachers, particularly those founded around Spirit Rock on the West Coast.[37]

There are also, increasingly, a number of rituals inside CIMC as an organizational container. Larry Rosenberg and other early white Theravada Buddhist teachers initially focused on the meditation, which they perceived to be the core of the Theravada Buddhist tradition, and left all that they considered to be ceremonies and rituals behind. They consciously rejected these aspects of Theravada Buddhism in Southeast Asia, arguing, like the early Protestants, that these rituals and ceremonies were obscuring or even replacing the Buddha's teachings. Gradually, however, the teachers at CIMC learned that some rituals are helpful in supporting people's meditation practices. At the most basic level, classes and meditation sessions follow the same general format at CIMC and end in the same ways each time with three bells and sometimes a bow to the teachers or Buddha statue at the front of the meditation hall. Additional rituals were started at CIMC around ethics and bereavement. Fairly early on, the teachers there and elsewhere realized that ethics were an important component of meditation practice, and they posted the precepts or guidelines for behavior.[38] More recently, they began to have ceremonies in which practitioners are invited to take the refuges and precepts responsively from the teachers. While practitioners at Wat Phila are invited to take the refuges and precepts every time they come to the temple for a ceremony, practitioners at CIMC are invited to do so in particular ceremonies for that purpose once or twice a year. In July 2001 about forty-five people gathered at CIMC on a Friday evening to take the refuges and precepts. Narayan first taught that by taking refuge in the Buddha, dhamma, and sangha, practitioners take refuge in the fact that freedom is possible and that the teachings and community will support you in your efforts to attain it. She then administered the refuges and precepts, one at a time in Pali and in English.[39] In addition to the precept-taking ceremony,

CIMC also holds a yearly bereavement ceremony to remember relatives and friends who have passed away.

A number of additional, largely unspoken, ideas and assumptions related to the teachings inside CIMC as an organizational container are important to mention. First, the teachings at the center are presented within a physical space that privileges an ascetic of tasteful simplicity. With the center's renovations, the walls were painted a unified neutral shade, and floors covered with neutral carpets and hardwood. Images of the Buddha on the altars and walls throughout the center are medium-sized and elegant, unlike the large, shiny gold Buddha's on the altars at many Thai temples. CIMC would look very different if, as at many Thai temples, everyone were welcome to bring Buddha images and pile them on the altars in mismatched collections that are highly communal but sometimes less than artful. This simplicity creates a serene environment that complements the direct, simple way the teachers try to present the teachings. Second, although it is not always presented this way, the teachers and practitioners are comfortable drawing from a somewhat eclectic group of spiritual teachers. The photos of Ajahn Chah, Buddhadasa Bhikkhu, and others in the center's library show the center's many influences in addition to the range of teachers with whom all three teachers have studied. More concretely, the altar at CIMC was carved by a Korean monk and the bell used is from a Japanese Buddhist tradition although the center officially places itself in the Theravada Buddhist tradition. And third, the teachings at CIMC are presented in an environment in which people are asked directly to pay for them through class and membership fees. Unlike at Wat Phila where the teachings are offered for free and practitioners make voluntary donations to the monks, membership and class fees are listed on CIMC's brochure and money is collected at the beginning or end of classes and sessions at CIMC (though scholarships are available). While this approach is practical and needed given the realities of the center, it is different from Wat Phila's voluntary approach, and shapes how people hear the dhamma at CIMC.

## IN COMPARISON

The contents of Wat Phila and CIMC as organizational containers overlap and diverge largely as a result of each center's particular history and struggle to find an authentic teaching and practice in the United States. The centers share a commitment to the dhamma which includes teachings about the Four Noble Truths, Noble Eightfold Path, and core teachings about impermanence and selflessness. They also share a commitment to meditation instruction although the content of that instruction differs somewhat as do most practitioners' beliefs about the likely outcomes of that process in this lifetime. Some of the rituals, particularly around the refuges and the precepts, are common at both centers while others, like ceremonies held at Wat Phila on Buddhist holidays, are not. The cosmologies that undergird the teachings at Wat Phila and CIMC differ as do other components of the organizational containers like the veneration of monks and the wearing of amulets.

The contents of each organizational container differ because they were developed as the centers constructed what teachers and practitioners at each understood to be authentic interpretations of the Theravada Buddhist tradition in the United States. At Wat Phila, Taan Ajahn was at the center of this process and practitioners supported him and the temple because he and the developing temple looked authentic to them based on their experiences in Thailand—it looked like a temple in Thailand. While some of the contents of the container have certainly changed as they adapted in the United States, the changes at Wat Phila have been small enough not to threaten practitioners' sense that this is an authentic Thai Buddhist temple based on their experiences in Thailand. In pulling together the contents of Wat Phila as an organizational container, practitioners at Wat Phila illustrate what Robert Wuthnow calls a "dwelling" approach to spirituality that emphasizes habitation, creating a kind of sacred space in which practitioners can dwell and feel secure.[40]

Not having been born in the Theravada Buddhist tradition, practitioners at CIMC have little sense of what an authentic Theravada Buddhist organization or teaching includes. The teachings, ideas, and practices included in CIMC as an organizational container therefore initially resulted not from what practitioners judged to be authentic based on their experiences in Thailand or in other Buddhist centers but based on the aspects of the Theravada Buddhist tradition, and the meditation practice specifically, that seemed most practical and useful to them. Larry Rosenberg, like other early white Buddhist teachers, was highly educated and found the practice of meditation rather than the rituals or ceremonies in the Theravada Buddhist tradition to be the most compelling and accessible to him. As a result, he initially embraced meditation practice as the core or heartwood of the center and it was only later, after the center had existed for awhile, that rituals and other aspects of the sapwood were brought into the center. Interplay between aspects of psychology evident in practitioners' lives and in the culture more broadly as CIMC and other Theravada Buddhist centers developed are central to how the Buddha's teachings have been interpreted and packaged. In contrast to Wat Phila, CIMC illustrates a "practice-oriented spirituality" that Robert Wuthnow describes as spirituality characterized by deep inward reflection about who people are and how they experience their worlds. [41]

Despite differences, it is important to point out that the dhamma and contents of both organizational containers at Wat Phila and CIMC are syncretic on two levels. [42] The dhamma imported from Asia is syncretic. As Maha Nom's story that began this chapter illustrates, Buddhism was started in India, and Indra and other Hindu gods have been a part of Buddhist history and practice over thousands of years. Buddhist stories and practices in Thailand and brought from Thailand to Wat Phila are embedded with this kind of syncretism. Once the dhamma arrived in the United States, it also immediately began to mold and change, picking up new ideas and practices from its environment and leaving behind those not of interest to practitioners. The teachings at Wat Phila, for example, likely emphasize different themes than teachings at similar temples in Thailand, though a comparative study is needed to fully understand these differences. The dhamma at CIMC has also picked up many new ideas, like those around psychology, and developed new forms.

Despite differences in the content of Wat Phila and CIMC as organizational containers, both are labeled "Buddhist" by the organizations themselves. Wat Phila is called a Buddhist temple by the monks and lay practitioners and there is little doubt in anyone's mind that Buddhism and the Buddhist religion is what is being taught and practiced there. At CIMC, the teachers label the center "Buddhist" although neither "Buddhist" nor "Buddhism" is in the name. The early teachers decided to include "insight meditation" in the name to emphasize the meditation practice, but felt that Buddhism clearly underlies the meditation teachings. I talked with Larry Rosenberg about the Buddhist-ness of the center.

"People ask me," I told him, " . . . why isn't it called a 'Buddhist' meditation center?"

"But it is," he replied.

"But why is that phrase not in the name? . . . Is it symbolic of something?"

"It wasn't for me," he replied. [43]

The possibility that people might not consider CIMC a Buddhist center had hardly entered Larry's mind. An image of the Buddha is on the front of the center's brochure, and images of the Buddha hang throughout the center as well as on the altar in the main meditation hall. The emphasis on meditation and lack of Buddhist cosmology at many insight meditation centers have led some commentators to argue that centers like CIMC are teaching vipassana meditation largely independent of the Theravada Buddhist tradition. [44] While this may be true in some cases, at CIMC the teachers consciously link their teachings to the tradition.

## Personal Worldviews

The contents of Wat Phila and CIMC as organizational containers are one way to understand the teachings and practices central to the two organizations; the specific beliefs and practices of individual practitioners are another. As in all religious groups, practitioners at Wat Phila and CIMC come to the organizations with different beliefs and practices and pick selectively among the ideas and practices inside the organizational containers in constructing their individual ways of understanding and being in the world. I view the relationships between practitioners at each of these two centers and the centers themselves as ultimately cyclic, in which people are influenced by the ideas present in the organization and influence those ideas in turn as they learn, challenge, and talk with teachers and other practitioners. Through their participation in classes and ceremonies at Wat Phila and CIMC, practitioners bring the contents of the organizational containers into their daily lives in a wide range of ways and see their lives change through the process.

### WAT PHILA

Næn, a Thai woman in her forties, comes to Wat Phila at least once a week and has a small altar in her home where she goes every day. A Buddha sits at the top of the altar, and candles, incense, photos of Luāngphō Sot, and amulets sit below the Buddha. Every morning or evening she kneels before the altar and bows three times to the Buddha. She lights candles and sometimes incense, and chants the *Namo Tassa* and Homage to the Buddha in praise and respect.[45] Sometimes she meditates, especially if something is going wrong in her life, often promising Luāngphō Sot that she will do a day or more of quiet meditation and chanting at the temple if her problem is solved. She has a photo of Luāngphō Sot in her wallet and almost always has one of several amulets with her when she is away from her house.

Like Næn, Dr. Chan, a Thai-born physician, comes to Wat Phila regularly and also goes to his family's Buddha room, an upstairs bedroom in his home, at least once a day. The room is a rectangle, and in an alcove cut into one of the long walls stands a floor-to-ceiling altar that holds Buddha statues, photographs of Luāngphō Sot, several vases of flowers, and a glass of water. On the ground below the altar is a large crystal ball like the one at the temple used for meditation. Dr. Chan's wife and sister-in-law take care of the altar, bringing and removing flowers and other offerings daily, and he uses the room for chanting and meditation. He described the ways he practices Buddhism every day by showing me a laminated color photograph of the cycle of dependent origination.[46] "You have *lobha* [greed], you have *dosa* [hatred], you have *moha* [delusion]," he explained, pointing to the cycle. "So you go from one thing to the next like a chain. . . . That is what is going on for everyone, me included. I'm greedy. I buy a lot of stuff. I want to be rich." To try to escape from this cycle, Dr. Chan recently started to meditate after visiting a Thai monk at a temple in North Carolina.

In addition to practicing at home, Dr. Chan brings Buddhist teachings and practices into his work as a physician. "One of the principles in Buddhism is that you have kamma. That kamma you carry now is basically what you have done from the previous being. . . . So it is my job to reduce the weight of the kamma [in his patients]. So I try to use what I have in the other part of me. My *punna* [merit]. Take some of mine and give it to the patients so it will help reduce the kamma." In addition to this exchange, Dr. Chan uses what he has learned about meditation to take care of himself as he cares for patients: "Many times when I see difficult patients who have difficult problems I do meditation at the same time that I am seeing them."

Like Næn and Dr. Chan, the majority of practitioners at Wat Phila practice Buddhism regularly through chanting and meditation in their homes, and some talk about bringing it into their lives outside the temple and their homes by following the precepts or guidelines for moral behavior and through small acts of generosity. Most have Buddha rooms or altars where they light candles and incense, kneel and pay respect to a Buddha image by bowing, and do their chanting and meditation. Many of these practices are devotional, as people chant the *Namo Tassa*, prayers to the Buddha they learned as children, and sections of the chanting service recited every Sunday at the temple. About half of the people at Wat Phila meditate between ten minutes and an hour every day. Some do the dhammakaya form of meditation taught at the temple, while others do kinds of meditation learned from books or at other temples. (Wat Phila is unique among Thai temples in the States in its emphasis on dhammakaya meditation, though not necessarily on meditation itself, which is taught, in different ways, at many Thai temples across the country.)[47] People also read dhamma lessons in newsletters printed regularly by Wat Phila and other Thai temples in the United States.[48] On *wan phra* or days that correspond to the phases of the moon, some practitioners do special things in their homes. Kanyā, a Thai woman in her forties who owns a small business, told me that she is grateful every day and especially on Buddha days. "I wake up, get in the shower, make myself feel fresh and go into my Buddha room. I go in and do meditation or prayer or if it is a Buddha day I wear white and take the Eight Precepts. On a Buddha day I sleep in that room and I do not touch my husband or son. I do not talk to them if it is not necessary. . . . I'm peaceful. . . . I want to train myself for purity."

Several practitioners spoke with me about practicing Buddhism by following the precepts and through acts of generosity like giving money to people begging on the street or to food drives in their workplaces. "If I am walking past the Salvation Army and they ask," Dr. Malin told me, "I give." When she goes to the grocery store, Dr. Nūang always buys something to donate to the temple or someone else. "I buy food, fruit, paper towels, Ziplock bags. . . . I buy things to bring to the temple." In addition to donating to the temple, Mū also emphasized how important it is to make donations to different groups. "There are many times when different groups of people call, like the Police Academy, and we donate. . . . We try to help as much as we can."

Despite similarities in their practices, people at Wat Phila interpret the Buddha's teachings and Buddhist tradition in a wide range of ways. I conceptualize this spectrum of interpretation as a long continuum between rational understandings that do not assume the existence of gods or other higher powers, and supernatural understandings that do.[49] Regardless of where they fall on this continuum of belief, everyone at Wat Phila believes in samsara, or the endless cycle of birth and death, and the importance of accumulating kamma and merit through good works and donations to the temple. Dr. Chan and people like Kop, a practitioner in his fifties at Wat Phila, fall near the rational end of the continuum. Sounding much like the practitioners at CIMC, Kop believes that Buddhism is largely a scientific philosophy and that practitioners need to accept the teachings only when they can prove to themselves through their own meditation practice that the ideas are true. Næn and Kung, a Thai nurse in her fifties, fall more toward the supernatural end of the continuum. Kung meditates daily, and when she dozes off and wakes, often to the sound of the amulets she wears around her neck clinking together, she believes Luāngphō Sot is speaking to her. Her meditation, she believes, causes a plant she keeps inside a glass globe on the altar in her Buddha room to grow. Despite the fact that her husband Dr. Chan calls this idea "vodou," she holds fast to this belief as truth. As I sat in her Buddha room looking at her plant with a magnifying glass she told me, "It's amazing . . . some things you never know and you've never seen but they are real. That is why I say it's growing. I pray every night. I believe." Like these four people, practitioners at Wat Phila fall in many places along this continuum.

## CIMC

David, a white American-born man in his forties, is a therapist and group leader in the mental health field in Boston. He has been coming to CIMC for many years. At home, he meditates for twenty minutes every morning and evening, either in his den, which is filled with mats, cushions, and a Buddha statue, or on a cushion in his bedroom. Outside of these formal sitting periods, he tries to practice all the time. "I've really been trying to bring it more into daily life and to bring mindfulness into whatever I'm doing, whether it's talking on the phone, washing the dishes, or driving my car." Anissa, a white woman in her forties, describes herself as a "rebel at heart," and says she was drawn to Buddhism initially because the Buddha said, "Don't believe me; try it out and see." "Well, that's perfect for me," she told me, "because I'm not going to believe you anyway." She has been practicing now for more than fifteen years and begins her practice every morning by saying the precepts out loud and then meditating. She does metta or loving-kindness meditation in her head when she goes for a run later in the day and has also worked practice into many daily tasks. "I try to break tasks, chores, or things I have to do. So that's my practice, like making my bed for example or brushing my teeth or washing dishes. Any little task like that. Or driving. I try to drive mindfully."

Practitioners at CIMC center their regular practice around meditation, and the use of the word "practice" implies something based in meditation. Almost everyone I interviewed tries to have a regular meditation practice and several people described losing their practice and getting it back over a number of years. Like David and Anissa, people meditate from a few minutes to more than an hour every day. While some people have Buddha images in their homes, many do not sit in front of them or bow to them, generally considering these kinds of devotional practices as part of Buddhism left behind in Asia. Several people combine their meditation with various kinds of yoga, usually doing the yoga as a preparation for meditation to calm the mind.[50]

Practitioners at CIMC are often eager to bring meditation into their daily lives, particularly in ways that will change their day-to-day experiences. Like David and Anissa, many try to walk or drive "mindfully," which means they try to be present and aware of the experience of walking or driving as it is happening rather than allowing their minds to wander. Some people have worked signals into their daily lives that remind them to be present. In a talk about right livelihood, Larry encouraged a student to find five or ten minutes at work during the day to sit quietly. "Does the clock bell every hour or does the telephone ring?" Larry asked the student. "If you reeducate yourself, it's possible that it can be a reminder." Like David and Anissa, practitioners describe practicing in daily life as they walk, drive, sit at their desks, type on their computers, or hear telephones ring. One practitioner heeds Larry's teaching and describes himself as practicing at work by taking a deep breath, centering himself, and preparing for the next moment every time he hears the telephone ring.

People at CIMC also interpret the Buddha's teachings toward the rational end of the continuum described above. A few people believe in kamma, but most interpret it in the context of their present, rather than future, lives. People who come to the center with other ideas, particularly with supernatural ideas that require belief in gods or powers, tend to go elsewhere rather quickly. One man in his thirties, for example, visited CIMC several times as part of developing his own theory about the flow of energy and light movement between people. He was hoping to find a group of people or a center where people could do dance and meditative rituals to access and share this energy, but quickly became frustrated with the people at CIMC, whom he found to be polite but not interested in his ideas. He stopped coming to CIMC after just a few visits.

While the teachers at CIMC label what they teach "Buddhism," the practitioners themselves give it a wide range of labels, including the label of "no label," and sometimes no label at all. In their teachings, the teachers consistently deemphasize all labels, saying that what is ultimately important is the meditation practice. Despite the Buddha on the altar and the Buddhas around the center, it sometimes takes new practitioners several visits to grasp the Buddhistness of the center. Katie, a longtime practitioner, explained, "I was midway or maybe almost done with the first course with Larry before I realized, I really got it, that he was teaching Buddhism. He does it very subtly and doesn't say it's Buddhism. Maybe he does once or twice."

## LOOKING AT EACH OTHER

To fully understand how people at Wat Phila and CIMC understand their personal practices, it is helpful to listen to what they say when they describe each other. White Buddhists have been quoted as saying that Asian Buddhists do not practice. What they mean when they say this is that Asian Buddhists do not meditate, because for many white Buddhists, as evident at CIMC, Buddhist practice equals, or at least starts with, formal sitting meditation. Bob, a practitioner at CIMC for several years, told me in an interview that "Buddhism is meditation." Jack Kornfield writes, "I saw that the majority of Buddhists in Asia do not actually practice. At best they go to the temple devotionally like Westerners go to church. They go once a week to hear a sermon or a few moral rules or to leave a little bit of money to make some merit for a better rebirth in the next life."[51] This emphasis on meditation as the core of Buddhist practice for lay people, as articulated by Kornfield here and at CIMC, is new and developed in America.

Practitioners at Wat Phila are generally quiet about the activities of white Buddhists. Many say that all Buddhists are the same, but occasionally express genuine puzzlement at the activities of white Buddhists. "It seems pretty much lately that more and more people are interested in Buddhism," Noo, a middle-aged Thai engineer, told me over lunch, "but most of the time I can see that they are modifying it [from] the real Buddhism. . . . Some of them like meditation, so they just chose that part, the meditation. But if you do the meditation and you say 'I am a Buddhist,' you're not a total Buddhist you know. . . . It's like halfway. Just like when you go to school to learn to be a programmer you can't say, 'I'm a computer engineer.' You're just a programmer." While people at Wat Phila recognize what white people are doing as meditation, some view it as only one of the practices central to Buddhism.

White practitioners' attitudes toward Thais' practices were evident one evening when I was driving home from CIMC with a friend after a meditation class. We talked about a Thai temple in Boston that I had visited the Sunday before and she had visited some weeks earlier as part of a Buddhism class she was taking.

"We met the Abbot and he showed us his path for walking meditation outside; it was just beautiful, that he can walk there between the trees," she told me.

"What about the lay people?" I asked. "How do they practice?"

She seemed a little confused at the question. "They mostly seemed to be practicing generosity through *dana*," she told me. "They come and cook and serve the food."

"So this is their practice?" I asked.

She was silent for a few moments and then spoke carefully, reflecting on the time she spent working as a cook at a Buddhist retreat center. "Yes, I guess that could be their practice. When I was working at IMS, cooking was a large part of my practice and the teachers worked with me a lot around that." Considering the cooking done in Asian temples as a part of Buddhist practice was a stretch for my friend, who, like many at CIMC, view practice as starting on the meditation cushion.

Approaches to food presentations also clarify the various meanings given to practice at Wat Phila and CIMC. Lay people regularly bring food to Wat Phila, and the exchange of food between monks and lay people is central to merit making and lay practice. When retreats are held on weekends at CIMC, people sign up to prepare food for the retreatants. While some may consider generosity in the act of bringing the food a part of the practice, they are more likely to talk about practice in the food preparation. Becky told me that when she brings food, she treats the experience as practice not because of her generosity in volunteering her time and buying the food but by being aware and mindful as she stirs the couscous and lays the dishes on the table. The practice for her is in her relationship to the act of cooking the food, while for those offering food to the monks at Wat Phila, the practice is primarily in their relationship to those who are eating it. While the way that one does something, like housecleaning or cooking for a retreat, may be viewed as a component of practice at CIMC, the act of doing it and the attitude of generosity behind it generally count at Wat Phila.

## FAITH

Through their differing understandings of practice, practitioners at Wat Phila and CIMC both demonstrate their faith, though their faith is in different things. At Wat Phila, people have faith in the Buddha, Luāngphō Sot, and meditation, in varying degrees depending on where they fall on the continuum of interpretation described above. Ō, an eighty-year-old Thai woman who comes to Wat Phila during the six months she lives with her son in New Jersey each year, falls toward the supernatural end of the continuum. She said goodbye to me as she prepared to return to Thailand, saying, "You keep coming here . . . and Buddha will take care of things." Some people believe the Buddha or other gods can help them supernaturally, while others closer to the rational end of the continuum have faith in the Buddha's example: "While you can't be like the Buddha," one man told me, "you have to follow his step." In addition to faith in the Buddha, many people like Næn, described earlier, have faith in Luāngphō Sot as someone who can help them in their lives directly and through his meditation teachings. When Næn sends her daughter to school with a Luāngphō Sot amulet or people bow to images of Luāngphō Sot before they leave the temple for the day, they have faith that Luāngphō is watching over them and will protect them when they need it. Some people also have faith, in different ways, in the practice of meditation. Ku*ng*, described above, has faith that her meditation practice causes the plant in the glass globe in her Buddha room to grow. Sam, an engineer in his forties, continues to have faith that meditation practice will improve his life even though he says he has not seen any tangible evidence of it doing so yet. "I still have not gotten anywhere because it is not coming to the point where I can calm my mind and keep it in a calm state," he told me. "I try to do it for ten minutes or fifteen minutes. And then I chant and then meditate for ten or fifteen minutes. I try to keep up with the good habit. The more you keep up with it, the easier it is going to be. . . . I try to create the discipline. No matter how tired I am or how late, I try to keep it up."

Practitioners at CIMC tend to have less variation in their definitions of faith, which focus on their belief that the meditation practice will decrease their suffering and improve their lives.[52] Practitioners can trust the teacher and the teachings for a short time, Larry told me, but if they do not experience for themselves the benefits of meditation practice, that faith will wane. Michelle, a woman in her thirties who has been meditating for ten years, emphasized the importance of faith in her meditation practice by talking about her attempts to bring the practice into her daily life. "When I first started meditating," she told me, "I was in such a rush to make it a part of my life. If somebody could have just told me, 'You know what? If you do it long enough, you're not going to have to work at it. It will automatically bleed in.' Maybe somebody did say that and maybe I didn't hear it because I wasn't ready to hear it. I didn't have faith." Despite her initial lack of faith, Michelle stayed with the practice and believes it has had a dramatic influence on her life. Becky spoke also about faith in the practice. "It's huge," she told me. "That's been a giant shift for me . . . faith that the practice works." Narayan emphasizes that faith often becomes important in the fifth or sixth year of meditation practice when, she has often observed, practitioners seem to have crises of faith. "It's kind of like as the teacher, I hold the faith," she told me. She is the one who knows that if practitioners stay with it through the difficult points, their lives will improve in the long term.

In the most general sense, practitioners at Wat Phila and CIMC have faith that by coming to the centers and chanting, meditating, make offerings to the monks, and practicing—in all of the ways they define practice—at home they will have less suffering and more peace in their present lives. Their more specific aims differ, with practitioners at Wat Phila mostly hoping for a better rebirth and practitioners at CIMC primarily focusing on reducing their suffering and attaining freedom and liberation in this one.

## CHANGED LIVES

Through their involvement with Wat Phila and cimc and their own personal practices, practitioners at both centers describe their lives as changed.[53] People at Wat Phila tend to describe less dramatic changes than people at cimc. Practitioners at Wat Phila say that coming to the temple helps them to "calm down my mind," "find peace with myself," "calm down and clean up inside." Phæm believes going to the temple and practicing Buddhism at home has helped her in her job because it taught her not to be impatient with people. "Before, I used to get quick-tempered with people and irritated so easily. And now . . . when I don't understand why they do something I walk away instead of getting mad at them. I don't argue with people like I used to argue with them. It made me calmer." Dr. Nūa*ng* spoke about how Buddhism taught her how to disagree with other people. "The Buddhist way is that we, each of us, control our own minds. We do not allow another person to upset us. We do not allow their world to enter our minds. We have to be responsible for our own well being." A few experience dramatic changes in their approach to the world, generally through meditation practice, though the majority experience slight reorientations to themselves and to the world around them as a result of their involvement in the temple.

Practitioners at cimc, on the other hand, describe themselves as dramatically changed through their practice and experiences there. Peter thinks the practice "changes everything. It's just a matter of how radically or how minimally." Some people describe minimal influences and others, like Sara, say that the practice "has had a huge impact," leaving little in her life not affected. Almost everyone I spoke with at cimc said that the practice taught them or helped them to be "more present" and aware of their experiences rather than lost in daydreams, worries, and concerns about the past or the future. David says the practice "helped me be a lot more present for whatever is happening." In a practical way, it has helped him live more effectively by "being more mindful and more present. . . . [It] has really made my life richer and more alive than it was before." Lucy echoes, "I have the ability more to live in the now and to have an open mind instead of coming to this moment with all the ideas of what this moment is."

Some people at cimc also said that practice influences not just their experience of this moment, but the way they see the world. Some practitioners described the practice as bringing a framework of meaning to their lives that was not there before. David says that "in terms of the bigger picture, the Buddha's teaching on impermanence and selflessness and the Four Noble Truths and all that—I think it has given me a framework for just giving my life some meaning. It's something that I feel I can embrace and . . . it feels right to me." Helen, in large part, agreed: "I think that practice gives me a foundation of meaning in my life which is kind of essential. I lose perspective, but if I come back to my practice then I recover perspective. . . . It's so rare to take human birth [i.e., to be born as a human], to hear the teachings, and to practice." And Nancy agrees, "I think it was a combination of a spiritual discipline which I had wanted but had not succeeded in either finding or sustaining and the philosophical framework that it gave my life. . . . I knew from the start that this would actually allow me to continue my life—which I was happy with . . . but I knew something was missing and I knew I needed to change internally, so I felt that the practice offered all those things and I saw it very clearly from the beginning, all the rewards." For David, Helen, and Nancy, practice is not just about being in the present but has also allowed them to create frameworks based in the Four Noble Truths and Eightfold Path taught by the Buddha through which they now approach all aspects of their lives.

Many people at both centers describe changes in their lives specifically around how they make moral decisions and know right from wrong. The ways they describe knowing right from wrong are best understood on a continuum, with authoritative or regular ethics on one end and expressive ethics on the other. Practitioners at Wat Phila tend to cluster at one end of the continuum, seeing in Buddhism an authoritarian or a regular ethic. They see clear guidelines about right and wrong determined either from the Buddha's teachings or from rules and principles directly based on those teachings and known by reason. Many of these lessons are described in relation to the precepts as moral teachings. Nū, a fifty-year-old Thai woman, says she thinks about the Five Precepts daily as guidelines for telling good from bad. Chāng, a Thai man in his forties, also spoke about precepts guiding his behavior. The precepts are like a filter, he said. "If you have five things, your mind is very good and pure," but without the five things your mind is "heavy, thick, and dark." Kop, a practitioner in his fifties, says that through meditation he develops *sati*, or mindfulness, which allows him to know his duties, and "discharge them appropriately at any moment. . . . There are duties I need to perform as a son, father, husband. . . . It helps me to do the right things right." It is interesting to contrast Kop's definition of mindfulness, which helps him know his duties and discharge them correctly, with the definition of mindfulness as used at CIMC, which tends not to emphasize responsibilities or the correct way to act on them, but rather emphasizes being in the present to experience and pay full attention to whatever is taking place around you.

Practitioners at Wat Phila also see in Buddhism clear lessons about the values, like honesty, that should guide their lives. In her business as a florist, for example, Mai says because she is a Buddhist she has been generous and honest with her customers. That honesty has led to her success. "We started with almost nothing," she explained. "People came in and wondered what kind of a business are these people running, because they couldn't tell from outside. And little by little we built up by being nice to people. We wouldn't let them leave the shop empty-handed. We would wrap up stems of flowers and give them for free at the beginning . . . and being honest, that's the most important thing. I would say that has to do with being a Buddhist." Sam changed how he values life, particularly the lives of animals, since he started coming to the temple. "I used to go crabbing all the time in the summer. . . . Now I don't do that. I don't go fishing. . . . I don't think it's the way to have fun."

Practitioners at CIMC also talk about the practice leading them to rethink how they make moral decisions, but overall they do not see in Buddhism an authoritative or regular ethic that leads to clear moral guidelines or values. They tend instead to cluster closer to the other end of the continuum, seeing what sociologist Steven Tipton describes as an "expressive ethic," in which they evaluate behaviors based on personal feelings and intuition.[54] While practitioners at Wat Phila see in Buddhism clear moral guidelines, practitioners at CIMC say that Buddhism, and the practice of meditation specifically, leads them to discover their *own* understandings of right and wrong experientially. This relative sense of right and wrong is particularly evident at CIMC with regard to precepts. While the precepts are presented at Wat Phila as rules to be followed, they are presented and interpreted more relatively at CIMC. Larry describes precepts as "not simply ethical commands like the Ten Commandments; they are more like intelligent guidelines to warn us of the areas where we typically create problems for ourselves." A few people take all five precepts and agree to follow them, but many others take the precepts and view them as guidelines within which they can make their own decisions. Dawn, who has been meditating for more than fifteen years, describes precepts as a "touchstone." "It's not like I take the precepts and suddenly I try to get really good in my behavior. It's kind of just to remind me in a way that I might lose track of. For me the precepts are really more about exploring what ethics is to you . . . versus this is how you behave." Tom, a relatively new meditator, does not disagree with any of the precepts but sees them, ultimately, as a relatively limited set of rules. "What you are really cultivating," he explained, "is the ability to ascertain what right conduct is in any moment, and the precepts can't do that." The precepts do not tell Tom what right conduct is, but give him a framework within which to evaluate for himself, based on his own experiences, what he thinks right and wrong action is.

The expressive ethic many practitioners at CIMC develop through their meditation practice does lead some to significant changes in their own moral behaviors. Gary, a forty-five-year-old man, has been practicing meditation at CIMC for a few years. Through meditation practice, he came to different ideas about what he wanted to eat and now only buys organic products: "It's not just because I think it is healthier for me, but because I think more and care about the effect of pesticides on the water table." Gary did not come to this understanding primarily by hearing the Buddha's teachings and interpreting those teachings as instructing him to purchase organic vegetables or care more about all life forms. Rather, it was through his experience of meditation and internal self-examination that he felt and knew intuitively that it would be best for him to change his eating and purchasing habits. Through a similar process, David came to a new understanding about his work. He was working in advertising when he started to practice meditation and gradually became more conscious of what he was doing as an advertising copywriter. "I began to see more and more that I was kind of helping spread greed, hatred, and delusion. I mean I really came to believe that. And sitting on the cushion, my goal, if you will, is to diminish greed, hatred, and delusion." He continued, "I really felt this conflict between the spiritual values I was developing as a practitioner and the values that were kind of informing my work in the business world. And eventually it became this irreconcilable conflict and I felt like I had to do something that I felt was more in line with my spiritual values." With the support of the teachers at CIMC and his wife, David went back to school and now, several years later, is working as a therapist in the mental health field. Like Gary, David changed his behaviors not because he understood the Buddha's teachings or the teachers at CIMC to be instructing him to do so, as many practitioners at Wat Phila believe. Rather his personal meditation practice led him to an intuitive sense of right and wrong, and it was this experience that led him to leave his job and go back to school to pursue a more right livelihood.

## Conclusion

Wat Phila and CIMC include the dhamma and meditation in their organizational containers as well as a range of other practices, rituals, ceremonies, and ideas. Meditation is at the heartwood of both organizational containers, although who has best access to this meditation and the likely effects of meditation practice in this lifetime differ between the centers. There is variation among practitioners, more at Wat Phila than at CIMC, in how people interpret the teachings and ideas present at the centers, and both organizations are relatively flexible in enabling people with a diversity of interpretations to participate and feel welcome. People at both centers describe, in different ways, their lives as changed as a result of their practice and involvement. The emphasis on lived experience continues in the next two chapters, which examine respectively how people at both centers construct communities and identities.[55]

*Chapter 5*

# REFUGE IN THE SANGHA: THE SHAPE OF BUDDHIST COMMUNITIES

It is the first Thursday of the new year (2001) and nine women in the New Jersey group are moving swiftly around the kitchen at Wat Phila preparing lunch for the monks.[1] Between Happy New Year's wishes and conversations about how people spent New Year's Eve, Phim is washing grapes and arranging them on a plate, Mū is frying chicken, and Thip is mixing cabbage, fish sauce, and spices in a gray stone mortar on the floor. I peel apples and pears at the long, stainless steel counter in the center of the kitchen and arrange them in a circular pattern on a glass plate so they can be presented to the monks. I have learned, after several months of cooking with the group, that fruit should be carefully peeled, not placed directly on the counter, and not sampled by me (or anyone else) before it is offered to the monks. Two silver trays in the center of the counter hold bite-sized samples of each food prepared today that will be offered to the Buddha image before the food is presented to the monks. As I cut the apples, I add a piece to each silver tray and chat with Næn about her daughter's school project.

A few minutes before eleven, Taan Ajahn, the head monk, and the four other resident monks file into the main hall of the temple and move to their places on the elevated platform that runs along the right-hand side of the room. Before they sit down, each monk kneels and bows deeply three times to the gold Buddha on the main altar, placing his elbows and palms on the ground with each bow. Thip wheels two carts filled with food from the kitchen to the platform where the monks sit and tells me to bring the rice. Næn and Phim present the silver trays of food to the Buddha image on the main altar and all of us kneel in front of the altar and bow to the Buddha image and the monks. In Pali, Phim, the leader of the New Jersey group, requests the refuges and precepts and Taan Ajahn administers them to the group, line by line. The monks then move to the other end of the platform where they take their meals and we serve the dishes of food, one by one. Taan Ajahn lays a piece of shiny orange cloth next to him and Phim places the plate of grapes she arranged on the cloth. She places her palms together and bows to the abbot as he picks up the plate to make room for Næn to present the seafood soup she made. The food presentation continues until the monks are literally surrounded by dishes of food.

Once the food is served, I kneel with the other women in front of the altar. Phim begins to chant in a high voice "Yo so bhagava araham sammasambud-dho."[2] As soon as she begins to chant, the monks start to eat. For the next thirty-five minutes, we chant in Pali in unison. Each woman remains kneeling on the red carpet during these eight chants and reads from a paperback book with each of the Pali chants written out in Thai script. Three quarters of the way through the service, the monks finish eating and quietly leave the main hall. After the chanting, Phim announces "fifteen minutes of meditation" and sets the alarm clock next to her. All is quiet. When the timer beeps after fifteen minutes, the monks have returned to their places on the raised platform.

In honor of the New Year, Taan Ajahn says the monks will give a special blessing today. Each of us gives some money to Phim as a donation and a way to make good merit for the year, and Phim sorts the money into five envelopes, one for each monk. We then sit with our palms together, our eyes closed, and our heads lowered slightly. The five monks begin to chant the blessing, which includes the names of each person present. I am sitting next to Thip and, at the few points in the chant when the tone drops, she whispers "sāthu" under her breath. The envelopes of cash are then presented to the monks.[3] The service concludes when Som motions for me to pass a small silver container of water to each woman for a *trūat nām* ritual. Under the monks' chanting and the trickles of the streams of water, I hear a few of the women reciting, almost under their breath, prayers that dedicate merit to their ancestors.

The service concludes, and Phim and Som linger to talk with the abbot while Næn and Nūan hurry to the kitchen to have their lunch. I fill my plate with rice, curries, and other food left from the monks' lunch, and, for the next thirty minutes or so, we stand around the stainless steel counter in the kitchen eating and talking, mostly about the food and plans for an upcoming festival at the temple. Mū hands out amulets that are a New Year's present from Maha Nom, one of the monks, and a few of the women exchange small gifts. After everyone has finished eating, we clean up the kitchen.

Before leaving the temple for the day, Thip tells me to come with her to say goodbye to Luāngphō Sot. We go back into the main hall and sit on the red carpet chatting. "People think life here is easy," she tells me, "but it's not.

You have taxes and a house and a car and bills. At least in Thailand you have some property and some land you can farm. . . . You have to buy your food here and it's not easy. And when you have kids, it's not easy." Thip grew up in northeast Thailand and has lived in the United States with her American husband and daughter for twenty years. Mū joins us a few minutes later and we talk some more before bowing three times to the Buddha image and the image of Luāngphō Sot to say goodbye. Some Thursdays a few women stay after lunch to stuff envelopes for temple mailings or gather at Nim's house nearby for makeovers. Today everyone is tired and heads home. This group of women has been preparing lunch for the monks several Thursdays each month for a number of years. Several of the women work outside their homes and carefully arrange their work schedules so they can have this time free.

Activities at CIMC on the first Thursday in January 2001 were probably much the same as when I participated several months later. For more than ten years, a group of practitioners has gathered on Thursday mornings from nine to one for a short meditation retreat. Narayan Liebenson Grady leads the retreats and meets individually with students for interviews about their practice once or twice a month.[4] On the Thursdays when she is not there, practitioners gather without a teacher and one of them rings the bell to signal a movement from sitting to walking meditation and vice versa. The participants gather for lunch at one when the session ends. While some practitioners stay the whole morning, others join and leave the group during the periods of walking meditation.

On a Thursday in mid-May, I stand outside the door of the main meditation hall just before noon waiting to hear the bell that signals the beginning of walking meditation and the time when people can join or leave the group. When the bell rings, Lucy, a practitioner in her thirties, carefully opens the door and moves slowly and deliberately down the stairs. I go through the open door into the meditation hall and join four women and one man who are walking slowly and carefully in stocking feet in a big circle around the perimeter of the room. A few more people enter the room during the next fifteen minutes, and then George rings the bell again and we sit down facing the Buddha on the altar. For the next forty-five minutes we sit in silent meditation. The windows are open and the sounds of cars and trucks passing outside are interspersed with the occasional bird call. Ten people sit during this session and a comfortable stillness pervades the air inside the room.

FIGURE 18. Walking meditation at CIMC. Photo courtesy of Posh Voynow.

At one, George rings the bell three times and several people put their palms together and bow their heads gently forward toward the Buddha as the third bell sound disappears into the distance. I stretch and join the others moving downstairs for lunch. People start to chat on the stairs, and three or four people head to the Whole Foods store around the corner to get some lunch. The rest of us prepare our food in the kitchen. While her lunch warms in the microwave, Amy tells me about the Compassion Arts group that she and several other artists from CIMC formed and the benefit for the group they held last night at the Somerville Museum. She brought strawberry rhubarb cobbler left over from the benefit to share with the group today. When Amy is finished with the microwave, Lucy heats up a stew that Jean, a practitioner and cook, left in the fridge.

A little later the group comes back from Whole Foods with sandwiches and snacks to share. Everyone pulls folding chairs up to the tables in the dining room and we begin to eat lunch. Conversation is free-flowing, with several conversations initially going on at once. Carol tells Amy that she was accepted for a one-week stay at Plum Village, Thich Nhat Hanh's center in France. Anissa asks what people thought about a recent speaker at CIMC and Lucy mentions a book she has been reading called *The Power of Now*. George inquires about Brenda, a woman who usually comes on Thursdays, and Mike asks about another practitioner's health.

As Amy heats the rhubarb cobbler, George says he has something he would like to discuss with the group. Since he came back from a ten-day retreat a few weeks ago, he says, his practice has been a mess. He wonders if anyone else has had this experience. The group is silent for a few minutes and then Art asks quietly, "Has your practice changed or have your expectations changed?" "That's a hard question," George replies. Carol says she has been living with a lot of doubt since her last retreat and has started to read *When Things Fall Apart* by Pema Chodron. "I'm trying to make friends with doubt. To invite it in and give it a cup of tea—though not a good cup—and to work with it," she says. Several other people identify with George's concern, and Anissa suggests he try equanimity practices or metta meditation. "It's often helped me," she says. George seems relieved and encouraged by this conversation and when I interview him later in the day he tells me that these gatherings and conversations are very important for him. He has been coming to CIMC on Thursdays for nearly ten years and, like most others in the group, has arranged his work schedule to have this time free.

Lunch concludes a little after two and people leave the center and head into the rest of their day. Narayan did not lead the retreat this morning, but when she does, she often concludes the last meditation session of the morning by saying, "In a few minutes you will be invited to bring your mindfulness into your daily living. Take your practice into your daily life by being in the present. Remember to keep things simple because the practice is simple . . . to be patient . . . and to be compassionate for those who are suffering in any way. May all beings be mindful, may all beings be patient, and may all beings be compassionate towards those who are suffering."

Thursday mornings are one of several times each week when people come to-gether at Wat Phila and CIMC. In their regular interactions with the monks, teachers, and each other, practitioners at Wat Phila and CIMC have created small groups or communities in these gatherings in which they engage with each other in ongoing conversations in the context of their Buddhist practice.[5] As Phim served grapes to Taan Ajahn, led the chanting, and had lunch with her friends, she engaged with the Thursday morning group in ways similar and different from how George did when he sat in silent meditation, went to Whole Foods, and talked about practice over lunch. While the communities or groups of people who gather regularly at Wat Phila and CIMC appear quite different when looked at casually from the outside, an examination of the structure and purpose of these groups from the inside will help us understand how practitioners organize themselves into groups at each center and relate to these groups religiously or spiritually and socially.[6]

The importance of communities or groups of people who gather regularly around a shared idea or purpose have been discussed by social scientists since Emile Durkheim.[7] Small groups, associations, and communities have been described in the American context since Alexis de Tocqueville wrote about them in the nineteenth century, and recent research has focused on small groups and the changing nature of people's ties to each other.[8] Today, many Americans, sociologist Robert Wuthnow argues, are bound together by loose, ad hoc connections that take flexible forms rather than by life-long commitments and connections, as they were in the past.[9] At Wat Phila and CIMC, this is evident in the fact that most practitioners, like many people in America more generally, live at distances from their families of origin in a society characterized by fluid ties between individuals and the breakdown of traditional networks. The Buddha himself thought some kind of communal life was central to his teachings, and different kinds of groups and communities have been important to Buddhist practitioners in the United States as well in different time periods and historical locations.[10]

This chapter describes how in the Buddhist tradition, people historically gathered in groups or communities, sometimes called sanghas, and how sangha and community are defined at Wat Phila and CIMC. I argue that practitioners at both centers value communal life, but that the ways they understand it and the forms that it takes differ due to family, language, and ethnic differences between the centers and because of the kinds of religious or spiritual and social support people seek. At Wat Phila, public merit-making rituals between the lay people and monastics are the glue that holds the community together. At CIMC the glue is also public, but has three components—support for meditation practice, example in others, and a sense of interconnection—that are invisible to the naked eye but still a powerful adhesive. These glues lead practitioners at each center to develop spiritual and social ties with each other, based on varying degrees of speaking and silence. Ultimately, it becomes evident that very different kinds of groups and communities exist in Theravada Buddhist America, even within the same organizations.

## History and Definition of Sangha

The word "sangha" is translated literally as "an assembly of *bhikkhus* or *bhikkhunis* [monks or nuns]" and has often been used more generally to describe a Buddhist religious community or monastic order.[11] In the Buddha's lifetime the sangha was described in an ideal sense and in a conventional sense. In the ideal sense, the Buddha's sangha includes all people, monastic or lay, who have "acquired the pure Dhamma-eye, gaining at least a glimpse of the Deathless."[12] Everyone who has experienced a true glimpse of what the Buddha taught is a member of the ideal sangha. In a more conventional sense, the word "sangha" refers to the community of monks and nuns ordained by the Buddha or by monks and nuns in lineages started by the Buddha. While members of the ideal and conventional sanghas may overlap, there are members of the ideal sangha who are not monks or nuns, and there are members of the conventional sangha who despite being monks or nuns have not had a glimpse of the "Dhamma-eye."

The Buddha generally used the word "sangha" to refer to ordained monks and nuns. Shortly after the Buddha attained enlightenment, he met five mendicants whom he had traveled with some years before. They prepared a place for him to teach and in this, his first sermon in the Deer Park, he spoke of a middle way and a Noble Eightfold Path. The mendicants welcomed the teachings, and one of them, Kondanna, understood immediately. He asked and received full ordination with the Buddha's words, "Come, *bhikkhu*, the Dhamma is well proclaimed. Follow the chaste course to the complete termination of suffering."[13] Kondanna was the first member of the *bhikkhu-sangha*, or the order of monks, and several other men were accepted in the days that followed. The Buddha accepted the first woman into the *bhikkhuni-sangha*, or conventional sangha of nuns, many years later at the request of his aunt and foster mother, Mahapajapati.[14] While the *bhikkhu-sangha* was maintained in the Theravada tradition from the Buddha's time to the present, the *bhikkhuni-sangha* ended in the eleventh century, the reasons for which are debated by scholars.[15]

The Buddha recognized lay people as members of the ideal sangha shortly after he gave his second sermon, a sermon about nonself. After this sermon the Buddha was approached by Yasa, the son of a rich merchant of Benares, who was experiencing considerable anxiety. The Buddha taught Yasa a dhamma suitable for lay people, but after hearing the higher dhamma, Yasa became an *arahant*, or enlightened one, and took ordination as a monk. Shortly thereafter, Yasa's father came looking for him, and when he heard the Buddha's teachings, he attained the dhamma-eye and became an *upasaka* or male lay devotee, committing himself to the Buddha, dhamma, and sangha. Later, Yasa's mother and sisters also attained the dhamma-eye and took the three refuges, becoming the first *upasikas*, or female lay people. Throughout his lifetime, the Buddha's followers included male and female lay people and monastics. Everyone who took refuge in the Buddha, dhamma, and sangha (the triple gem) became a part of the Buddha's fourfold *parisa*, or assembly of followers.

At Wat Phila, the word "sangha" is used in its conventional sense to refer only to members of the *bhikkhu-sangha*, or order of monks. The five resident monks are referred to as the sangha and are clearly distinguished in dress, behavior, and lifestyle from the lay people. While lay people work and marry and have children, monks do not marry. They live at the temple studying and teaching about dhamma. In a dhamma talk, Maha Nom distinguished between four different types of monks. Some monks are good only for ceremonies. Others are good for ceremonies and to study dhamma. A third kind is like the second but can also lead people toward liberation and teach about kamma. And a fourth kind of monk is like the second type but can also lead people away from the Buddha's teachings and toward power, greed, and delusion. "Good Buddhist monks must evaluate, analyze, and figure out whether the teachings are true to their own satisfaction, beyond any doubts, before accepting them as truths," Maha Nom taught.[16] The monks are guided in their conduct by the *vinaya*, a set of guidelines outlined by the Buddha.

In a dhamma talk one Sunday, Maha Nom told the people gathered that monks as well as male and female lay people are all involved in the Buddhist religion, but they are not all necessarily involved in the sangha. To explain the differences between monastics and lay people, Maha Nom told a story about a monkey who saw a fisherman throw a net into the river to catch fish. When the fisherman was not around, the monkey went to the net and tried to do what the fisherman did. Instead of throwing the net into the river, however, the monkey fell into the river and drowned. There are certain things, Maha Nom said, that monks can and should do like chanting, studying dhamma, meditating, and helping other people, and certain things monks should not do, like sing. The same principle applies to lay people. This is not to say that lay people should not chant, study dhamma, meditate, and help others, he said, but it is important that lay people and monks do not get their duties confused. Monks and lay people at Wat Phila must discharge their duties, roles, and responsibilities appropriately, he stated.[17]

While the lay people at Wat Phila are not part of the sangha as the word is used there, they are a part of a community, defined most generally as a group of people who regularly gather together around a set of common or shared interests. Lay people and monks gather as a community at Wat Phila around both their common Thai background and their shared interest in Buddhism, although there are a few Thais who are not Buddhists and a significant minority of people who are non-Thai Asians interested in Buddhism. Rather than having formal members, the center keeps a list of people who receive the temple's newsletter and are notified of upcoming events. The community is grounded in the dhamma; as outlined in temple newsletters, "The temple is an important place where the dhamma sets its roots in generosity, morality, and mental development (*bhavana*)." It is a place where Buddhists meet, under the guidance of monks, to investigate these qualities for themselves. "One can examine oneself to see if one needs to improve. . . . It is the most sacred place."[18]

At CIMC the word "sangha" is used more loosely to refer to everyone who is involved with the center.[19] While the sangha and lay members are two different parts of the community at Wat Phila, there are no monastics at CIMC, and so the word "sangha" refers to everyone who attends the center. After a Saturday morning of spring cleaning at CIMC, Mike, one of the regular practitioners, tapped me on the head with a feather duster and, with a twinkle in his eye, said "I knight you a member of the sangha of the triple gem."[20] "With a specialty in cleaning," I joked in response. While "sangha" is used most often at CIMC to refer to the community, Narayan also spoke about the sangha as the people, primarily male monastics, who carried this tradition to the present. She expressed great appreciation to these monastics and described the changing definition of "sangha" in the United States as one of the primary ways Buddhism is adapting. "Sangha today is inclusive and embraces anyone who wants to practice," she said. "To me, this is one of the beauties of Buddhism. It can go into a culture and fit into that culture. . . . Sangha in the West has shifted from a monastic model to a lay model of deeply committed practitioners who have not chosen to ordain and yet are living lives devoted to the teachings of the Buddha."[21] The changing definition of "sangha" among convert practitioners in the West has also been discussed at meetings of teachers in all three branches of Buddhism who teach American-born, largely white Buddhist practitioners in the United States.[22]

The sangha or community at CIMC is not built around upbringing or shared ethnic characteristics (although most of the practitioners are white), but around an interest in the Buddha's teachings and ideas and a commitment to practice those ideas as a path toward freedom from suffering. In describing the community at CIMC, Narayan emphasized this shared focus on practice as the glue that holds the group together: "One thing that is so wonderful about sangha is that we are all here for the same purpose. It is very much a family. It is just not the same kind of birth family which one doesn't choose. . . . But in this kind of a family we do choose to be here. And it is quite lovely because of that. We are all here because of the same aspiration, the same commitment to waking up."[23] In this way, the sangha at CIMC is an intentional community in which practitioners are invited to participate as they feel comfortable. Some people formally join the organization as members, which gives them reduced fees for courses, permission to borrow books from the library, and a combination to the lock on the front door so they can use the center during day and evening hours. Others are regularly involved, but have decided not to become members. Practitioners themselves tend not to know or care who is and is not a member of the center. In describing the way she would like the sangha at CIMC to work, Narayan told me that she wants the center to be as welcoming to people who want to come in silence and not speak or share anything with others as to people who want to connect with others and practice in community.[24] The different approaches practitioners can and do take toward the sangha has led it to be multifaceted and adaptable.

## The Shape of the Sangha

### WAT PHILA: ONE GROUP

In addition to defining and using the word "sangha" differently, the people who gather at Wat Phila and CIMC organize themselves into groups in distinct ways. First, apart from the five monastics, the lay community at Wat Phila conceives of itself overall as one large group. While smaller groups, like the New Jersey group described at the beginning of the chapter, certainly gather at the temple, lay people have the sense that these smaller groups are part of the larger one, and these small groups often orient their actions toward the larger temple community. When women from the New Jersey group, for example, took home enormous pots before a festival to "cook for the temple," they were cooking not just for the monks or their small group but for everyone who would come to the festival. Small groups of people who work in the gardens around the temple want the gardens to be beautiful not just for themselves or to please the monks but so that everyone has an attractive place to visit. And the inside of the temple buildings are also kept clean by small groups and individuals who want the temple to look nice for everyone.

A sense of one large community at Wat Phila is created, in part, by common routines that govern temple life. While the New Jersey group that gathers on Thursdays has its own culture, it is governed in its activities by a clear set of overarching guidelines about how things are done at the temple. Lunch is served for the monks at eleven, the kitchen needs to be cleaned in a certain way, the dishes and silverware go in certain cabinets. Someone who usually prepares lunch for the monks on Wednesdays but arrives on a Thursday would easily fit into the group's routine because these mealtime routines, like other temple routines, are common across the small cooking groups at Wat Phila.

The sense of Wat Phila as one large group is further reinforced at Sunday gatherings that include a meditation class, *tak bāt* ceremony, lay chanting service, and dhamma talk and other merit-making rituals Lifecycle rituals at Sunday services also create a feeling of one community: after the chanting service and a brief period of meditation, financial donations are often made to the sangha by a person or family in honor of a birthday or on the death anniversary of a loved one. The person wishing to make the donation goes forward and offers it to the monks. Everyone at the temple sits together in front of the monks during these donations, which reinforces a sense of cohesiveness among those gathered, particularly because practitioners believe that the blessings that follow the donations come to everyone in the group. "Even when you do not make the donation," one woman explained to me as I sat quietly while an offering was made, "you sit like this [hands palms together in front of the chest] and pay attention because the blessing comes back to everyone." One Sunday in December, the monks chanted for a man who had passed away a few days before. A large photograph of the man, a member of the Air Force, was displayed in a gold frame covered in small purple flowers in front of the altar. The man's wife, daughter, and a few other relatives had come to the temple for this ceremony and after the morning chanting service and dhamma talk, the monks did special chanting for him. These blessings are often repeated, in this same group setting, at certain intervals after an individual's death.

Weddings are often celebrated at Wat Phila in the context of the whole community. By monastic guidelines, Thai monks are not officially allowed to marry a couple, but they are often asked to give a blessing. Dr. Nūa*ng*, a Thai woman, was married to Don, an American man, in February 2001. Don had started to come with Dr. Nūa*ng* to the temple several months before and often sat quietly in the back watching and participating in some of the ceremonies. They were officially married by a judge on a Tuesday and had come to the temple the previous Sunday for a blessing from the monks. They sat in front of the monks, with most of the others seated behind them. Together they lit a candle, which the abbot then took and dipped into a bowl of water as part of the blessing for the couple. After the blessing, Dr. Nūa*ng* and Don sat next to each other on stools. Crowns of string were placed on their heads and the crowns were connected by another piece of string. A large, gold bowl of water with flowers floating on top was prepared next to the couple. Everyone at the temple was invited to pour some of the water from a gold cup over the couples' hands to wish them well. The normal chanting service and dhamma talk followed this ceremony, and at the potluck lunch that concludes every Sunday morning gathering, a friend of the couple brought a cake with "Congratulations" written in icing. In Thailand, this ceremony likely would have been held at home or in a rented ballroom. In the States not only did it take place at the temple, but rather than being a separate event performed on a day and time apart from routine activities, the monks blessing for the couple occurred within the context of a regular Sunday gathering and served to reinforce a sense of the larger community.

Small groups of practitioners also often dress in white and take the Eight Precepts at the temple on Sundays in the context of a regular service. Practitioners vow to abstain from killing, lying, stealing, engaging in sexual acts, drinking, eating after noon, entertainment, and wearing perfume and jewelry. In taking the Eight Precepts on their birthdays or on *wan phra* days that correspond to the phase of the moon, practitioners make merit for themselves and are recognized and affirmed in the context of the community.[25] While the reasons that people take the Eight Precepts on Sundays rather than on their actual birthdays or *wan phra* days are normally related to their work schedules, the result is a greater sense of one temple community. On other occasions, people take the precepts to try to strengthen the community as a whole. The abbot of the temple was ill throughout this research, and groups of people periodically decided to take the Eight Precepts because they wanted to donate the merit gained through their meditation and good works to the abbot to improve his health. A similar communal or group motivation is evident in December of each year when the king of Thailand's birthday is celebrated at the temple. People take the Eight Precepts on the Sunday closest to his actual birthday as a way to dedicate their merit to the king and reinforce their membership not just in the community at Wat Phila, but in the Thai community in the United States and Thailand more generally.

A sense of belonging to one community at Wat Phila is further constructed and reinforced through festivals held at Wat Phila about eight times every year. Festivals such as *Kathin* and *Āsālahbūchā* celebrate Buddhist holidays while

FIGURE 19. Thai food being served at a festival. Photo courtesy of Thira Thiramongkol.

festivals like *Wan Chāt* celebrate Thai holidays. Festivals provide opportunities for many people who do not often come to the temple to gather and celebrate their common Thai Buddhist identities and backgrounds. Some temples also have smaller gatherings on American holidays like Thanksgiving and Mother's Day. On all of these occasions many people involved in Wat Phila comes together, and this cycle of festivals is one of the primary ways practitioners come to conceive of themselves as one large community.

FIGURE 20. People donate rice and other items to the monks on alms rounds at a festival. Photo courtesy of Thira Thiramongkol.

## CIMC: MANY SMALL GROUPS

Unlike at Wat Phila, practitioners at CIMC generally gather in a series of small groups, conceiving of themselves as a series of small interlocking communities. When I asked Narayan to describe CIMC as a community, she talked about it as "many groups." In a typical week during my fieldwork, practitioners gathered more than twenty scheduled times.[26] On Mondays, for example, practitioners could attend the morning sitting (from seven to seven-forty-five), the evening sitting (from six to six-forty-five), the chanting group (from six-fifteen to seven o'clock), an evening class (from seven-fifteen until nine), or the Engaged Buddhism discussion group. While some practitioners are involved in more than one group, these groups meet at separate times and there is no time during the week or the calendar year when everyone gathers at CIMC as at the festivals at Wat Phila. This configuration of gatherings may be partially related to the difficulty of coordinating the schedules of many individuals, but is more related to the spiritual and social connections people are looking for.

Practitioners at CIMC tend to describe themselves as primarily involved with one particular group.[27] At my first class at CIMC, I heard one woman describe herself to another as a "Larry groupie." "I just attend every class he gives," she said. Rick, another practitioner, told me he only attends the Tuesday night drop-ins with Narayan. Timothy comes only to morning meditation sessions. When I interviewed Donald, he told me that his home at CIMC is in the Old Yogis class.

On Wednesday nights the largest number of people gather at CIMC for a meditation session (from six-forty-five to seven-thirty) and talk (from seven-thirty to nine). While these gatherings have a consistent structure, like Sunday mornings at Wat Phila, there is not a regular group of people who attend. Every week the talk is given by a different person, and of the teachers, only the one giving the talk attends. Different people also lead the meditation sessions that precede the talks and serve as greeters. Before the evening meditation session and talk, practitioners are invited to do "mindful housework" (between five-thirty and six-thirty) around the center. Three or four people usually come for community housecleaning, only one of whom came regularly while I was at CIMC.

While lifecycle rituals at Wat Phila include everyone and reinforce a sense of one community, these rituals at CIMC take place in times apart from regular events. A religious or spiritual sense of connection among practitioners, however, does result from these events. Several times each year practitioners at CIMC are invited to a special ceremony, often on a Friday evening, to take the refuges and the precepts. In July 2001, practitioners joined the teachers in a "Celebrating the Dharma" ceremony. About forty people gathered to take the refuges and precepts, rededicating themselves to their meditation practices. Of the four hundred people who belong to CIMC, it is telling that only forty attended this ceremony, which is one of only a few times during the year when such a community gathering is held. Weddings, commitment ceremonies, and memorial services are also held at CIMC, usually as small private affairs not announced to the community at large and normally attended only by the people being committed or wed and a few family members and close friends.[28] For a number of years, Narayan has also led a bereavement ceremony every year as a "simple remembrance of our loved ones who have died, both recently and further in the past."[29] While a few of the people being remembered are members of the community, the majority are not. For this reason this gathering, while unifying people around their losses, does not unify people around shared history or memory.

The cycle of Buddhist holidays celebrated in festivals at Wat Phila are not recognized or a part of practice at CIMC. In fact Carol, a practitioner in her forties, told me she does not see in Buddhism "any real celebrations" and relies on her pagan community to celebrate humans' connections to the earth and other beings.[30] On the full moon day in May, Buddhists around the globe celebrate the birth, death, and enlightenment of the Buddha. After a Thursday morning retreat near this date, Jaspar brought a chocolate cake from Whole Foods with his lunch. He put the cake on the table and offered it to everyone, saying it was for the Buddha's birthday a few days ago. "It's not too late now to celebrate." Although Jasper is a regular and well-liked participant in the group, few people looked up from their conversations, and no one responded to his comment. Their silence conveyed the message that these "traditional" Buddhist holidays are not recognized or important to them and others at CIMC.

The teachers and center directors have tried various things over the years to create times when people can come together in one larger community at CIMC. They hold potluck gatherings, gardening days, fall and spring cleaning days, storytelling days, a gratitude gathering on Thanksgiving, a holiday gathering in December, and a New Year's Eve gathering. When these occasions mark holidays, they are American rather than Buddhist holidays. While people turn out for these events, they are rarely attended by large numbers of people, suggesting to me that the small groups in which people gather at CIMC fulfill their needs. During 2001, the holiday gathering was one of the most highly attended events, with more than eighty people in attendance. While people at CIMC told me over and over in interviews about how much they value the

FIGURE 21. People eating at a Celebration of the Dharma gathering at CIMC. Photo courtesy of Ruth Nelson.

FIGURE 22. Larry Rosenberg and Pash Voynow talk at a gathering to celebrate the dharma. Photo courtesy of Ruth Nelson.

community, they do not value or relate to it primarily in a way that leads to high attendance at these kinds of large social gatherings.

## SILENT AND SPEAKING COMMUNITIES

To fully understand the shape of the communities at Wat Phila and CIMC it is important to consider what it sounds like when people gather together at each place. Researchers have tended to conceive of communities in ways that involve conversation, discussion, and sometimes debate about issues of common concern. While both Wat Phila and CIMC include these kinds of speaking communities, they also include very quiet, even silent, communities. Developing speaking and silent communities and finding the balance between them has been challenging for the founding monks, teachers, and lay people at both centers.

While practitioners at Wat Phila consciously lower their voices when they enter the temple, the community there is primarily a speaking community. Practitioners recite chants, listen to the monks chant, and hear a dhamma talk from a monk almost every time they go to the temple. They chat with each other socially as they prepare food for the monks and while eating lunch with friends after the services. At festivals the meditation hall is often filled with the sounds of practitioners or monks chanting, and the area outside where people have their lunch is loud with many layers of conversation. While the monks at Wat Phila can support silent practice, more often than not communal practice does not take place in silence. The meditation class on Sunday mornings is held in silence, and occasionally one or two practitioners meditate together after the services on Sunday conclude, but most of the communal gatherings involve voices. In founding the temple, the abbot and some lay leaders were concerned that the social voices could overcome the religious purposes of the gathering, and that is partially why the abbot established clear informal expectations about how people are to behave at the temple. "People must be aware of their thoughts, speech, and actions while at the temple and must help to keep peace, cleanliness and orderliness," says an article in a temple newsletter.[31] Noise, especially during periods of silent meditation, has often been an issue at the temple. The kitchen is right next to the hall where meditation takes place, and people often speak loudly in the kitchen or allow the doors to slam between the rooms in a way that interrupts the silence. The monks and lay leaders at Wat Phila have recently decided to build a new building, in part to create a place where silent practice can take place away from these sounds.

While the communities at CIMC are both silent and speaking, the teachers and long-term practitioners create an environment where the speaking must develop from, or at least respect, the silence. In founding CIMC, Larry Rosenberg was very concerned about how to balance a place for silent contemplation with the development of a community. He decided to organize the center around meditation practice and at first was less concerned with developing a community or social group. At CIMC's tenth anniversary celebration he explained, "What I learned before CIMC started, having been in a number of sanghas . . . [is that] unless the commitment to practice is central there will be a community but what people are communing over is unclear. . . . I saw it fall apart many times. And so what we really emphasized when we started . . . was to defend the meditation hall with our lives, to put it mildly. We built a moat, submachine guns, barbed wire around the meditation hall. In other words, although community is very important, the feeling was, and we all agreed on this, . . . that unless there was a core of people who had tasted some of the fruit of contemplative life that any rush to create a community would be based on something that wouldn't be all that stable."[32] "Community," as Larry used the term here, referred to socializing that he at least initially assumed was antithetical to real practice, which happened in silence and was the basis around which the initial group of people at CIMC gathered.

The silent groups that formed in the early years of CIMC became speaking communities gradually as a core of people developed around the practice. In outlining his vision for the center in 1985, Larry spoke of the value of silent communal practice: "So every time you do something like that [sitting with a group] we are all bringing each other along. It's not an isolated kind of thing. That's the power of sangha, of community. It's not just to be dependent on each other. It's actually to take each other beyond where we could go individually."[33] Gathering together silently to support each other's practice was important in the early years. In the early 1990s, the center began to hold more communal gatherings that involved speaking. In 1991, Larry said in an interview that this greater emphasis on community was a conscious change at the center that came out of having a group of people convinced of the value of practice.[34] Community at CIMC no longer meant just social conversations, but support in contemplation and daily life that comes through friendships. The speaking community "has developed," Larry explained in 2001, "as people have developed in their practice."[35] While silent communities were central in the early years of the center, speaking communities developed gradually when their volume would not threaten to overtake the center. And the decision to renovate the center in 1999 was motivated, in part, by a desire to create more spaces for speaking and socializing away from the meditation hall.

Practitioners are divided in how they value the silent and speaking communities. While Ken says he has made a few friends at the center, he particularly values the silent support he gets from other practitioners: "Having people to sit with on a regular basis is tremendously supportive. . . . There are people that I see almost every night at the six o'clock sitting [and I doubt that] we've exchanged five words in ten years, . . . but I feel a lot of comfort in terms of their regularity. . . . It's people on the same path, doing the same thing, having the same commitment." John explained the silent bonds that many practitioners described to me, saying, "Metals don't meld because aluminum speaks to the copper. . . . The sangha bond is that—absolutely nondogmatic and unsentimental."

The second group of people at CIMC, which includes most of the practitioners, values silence and speaking in varying proportions. Members of the Old Yogis class practice together silently and then talk about their practice in small groups or together as a class on Thursday nights. In a class I took with Michael, several of the participants said they were there both because they wanted to learn meditation practice and because they wanted to do it and talk about it with other people. While the Thursday morning retreat is silent, lunch that follows is not. In talking with George after the morning described at the beginning of this chapter he told me, "The groups are another helpful thing. Having lunch here and hearing about how other people's practice is going— it is nice to realize that I am not alone in this stuff. Sometimes I get helpful ideas, and I can see how things relate to my own practice." While many of these conversations happen at the center, it is important to recognize that as people have formed friendships and seen each other socially outside the center, the practice has been discussed in a range of settings. Becky, whose story begins this book, told me that the thing she values most about group practice is the discussions with other practitioners that result. "It is in these discussions, either about daily life things or sitting," she told me, "where I can be really open and we can look at really deep things that are hard to talk about with people who don't practice."

## Why the Different Shapes?

Wat Phila and CIMC have roughly the same number of people in their core groups and on the periphery and, as we saw in chapter 3, people get involved with these centers for the same three broadly defined reasons. They want to learn about Buddhism, they want to be with like-minded people, and often they are going through or have recently gone through a difficult life event. Despite these similarities, they gather in differently shaped groups at Wat Phila and CIMC. While this may be partially related to people's schedules and availability, as argued by Robert Wuthnow in *Loose Connections: Joining Together in America's Fragmented Communities*, it is more likely related to family, language, and ethnic differences between the centers and to the religious and social reasons why people gather in the first place.[36]

First, it is important to note that there is evidence at both centers that some people gather in groups, in part, to overcome a sense of loneliness or isolation they experience in their day-to-day lives. As first-generation immigrants, many practitioners at Wat Phila live at a distance from their families of origin. While some live with spouses and children, others live alone, and many described, in direct and indirect ways, feelings of loneliness or isolation. I chatted with Sit on a chilly winter morning before the services started and she told me, "I've lived in this country for thirty-seven years and I still get so cold. I'm cold in here," she told me, pointing to her heart. Plā told me directly one morning that he comes to the temple, "to overcome loneliness because I am far from my family." Several people have told me that if they lived in Thailand they would probably not be as involved in a temple because they would have more friends and more things to do. Some people also come to CIMC because they are struggling with feeling alone or disconnected in the world. Michael, one of the teachers, told me that "a lot of people feel very isolated in this culture. . . . It's a very individualistic culture. It's extremely fragmented, and people's lives are extremely demanding and self-involved and people can barely keep up with things. So it's very easy to feel isolated. And when you do come to groups here [at CIMC] there are usually discussion periods where people begin to share things that they're working with. And it's really valuable."[37]

Factors related to family, language, and ethnic background also help to explain the configuration of the groups at Wat Phila and CIMC. First, the fact that practitioners meet in one big group at Wat Phila is related to the fact that families are involved there. Very few families are involved with CIMC and, in fact, it would be difficult for a couple to be involved as a couple unless they were both interested in attending the same small group. The family bonds that underlie many practitioners' involvement in Wat Phila lead to large group gatherings everyone can attend rather than a series of smaller, more specialized groups.

Second, language and ethnic identification influence the shape of the groups at Wat Phila and CIMC. Shared language, history, ethnic background, and experience among practitioners at Wat Phila lead them to view each other as a more primary reference group than are groups at CIMC and to want to gather and identify with that group They are surrounded by majority white cultures in their neighborhoods, sometimes even within their families, and often in their workplaces. While it takes a little while for new practitioners to feel involved or part of the community at Wat Phila, the rituals and ceremonies are generally somewhat familiar, and they make friends, or at least acquaintances, with other practitioners relatively quickly. Practitioners generally describe the temple as more communal than temples in urban Thailand, meaning that the group plays a greater role. They also describe Thai people in the United States as more religious than those in Thailand. Dr. Nūa*ng* told me that many people in Thailand do not have as many opportunities to participate in ceremonies, hear the dhamma, or learn meditation. "When I told my mom and sister [in Thailand] about my activities here, they say I am so lucky. The temple is exceptionally better than most," she told me. Ku*ng* also sees Thai people in the United States as more involved with the group of Buddhist practitioners: "Over here you don't have many friends close by or next door. You have fewer activities and then you become interested [in Buddhism]. And you don't know what to do. So you go to the temple and try to practice," she explained.

While white American-born people who are involved with CIMC share the English language, they do not view themselves as sharing a history and culture in a way that would lead them to gather in one group for rituals and festivals. They do share holidays, like Thanksgiving and New Year's, though most celebrate these holidays in places other than at CIMC. Rituals and ceremonies that were a part of Theravada Buddhism in Asia were largely left there when the first white Americans brought it to the United States, and people at CIMC have formed small groups because they are better suited to their religious and social reasons for gathering.

The final reason the groups at Wat Phila and CIMC are defined and organized differently is that people come to them in search of different religious and social experiences. People come to Wat Phila looking to participate in religious practices that are communal by definition. While these practices could be done in small groups, practitioners' common backgrounds and views of each other as a primary reference group lead religious rituals to be performed publicly by the whole group. Practitioners at Wat Phila are also generally looking for social experiences outside of their religious practices. At CIMC, practitioners come to learn about the Buddha's teachings and to practice with a group. The group is public but often in silent ways that are then affirmed in conversation in small supportive groups. While some people come to CIMC wanting to socialize outside of the practice, they quickly find that socializing at CIMC develops directly out of the meditation practice and largely does not exist apart from the practice.

### WAT PHILA: THE GLUE IS MERIT

A community of at least one monk and one lay person is essential to Buddhism as understood at Wat Phila, and people go there to publicly perform religious ceremonies that require at least one monastic and one lay person. Merit is the glue that holds the community together through religious ceremonies based in exchange between the monks and lay people. The concept of merit evolved in the early centuries of the Buddhist tradition and was shaped in Thailand by the *Apadana* texts, which have not yet been translated into English. The idea of kamma, or consequences of actions performed in previous lifetimes, also developed from the Buddha's teachings as lay people learned that to accumulate good kamma they should "make merit" by acting virtuously and giving alms to the monastics in public ceremonies that legitimate its value.[38]

Lay people at Wat Phila gain merit through a process of exchange between lay people and monastics that is validated by the community. Lay people provide the monks with food, housing, and other physical necessities required to live. The monks provide the lay people with merit, spiritual teaching, and guidance in exchange. The centrality of this exchange requires that monks and lay people live in close proximity to each other and come together regularly in some kind of community. Even the forest monks in northeast Thailand, who go off to meditate alone, normally remain close to a village so they can receive their regular alms or food for the day.[39] Lay people make merit every time they come to Wat Phila and make any kind of donation to the temple or the sangha. Merit making also reinforces the differences between monks and lay people and a sense of one lay and one monastic community living in relation to each other. Dr. Malin calls merit the "heart of Buddhism," because it encourages practitioners to do good. Merit is central both to the purpose of the temple and to the future of Buddhism in the United States, according to practitioners at Wat Phila. "We give donations to the monks because the monks are the sangha and in order for the sangha to continue we have to *tham bun* [make merit]—to make the teachings of Buddhism continue for humans," one layman explained to me.

Practitioners at Wat Phila make merit primarily through giving, and Maha Nom explained the merit gained through giving in a talk he gave one Sunday at the temple. In this talk, Maha Nom told a story about a time when the Buddha's stepmother, who was also his aunt, wanted to give the Buddha the finest robe for him to wear. She grew cotton plants, spun the thread, and hired the best weaver to make the cloth. When the cloth was finished, she went to see the Buddha and offered the cloth to him. The Buddha did not accept the cloth but told his stepmother to give it to the overseer of monks as a whole without specifying which monk would receive it. The Buddha's stepmother was upset and she left with the cloth and asked Ananda, the Buddha's assistant, why the Buddha would not accept the fine cloth. Ananda did not know, and when he asked the Buddha, the Buddha told him that there are different levels of merit generated by giving. The Buddha then told Ananda that the merit gained is the highest if the giver makes the donation without specifying which monk is to receive it. It is because the Buddha wanted his stepmother to receive the most merit that he did not accept her gift.[40]

Practitioners at Wat Phila also make merit by donating food, time, and money to the temple. The people who make breakfast and lunch for the monks every day make merit in their donations, as do people who make food for festivals or bring cases of bottled water or soda to the temple on their birthdays. While merit around food is normally made inside the temple, I accompanied several monks and laywomen to Red Lobster one weekday for lunch.

The monks ordered their food, and when the waiter brought the food to the table, the laywomen picked up the plates and presented them to the monks in a particular way, ritualistically offering the food so merit was made. Dr. Malin explained, "You prepare food, that's the first giving . . . and you give the monks things necessary for living . . . cloth, food, a towel, things to clean yourself, like soap and medicine." People also make merit by making donations to the monks and temple. People drop money in donation boxes at the temple, offer it to the monks in a ceremony, tape a bill to a money tree, or hand it to a woman at the donation table at a festival. Before festivals, announcements of the event are mailed to everyone at the temple, and people who cannot attend are invited to mail in a donation as a way to make merit. A final way people can make merit and simultaneously add to the sense of the community at the temple is by helping out around the temple, especially at festivals. In preparing the building, making the food, and cleaning up afterward, people make merit for themselves and others through their actions.[41]

In addition to wanting to make merit, people come to Wat Phila to socialize with their friends, who often live some distance away. While the New Jersey group comes to the temple on Thursdays to make merit through their donations to the monks, the gathering is also a time for them to speak Thai and socialize with Thai people, something that may not happen in other parts of their lives. For most Thai practitioners at Wat Phila, the temple has a dual purpose of providing an opportunity for them to participate in religious ceremonies and providing a place where they can visit with friends and maintain their connections to other Thai people. Sam, a Thai lay person, explained Wat Phila's religious and social purposes for him, saying, "It is a place for socializing. We gather, come in, bring the food and offer it, have lunch together . . . but it has something beyond that. If you think you want to come and see that much, do that much, yes, this is a place for the social . . . but if you want to do more, it's up to you." Sam does a lot of work around the temple and also often meditates there on Sunday afternoons after other people have gone home. To get something out of his involvement in Wat Phila, he says he has put his heart into it. "I come here . . . I try to help get some work done here. . . . I want to look for something that means something to me. I put my life into it. Put my heart into it. . . . That is what I thought I should do."

After clearly acknowledging that the temple is a place she comes to see her friends, Kanyā also told me she sees herself doing religious work as she takes care of a flower bed in the parking lot: "About five years ago, I started to do the flower bed out there. And for me I think like the crystal ball is in me. It is my soul . . . and what happens is we coat it with our greed, our experience . . . and we can't see things—we see delusion. And to get that off I will do anything—volunteer work. To have a soft heart . . . to look at another person or life more compassionately . . . maybe I can train myself to be giving and not just give food and go home. I give my soul, my self, everything to gain wisdom." People come to the temple, she told me later in our conversation, because they want to have a better life.

### CIMC: THREE GLUES

While the first generation of convert Theravada Buddhists left the monastic sangha behind in Asia, they gradually returned to the idea that communal gatherings or some sense of community is an important part of Buddhist practice in America. A sense of community at CIMC developed not around exchanges between the teachers and lay people, even though they do occur, or around notions of merit, but around small groups as sources of support, as examples of people practicing, and as ways to experience a sense of interconnection with other people. While merit is the glue that holds the community together at Wat Phila, these three experiences (support, example, interconnection) are the glue at CIMC. Narayan defined the sangha as the community around you, and taking refuge in it as taking refuge in the fact that these people are here and supporting each other's practice.[42] These connections are particularly important, she argued, because much of what Buddhism teaches is so different from what the culture teaches. People trying to live a Buddhist path need support.

People come to the sangha or community at CIMC looking for support in their own practice. Some people strongly believe that individuals can go further, higher, or deeper in their own practice by sitting with a group and drawing on the group's energy, while others reject this approach and emphasize instead the pragmatic benefits that come from being with a group. Practicing alone is also difficult physically, Narayan acknowledged in a talk, and the sangha provides a group of people who support practice: "It is often more difficult to sit on one's own, especially in the first few years. The Buddha did not even particularly encourage it. Being able to sit alone is necessary and builds self-reliance. But in a lifetime of practice, we need one another and we can be supported as well as support others by practicing together."[43] Michael, another teacher, believes group support gets people to practice. "I always tell people that I benefit enormously from group practice, that I almost can't imagine having done this practice and sticking with this practice without the group support at some time or another. . . . I would say that most people wouldn't sit the way they do if they didn't have that group support. They wouldn't sit as long."[44] Catherine, a long-term practitioner, says that this support and discipline is what CIMC provides for her. Fred says he came to appreciate the power of sangha as he recognized that often he would not be practicing if it were not for the group. Other people "are keeping me from running out of the room right now . . . the supporting silence with other beings despite not knowing them, you share something important." There is a lot of energy in groups, many practitioners told me, and when they are having a hard time meditating and can open their eyes in the midst of it to see the others sitting around them, "like Buddhas," they are encouraged to continue.

Some people emphasize the examples for their own practice they see in the sangha at CIMC. David, a long-term practitioner, told me that CIMC is important to him on a day-to-day basis: "Knowing the sangha is there, knowing the center is there, knowing that people are sitting, knowing that people are practicing the dharma and trying to see things more clearly, live their lives in a more mindful way, I feel is something that I sort of carry with me." Christine described the center similarly as a "reminder" of people who pay attention to their practice and to other parts of their lives. She and a colleague at work are both involved in CIMC, and she told me a story of the two of them being in a very stressful meeting at work and signaling to each other across the table by taking deep breaths. "We would just do something mockingly," she told me, "but it was real. . . . It sounds very trite, but it actually had a very . . . great meaning." These deep breaths were for both of them reminders of the community and people's intentions to live in a mindful way. It is interesting to note that practitioners look primarily to each other, rather than to the teachers, for the examples of practice they describe. In few of my conversations did people talk about Larry, Michael, or Narayan directly as role models or as the examples they strove to emulate. Donald spoke about his fellow students in the Old Yogis class as examples or inspirations for him and his practice: "It's also very powerful, particularly in the Old Yogis class, to sit with a lot of people who are doing what you're doing. It's really wonderful to have these people with such, to me, really wonderful aspirations. To really be trying to see what this life's all about . . ."

While people often come to CIMC in search of meditation teaching and later support for their own practice, finally what many describe experiencing in the group is a sense of interconnection. While merit is the group currency at Wat Phila, this sense of interconnection ultimately is the currency at CIMC. By interconnection, practitioners mean a sense of connection to other people that they gain by sitting with those people in group practice. Becky says that for her this practice is about connection, not renunciation, as in a more monastic model. "To me, just sitting with others," Anissa began, "there is nothing better, because we're all doing this, . . . It's just a deep support and I feel so connected and so much gratitude and love pours out of me." During times when she was not able to be at CIMC, Anissa formed small practice groups with friends because she believes this sense of interconnection that comes from being part of a group is beneficial to everyone involved. Bob also pointed to this same sense of interconnectedness as part of the way he relates to groups at CIMC: "Whether people ever experience it or not, they're part of it . . . hopelessly part of this connectedness. You can either take part in it or not, but that's where the foundation is." This sense of connection has increased for David as he has been involved with CIMC over the years. "Now I feel there is more sangha," he told me. "There are a number of people who have been coming here for years. People know each other more. There is a greater sense of interconnection I think among the members." Jaspar says the practice leaves him with a wonderful sense of connection with other people on a lot of different levels. "What surprises me too," he said, "is connectedness with other people."

Narayan emphasizes the interconnectedness practitioners experience through their sitting meditation in a story she often tells at CIMC. The story comes from the opening section of a book called *Opening the Hand of Thought* by Kosho Uchiyama Roshi.

> Behind a temple there was a field where there were many squashes growing on a vine. One day a fight broke out among them and the squashes broke up into two groups and made a big racket shouting at one another. The head priest heard the uproar and, going out to see what was going on, found the squashes quarreling. In his booming voice the priest scolded them. He said, 'Hey, squashes! What are you doing out there fighting? Everybody meditation! Meditate right now!' The priest taught them how to meditate. 'Fold your legs like this; sit up and straighten your back and neck.' While the squashes were meditating in the way the priest had taught them their anger subsided and they settled down. Then the priest quietly said, 'Everyone please put your hand on top of your head.' When the squashes felt the tops of their heads, they found some weird string attached there. It turned out to be a vine that connected them all together. 'Hey, this is really strange,' the squashes said, 'Here we've been arguing when actually we're all tied together and living just one life. What a mistake! It's just as the priest said.' After that the squashes all got along with each other quite well. [45]

After telling the story Narayan concludes, "If a squash can do it, we can too. The inner stillness that the squashes came to through sitting quietly together allowed them to recognize their interconnection. We recognize our interconnection as well when we are willing to let go of our personal agendas in relationship and work with our attachment to having things be a particular way."[46] While this sense of interconnection may theoretically come from groups of any size, the small groups at CIMC provide the kind of supportive environment in which people can become familiar enough with one another to experience the kind of interconnection described.

The sense of interconnection practitioners describe experiencing at CIMC has developed largely since Buddhism arrived in the United States and points to an important way that the dhamma is changing and molding to its new organizational and cultural environments. As Thanissaro Bhikkhu argues in his recent article, "Romancing the Buddha," the idea of interconnectedness comes not from the Buddha's teachings but from Western culture, specifically from ideas developed by the German Romantics through which the Buddha's teachings have been interpreted. The Romantics' contributions to American culture have led, largely through psychology and psychotherapy to "concepts such as integration of the personality, self-fulfillment, and interconnectedness, together with the healing powers of wholeness, spontaneity, playfulness, and fluidity" to become "part of the air we breathe" and in turn part of Buddhism as taught and interpreted in the States.[47]

Like practitioners at Wat Phila, many people also come to CIMC in search of social connections. The Buddha taught refuge in wise friendship, Narayan said once in a talk, and having wise friends is an important part of being on the path. "Ananda, the Buddha's attendant," she said, "once asked the Buddha whether having good friends was half of the entire path. The Buddha replied that not only is having good friends half of the path, it is the entire path . . . if one wants to be patient, be around those who are patient . . . if one wants to be generous, be around those who are generous."[48] Practitioners are generally not interested in making connections with others, however, apart from the practice, and the people who are most disappointed with the interpersonal connections available at CIMC tend to be those looking for a more general kind of socializing. People who are serious about silent practice and are looking for others to talk with out of this silence fit into the social environment at CIMC. Carol, for example, came to CIMC specifically to socialize with practitioners: "I decided I needed to be around people who were also practicing, at least once in a while," she told me. "My own personal friends were not participants and didn't study Buddhism, so if I was going to have a group of people who did, I should at least hear their experiences. So I started going to Thursdays." It is only through the practice that the structure of CIMC encourages social bonds to be formed. Not everyone comes with these social intentions, but people who are involved with the center for a number of years normally develop at least casual friendships.

## The Results of Involvement in Wat Phila or CIMC

Out of their involvement with Wat Phila and CIMC, practitioners develop both religious or spiritual and social ties with the monks, teachers, and other practitioners. By religious or spiritual ties I mean those that people see as core or essential to their Buddhist practice. At Wat Phila these ties are the relationships between the monks and lay people through which merit is made, while at CIMC these are primarily the relationships people have with each other and the teachers that lead to their sense of interconnection. By social ties, I mean relationships of friendship and support that people develop that are not directly related to their Buddhist practice but that help them in their day-to-day lives. Practitioners at Wat Phila and CIMC form both religious or spiritual and social ties through their involvement with the centers.

### WAT PHILA: SIMULTANEOUS TIES

Religious or spiritual and social ties at Wat Phila are formed simultaneously through the rituals, ceremonies, and festivals that are at the core of temple life. Out of these experiences, practitioners gain merit and connections with the monks that they believe will lead to better lives. The community, at least of monks, is essential for these ties to be formed and the merit that practitioners accumulate, they believe, helps them in other aspects of their lives. People also draw on lessons they learn in dhamma talks and more generally as they go about their lives outside the temple.

In nurturing their practitioners, the community at Wat Phila, like immigrant religious communities in the United States more generally, also fosters the formation of strong social ties. Socially, people spend time together outside the temple on New Year's, other holidays, or in social groups like the Thai golf club. One Sunday morning when there were few people at the temple, one of the monks told me that everyone was golfing today in a benefit for children in northeast Thailand. Some people describe the temple as a family, and the communal weddings and funerals and frequent birthday celebrations make the community much like a large extended family. Particularly the male practitioners at Wat Phila and other temples across the United States have developed business networks with each other, and people occasionally do favors for one another by carrying small items back and forth for friends and family members between Thailand and the United States. The ties among practitioners and also between practitioners and the monks also occasionally help people in need of social services. I sat with a woman one Thursday, for example, as she asked the abbot to suggest people in Texas who could help a Thai friend of hers there who was having some personal problems. The abbot gave her several phone numbers, mostly trying to link her friend to a temple close to where she lives.

### CIMC: OVERLAPPING TIES

Strong spiritual and social ties also result from practitioners' involvement in CIMC, but these ties take different forms than those at Wat Phila and are more evident from inside than from outside the organization. Family members and friends who accompany me to Wat Phila often comment on the strong sense of community they observe there. People are speaking Thai, eating Thai food, and usually chatting in small groups after the service. While Wat Phila looks like a community to visitors, CIMC often does not. Practitioners at CIMC are often silent and rarely gather in large groups. While people at CIMC are always eating vegetarian food, outside observers do not see this as a symbol or indicator of community. By learning how to meditate and then sitting in silence with a group, an observer at CIMC might think practitioners are becoming more disconnected from one another. When I first came to CIMC I imagined the practitioners sitting on their meditation cushions in the main hall as a series of bubbles. Everyone came to CIMC, I thought, in his or her bubble in part to see about finding a way out of it. Instead of coming out of the bubble through group interactions, I saw practitioners taught to sit with other bubbles and silently examine the inside of their individual bubbles. While bubbles may brush together, individual examination rather than verbal cross-bubble communication was the goal.

As I spent time at CIMC, I learned that the spiritual bonds forged between practitioners in silent practice are stronger than the organizational configuration or my initial image of rows of separate bubbles suggests. While an observer might look at CIMC and see this silent community as the most individualistic form of community possible, the teachers and practitioners do not view their community as a bastion of bubbled individualism, or as a community that reinforces the separation some people feel in coming there. Rather, they define community more broadly than their groups at CIMC and they see their practice as leading them to be less self-involved and more available to engage with other practitioners and the world generally. "Taking refuge in community doesn't necessarily mean we are taking refuge in a specific group of practitioners," Narayan explained. "We need to hold a more inclusive view of what community is. . . . While being part of the Buddhist tradition that began with the enlightenment of the Buddha, we are also part of a much larger sangha that includes not only Buddhists but the greater community of those who seek friendship and truth. . . . We are part of this greater community simply through our commitment to being awake and choosing not to engage in harmful actions toward ourselves and others. We are immediately brought into this larger sangha with our willingness to be openhearted and with our intention to grow in discernment."[49]

Practitioners see themselves entering into involvement with larger communities by meditating and being present with their experience. While meditation leads people to greater self-reliance and free thinking, Michael believes, it simultaneously leads people to be less self-interested and self-involved. While individual practitioners certainly go through phases, "the teachings are really directing them to not be so self-involved and to be more available." Being available leads people gradually to become more social. Michael argues, "People become more compassionate . . . more able to be with people suffering, more available, more connected." The interconnection or interdependence people experience as a result of their group practice further leads to changed experiences in how they relate to others. Michael told me he sees changes in relationships as the result of practice: "In other words, there becomes a little bit more energy and a little bit more fluidity within that relationship; it becomes more workable. And I hear that all the time. . . . A lot of what we talk about is how to be in that situation in a more equanimous, more balanced, more compassionate, more wise way."[50]

In addition to the spiritual bonds forged at CIMC, some practitioners develop strong, though largely overlooked, social ties or friendships, based in the practice, with people they have met at the center. Practitioners have dated each other and married, and several have found roommates through people they met at CIMC. Practitioners at CIMC also offer each other general kinds of social support. When I was talking with Kevin about our similar make and model of car one Thursday over lunch, Mike laughed and told me, "You can get everything from the sangha. Help with your car, French lessons" and then told me how he found his last apartment via a friend at the center. Several practitioners also develop professional networks or referrals through people they meet at CIMC. Catherine, for example, gets referrals for counseling, yoga, and meditation through the center; and Nick, a psychotherapist and sometimes meditation teacher told me that he has come to make half of his livelihood through teaching referrals from the center. "It really saved me professionally," he said. While some practitioners at CIMC have had few social conversations with other practitioners, quite a few have formed strong social ties with other practitioners. When members of the community took care of one member during a sickness, she told me, "They come through in the meaningful ways. I have other groups of friends that I think really care about me, but when it comes to the more serious stuff they just don't get it. . . . I feel like that group of people [at CIMC] is probably my most reliable group of friends in terms of people that I can really count on and who really care about me."

## Conclusion

Practitioners at Wat Phila and CIMC define the word "sangha" and form communities within their organizations in different ways. While practitioners at Wat Phila view the monks as the sangha and tend to conceive of themselves as one large community of monastic and lay members held together by merit, practitioners at CIMC tend to view everyone involved in the center as the sangha and to conceive of themselves as a community of small groups joined by support, example, and interconnection between practitioners. Although quite different, the communities at Wat Phila and CIMC are both public and point to the different ways communities are being formed in the context of the Buddhist tradition in the United States. Despite recent concerns in the broader sociological literature about the strength and vitality of associations and communities in the United States, Wat Phila and CIMC further show that Buddhist and other religious groups continue to provide support through communities, though in different ways to different constituencies.[51]

It is interesting to note, in conclusion, that practitioners at both Wat Phila and CIMC occasionally described themselves and their communities to me as families, though the families they referred to are quite different from one another. At Wat Phila, two students told me the temple is more "like a family" than temples in Thailand because there are regular times to attend and practitioners see each other regularly. Early in my fieldwork, Sang referred to Mai as his sister one afternoon while washing dishes at Wat Phila. I was just getting to know them and asked if they were really brother and sister. "No," Sang told me, "but she is like a sister. The people here are so nice to me. They have taken me in as family. I hope Mai is my sister in the next life." Practitioners at CIMC also speak of themselves as loosely knit families, though the families they refer to, even in metaphor, are less cohesive than those referred to at Wat Phila. One staff member told me that CIMC "is kind of like a loosely knit family . . . you can tell by the way people come in and use the place and don't put things away. You can tell people feel at home here." And Mike, a practitioner, told me that CIMC is "as good a sangha as any sangha can get in this country. . . . It doesn't hang together like an intense family group . . . though the connections are solid . . . it's related to the seriousness people give to their purpose."

Despite the reference to families, the majority of people at Wat Phila and CIMC did not refer to themselves or their communities using the language of group membership. While people participate in, benefit from, and appreciate the communities at Wat Phila and CIMC, they tend to develop personal identities in relation to the Buddhist tradition generally rather than in specific relation to Wat Phila or CIMC as organizations. How people at Wat Phila and CIMC understand and construct their personal identities in and through the centers and the Buddhist tradition is the subject of the next chapter.

## Chapter 6

# ASCRIBED AND ACHIEVED
# BUDDHIST IDENTITIES

Næn slips her shoes off and places them on the rack by the door of Wat Phila in one fluid motion. She carries a heavy pot of soup into the kitchen and places it on the stove and then hangs her coat in the closet and gathers a few spices from a lower cabinet. After adding the spices to the soup she moves quickly into the main hall as the Sunday morning meditation class begins. Her stocking feet glide smoothly over the hard linoleum floor until she kneels on the red carpet at the front of the room. Facing the large adorned altar, she puts her palms together in front of her, closes her eyes and bows deeply, placing her hands and her forehead flat on the floor. She repeats the bow three times, facing the five-foot-tall Buddha and many smaller Buddha images on the altar. She then turns and bows three times to Taan Ajahn, who is sitting on the raised platform to the right of the altar. She turns to face the altar again, hands still together, as Taan Ajahn leads everyone in three bows to the Buddha that formally begin the class.

As he gets out of his car at CIMC, Chris removes his suit jacket and folds it carefully on the back seat. He takes off his tie and takes a few deep breaths as he rolls up his sleeves. He has been sitting at his computer at work since lunchtime, and his body feels cramped and strained. He walks slowly through the side gate and tries to focus on the sensations of his feet hitting the pavement as he moves along the slate steps through the garden to the front door. Inside, he breathes in the quiet stillness as he places his shoes on the rack by the door. The carpet feels thick under his feet as he pads up three flights of stairs to the meditation hall on the top floor, where evening sunlight is streaming through the windows. He enters the meditation hall and turns slowly to the two-foot-tall Buddha image sitting on the tall wooden altar. He puts his palms together, closes his eyes, and slowly bows his head to the Buddha image in greeting. He then picks up a meditation bench and walks slowly and mindfully to sit on a green cushion at the back of the room facing the altar.

꙳   ꙳   ꙳

As Næn and Chris arrive at Wat Phila and CIMC and sit before Buddha images on the altars there, their actions raise questions about who they understand the Buddha to be and how they view themselves in relation to these Buddha images and the Buddha himself. The Buddha's teachings are central to both centers and influence how the centers were created, what is taught, and how people form communities. Questions of how people view themselves and construct their own personal identities in relation to these teachings and the Buddha remain. Practitioners at both centers often told me that the Buddha encouraged people to "come and see." Rather than emphasizing identity, they say, the Buddha told people to take from his teachings what they find useful and to leave the rest behind. Following the Buddha's teachings or going to Buddhist centers, practitioners say, does not make them Buddhists, and many expressed ambivalence about calling themselves Buddhist at all. Further, many practitioners at both centers interpret the Buddha's teachings about nonself, or *anatta*, to say that human beings have no soul, self, or unchanging essence; that we are collections of elements that arise and pass away.[1] Because humans have no permanent self to identify, some practitioners suggest, we can make little sense of the ideas of identity in general and Buddhist identity in particular.[2]

This chapter examines questions of personal identity among practitioners at Wat Phila and CIMC by first asking who they believe the Buddha was and how they think about and treat his physical images. I then ask whether and how practitioners involved with these two centers identify religiously or spiritually.[3] The approach to religious and spiritual identity outlined here points to a new way of thinking about immigrants' religious identities and the development of minority religious identity in the United States more generally. Existing research about the religions of post-1965 immigrants tends to focus more on organizational than on individuals' identities. This chapter describes the ways practitioners at Wat Phila construct their personal identities, often as a result of many years of interacting with people from a wide range of religious traditions. More generally, the stories that people at Wat Phila and CIMC tell about how they became Buddhists or practitioners and what this means are an important counterpoint to Christian Smith's subcultural identity theory of religious strength. Smith argues that modern religious pluralism creates conditions in which some religions thrive by embedding themselves in subcultures that create clear distinctions from and significant engagement and tension with other relevant out-groups.[4] While Smith argues that religiously pluralistic environments lead to stronger identification among religious minorities, the Buddhist subcultures described here are loosely bounded and not in tension with other groups, suggesting that strong personal identities are not needed for Buddhist organizations in the United States to develop and thrive.[5]

## Who Was the Buddha?

Versions of the Buddha's life story are based on combinations of canonical suttas, *vinaya*, commentary, popular legends, and myths.[6] People at Wat Phila generally describe the Buddha through commentaries, subcommentaries, stories, and folktales. Some, like Dr. Malin, an administrator at a local university, view him as a proponent of a rational, empirically based philosophy, while others like Plā emphasize his supernatural powers.[7] Dr. Malin drew a picture of three lotus blossoms in and above a body of water as she described the Buddha to me as a teacher with enormous knowledge: "You know," she said, "there are some lotuses below the water, some just above, and some all the way up and blooming. The Buddha says humans are like the lotus. Some people never come above the water and are just fish food. Others come above the water but are far from blooming. And some blossom. This is the Buddha," she continued, pointing to the blooming flower. "When you get to the stage of full bloom then you know everything. I am maybe here," she said, pointing to the lotus above the water but not open. "I know some things but not everything. So if I keep improving, some day, I may bloom." Dr. Malin and others at Wat Phila describe the Buddha as an example to follow, and they see in his teachings a way for people to take care of and improve themselves. Other practitioners, like Plā, tend to focus largely on supernatural components of the Buddha's life. When Plā told me the story of the Buddha's birth, for example, he reminded me that "when most people are born, they just lie there, but when the Buddha was born he walked about because he had psychic abilities." Rather than focusing on what the Buddha teaches people about how they can improve themselves, those who view the Buddha through a largely supernatural lens tend to look to him, as many people look to Luāngphō Sot, as a powerful figure who provides them with help and protection.

At Wat Phila the monks describe the Buddha as a teacher who taught a system for overcoming suffering. They recognize the range of ideas and interpretations practitioners have about the Buddha and often tell stories in dhamma talks that allow for this. One Sunday morning Maha Nom told the people gathered a story about a woman named Patacara who lived in a province of India during the Buddha's time.[8] She was born into a rich family and fell in love with one of the servants. She married him and later became pregnant. When it was time to deliver the baby she wanted to return to her parents' house, but her husband (the former servant) did not like this idea at all. He was afraid because he knew he had taken away his former boss's most precious possession, his daughter. One day when her husband was not home Patacara decided to return to her parents' home. When her husband learned that she had left, he followed her and found she had been forced to deliver the baby on the side of the road. About a year later she became pregnant with her second child, and she and her husband and their first child set out together for her parents' home. Along the way, they encountered a big monsoon and her husband was killed. She delivered the baby, and the baby and her first child also died in the storm. She continued toward her parents' home and when she arrived there she learned from a villager that the monsoon had killed everyone in her family. Her mind was a blur, and she continued walking, not knowing where she was going. She ended up at a temple where the Buddha was staying, and he was in the middle of teaching his followers when she arrived. Some people tried to stop her from entering, but the Buddha saw her and asked her to enter. The Buddha told her to reestablish her *sati*, or awareness, and she did. She then stayed and became a follower of the Buddha. In commenting on this teaching after the talk, some people spoke about how the Buddha teaches all of us to use our *sati*. Others focused on the supernatural powers they said the Buddha probably used to "cure" the woman.

Unlike at Wat Phila, practitioners at CIMC describe the Buddha almost exclusively in rational terms and emphasize his teachings more than him as a person. Overall, they view him as a teacher of pragmatic lessons about suffering and the end of suffering. Larry Rosenberg described the Buddha in a dharma talk as an "extraordinary phenomenon; a very powerful human being," and explained that "although the Buddha can't do it for us, the presence of someone like that makes a great difference."[9] "It" here refers to waking up. Practitioners at CIMC view the Buddha as someone who recognized suffering and the end of suffering and "woke up," or became enlightened. He laid out a path for all of us to follow that can bring "more peace," "more love," "more connection," and "more kindness." They especially emphasize the Buddha's message to "come and see," to try out the path he described, and to judge its value for oneself. By coming and seeing, we can learn, as Narayan explained in a talk, that the Buddha "really simply discovered inside what all of us can discover."[10]

Regardless of how practitioners at Wat Phila and CIMC view the Buddha, all of the practitioners treat his image with respect. The meditation halls of both Wat Phila and CIMC are dominated by large Buddha images sitting above the heads of the monks, teachers, and practitioners. Practitioners at Wat Phila are careful that the Buddha image is the highest object in a room; they sit below the Buddha image and below the monks when they are gathered. They bow three times when they approach a Buddha image to show their *khaorop*, or respect, and they also bow three times after receiving teaching from a monk. The actual physical image of the Buddha is central at Wat Phila, and there are more than twenty statues of the Buddha as well as murals painted on the front wall of the inside of the meditation hall that illustrate scenes from the Buddha's life. The importance of these images became particularly clear to me one Sunday morning when I was talking with a Thai woman at Wat Phila who is a graduate student at a nearby university. We were talking about different kinds of Buddhism and she told me, "Zen Buddhism is a philosophy, not a religion, because there is not a Buddha you are taught to respect. It is just yourself and how you behave." The Buddha images that surrounded us as we spoke were central to how she understood the teaching and were a symbol for her of the Buddha and his teaching, both of which were to be respected.

Practitioners at CIMC have a much more ambivalent attitude toward physical images of the Buddha. Although the main meditation hall at CIMC is focused on a Buddha statue sitting on an intricately carved altar, people recognize and respond to the Buddha in different ways. Some, like Chris, bow gently to the Buddha as a sign of greeting and respect when they arrive in the hall and when they leave. Others treat the image more as a piece of art to look at closely before or after a class than as an object to be venerated or intrinsically respected. Other people ignore the Buddha image in the main meditation hall completely. Some people bow deeply to the Buddha after a meditation session to say thank you to the Buddha for his teachings and to the teachers who have passed them along. Others are intentional about not bowing, because they view bowing as part of devotional practices outside their understandings of the Buddha's teaching. People's interactions with the Buddha images at Wat Phila and CIMC are mirrored in their private practices.

In addition to bowing (or not bowing), respect is paid to the Buddha through chanting. The chanting portion of the gatherings at Wat Phila on Sundays begin with praise for the Buddha as practitioners face the image on the altar and recite in Pali, "Now let us chant the sublime praise of the Buddha," ending with "To that Exalted One I bow down my head."[11] At CIMC, chanting is held in the lower meditation hall every Monday evening next to a standing image of the Buddha, and praise is always recited in Pali and in English. While everyone who comes to Wat Phila on a Sunday morning participates in the chanting service, this chanting is a more marginal activity at CIMC, with only a few people participating.

At Wat Phila, though not at CIMC, lay people show their respect by regularly offering food, flowers, and fruit to the Buddha image. Before food is offered to the monks every day, small portions of each item are placed on a tray and presented to the Buddha image at the front of the main meditation hall. People also routinely leave fruit, flowers, and plants in front of the images. These offerings are generally made with the expectation of some benefit in return, which Donald Swearer argues reflects the power some practitioners project onto the physical image of the Buddha.[12] People at Wat Phila describe these offerings as things they do for good luck or to have a better next life. The concept of merit is central to understanding these devotional practices.

As another way to show respect to the Buddha, practitioners at Wat Phila and CIMC formally take refuge in the Buddha as one part of taking refuge in the triple gem.[13] At Wat Phila, people take refuge in the Buddha every Sunday by chanting in Pali three times, "Buddham saranam gacchami," translated as "I go for refuge to the Buddha." This is followed by taking refuge in the dhamma and the sangha with the words, "Dhammam saranam gacchami," or "I go for refuge to the dhamma" (repeated three times) and "Sangham saranam gacchami," or "I go for refuge to the sangha" (repeated three times). At CIMC, people have the option of taking refuge in the Buddha once or twice a year at a ceremony specifically devoted to taking the refuges and the precepts.

At both centers, what it means to take refuge in the Buddha is a deeply personal question. In a talk about the Buddha as refuge at CIMC, Narayan taught that taking refuge in the Buddha is part of "needing a sense of vision about the spiritual journey." She described three ways to look at refuge in the Buddha. First, there is taking refuge in the Buddha as an actual person, which means using the Buddha as an example of inspiration and looking to his life for ways to inform our own. The second is taking refuge in our own commitments to freedom and to waking up: "The Buddha is one who discovers what is true . . . and this commitment to awakening gives us true reason for being alive." The third interpretation emphasizes taking refuge in yourself.[14] Practitioners at CIMC tend toward Narayan's second and third interpretations. Practitioners at Wat Phila would not disagree with Narayan's three levels of interpretation, but they do not outline the meaning of refuge in the Buddha in this way. Instead they emphasize the physical person of the Buddha and refuge in him as a way to lead a good life. Dr. Malin said that for her, being Buddhist is about "refuge." It is about "faith that the Buddha can help us from his higher level." Formally taking refuge makes her "feel close to Buddha." Some feel that by taking refuge they will be protected. Others view refuge more as a reminder of their commitments to the Buddha, of growing up in Thailand, or of their families. Some commentators describe the act of taking refuge as akin to taking on the identity of "Buddhist," though none of the monks, teachers, or practitioners I spoke with at Wat Phila or CIMC made this connection.

## Who Is a Buddhist?

People in the Buddha's time were not called "Buddhists," although the Buddha had both monastic and lay followers. The word "Buddhist" first appeared in an English-language dictionary in 1828, and researchers have spent a lot of time, especially in the past ten years, discussing who counts as a Buddhist and how to count Buddhists in the United States.[15] Credible estimates of the number range from 1.4 to 4 million, though researchers have little reliable data, both because of the difficulty of determining who is Buddhist and the challenges of collecting data among an Asian, American, and Asian American population, many of whom do not formally belong to a Buddhist organization.[16]

In early research about Buddhism in the United States, Charles Prebish defined Buddhists as people who consistently claimed to be Buddhist when questioned about their most important pursuits.[17] More recently, Jan Nattier outlined a typology that describes forms of Buddhism according to how they came to the United States. Import Buddhism, described by others as white Buddhism, elite Buddhism, or new Buddhism, is demand driven, sought out by recipients who have the leisure time and money for spiritual investigation through teachers and retreats. Export Buddhism, also described as evangelical Buddhism, came to the United States with Buddhist missionaries. And baggage Buddhism—also called ethnic, cultural, or hereditary Buddhism—came with people during immigration.[18] This typology usefully clarifies three types of Buddhism but says little about who actually uses these terms or how these terms map onto people's self-descriptions. Religious historian Thomas Tweed points out that the usual ways of deciding who is a Buddhist, through beliefs and practices, membership, and attendance, do not take seriously enough the complexity and multilayered reality of religious self-identity. Previous studies, he notes, show that people functionally compartmentalize religions or draw on several religions crossing boundaries in different times and places. Conversion is a complicated process, and a straightforward definition of adherents may miss the hybrid identities of many involved with the Buddhist tradition. Looking only at adherents, Tweed argues, misses a large group of sympathizers or "night-stand Buddhists" who are not "luke-warm adherents," people who identify with the tradition but do not practice it regularly, but are those who have "some sympathy for a religion but do not embrace it exclusively or fully."[19] Particularly in the United States, these sympathizers have been central to the growth of Buddhism.[20]

Listening to how practitioners at Wat Phila and CIMC think and talk about their religious and spiritual identities led me to approach the issue here using the language of ascription and achievement.[21] While the people I interviewed did not use this language, the ideas framed the stories they told. I define *ascribed identities* as the religious or spiritual identities people inherit at their birth and often develop through their childhood or young adulthood. At different points in their lives, people choose to accept or reject their ascribed religious identities.[22] *Achieved identities*, on the other hand, are those that people may or may not construct, in response to the tradition of their birth or another religious tradition. These identities are generally constructed in response to a period of change or transition, and their defining feature is that they involve choice.[23]

This two-part classification scheme is particularly helpful when thinking about Buddhist identity because of the fuzzy boundaries around what it means to be Buddhist and who counts as a Buddhist. Unlike evangelical Christians and other religious groups with clear in-groups and out-groups, people at Wat Phila and CIMC do not make clear distinctions between themselves and people of other religious traditions, in part because they believe people can take as much or as little from the Buddha's teachings as they like without having to express total commitment. The monks, teachers, and practitioners at Wat Phila and CIMC also believe that people need to come to whatever part of the Buddha's teachings they are interested in on their own. "Buddhists do not believe you can force on someone what they should believe," a longtime member of Wat Phila explained to me. When Karen, a longtime practitioner at CIMC, introduced her partner Jeanette to Larry Rosenberg at the first meeting of a meditation course, he had a similar response: "Were you talked into coming here tonight in any way?" Larry asked Jeanette. "No," she replied. "That's good," Larry concluded. "People need to make their own decisions about coming here."

## RELIGIOUS AND SPIRITUAL IDENTITIES AT WAT PHILA

The issue of religious and spiritual identity is more straightforward for practitioners at Wat Phila than at CIMC, though a significant number of practitioners at both centers describe changes in their identities after arriving in the United States. People at Wat Phila describe their religious or spiritual identities in one of three ways based on ascribed and achieved categories. Some, like Dr. Chan, describe their religious identities only as an ascribed characteristic. They say they were born as Buddhists, have always been Buddhists, and are still Buddhists. Dr. Chan spoke for himself and his wife when he told me, "We are born with Buddhism. My parents always went to the temple like we do." He did not see any difference between the temple his parents went to in Thailand and the temple he goes to in Philadelphia, and he believes his three children were born as Buddhists and will always be Buddhists. This often leads him to be frustrated with his children, who do not see their identities in this way and rarely go to the temple. While Dr. Chan's understandings of Buddhism may have changed over time, his sense of himself as a Buddhist has been stable from birth.

The majority of people at Wat Phila fall into a second group of people, who both accept their ascribed religious identity and have constructed an achieved religious identity.[24] In describing how they learned about Buddhism and came to Wat Phila, they tell very similar stories of being born as Buddhists in Thailand but not knowing much about Buddhism or initially practicing when they came to the United States. After living in the States for some period of time, many realized they were not "real Buddhists" and took steps to become so. The stories they tell are about a movement to an ascribed and achieved Buddhist identity that, while still Buddhist, means something very different to them than the ascribed Buddhist identity of their birth.[25]

Dr. Malin, for example, was born into a Buddhist family in Thailand and came to the United States in 1972. "When you are born into a Buddhist family you just learn," she told me. Her mother went to the temple and cooked for the monks regularly and when Dr. Malin left home around age twenty, she says, "I was not very serious about Buddhism. And then I skipped twenty years before I became a real Buddhist again. In between I was in Oklahoma, where there was no temple. You don't need a temple to practice. You can pray in front of the Buddha at your house; I sometimes did that." Mai, whose story started this book, also describes herself as "born as a Buddhist," but after living in the United States for six years, she realized, "I took it [Buddhism] for granted because I was born with it. I was not really paying full attention." She got involved with the temple and now says her understanding of herself as a Buddhist has changed. Phæm tells a similar story: "We were born as Buddhists. My family always believed in Buddhism even though I went to boarding school in England and I had to go to church and things like that. In your heart you know you are still Buddhist." She lived in the United States for sixteen years with a non-Thai American-born husband, and it was not until her sister, a devout Buddhist, came to visit from Thailand and took her to Wat Phila that she began to construct an achieved Buddhist identity. "My sister came and she said, 'It's time to go to the temple.' I didn't want to go but I did." She continued visiting Wat Phila after her sister returned home, and now says "I learned so much about how to be a Buddhist." These three women articulate the relationship between their ascribed and achieved Buddhist identities in different ways, but all share an approach to Buddhist identity that distinguishes between their birth or ascribed Buddhist identities and the achieved or chosen Buddhist identities they developed in the United States.

A few people at Wat Phila also spoke about constructing their achieved identities as a result of learning about Buddhism in college in the United States and realizing that it was "theirs" but they did not know much about it. Nōi went to college in the United States twenty years ago and took a religion course in which she was asked about Buddhism. "I didn't know anything. I knew three things—to do good, not to do evil, and to purify your mind. And I thought, 'I have to learn about this from a *farang* [foreigner].' So I started to learn. I came to the temple and I started to learn about Buddhism." Kanyā had a similar experience when she took a college course in non-Western religions that she expected would be "an easy A." When the professor began to teach about the Buddha as a "rich landlord," she thought he was wrong and started to challenge him. Now, she says, "When we grow up in Thailand, we are born into Buddhism, it is the religion we grow up with. . . . I did my research in this class and I studied and, my god, you know I realized I took my religion for granted. There are a lot of things we can do and practice to help us understand why we are believing in Buddhism." Realizing that being Buddhist based on her birth was not enough for her, she says, "I came here to the temple to do the landscaping and devote myself to my religion—to be part of it. And for seven years now I have been practicing my religion. I am more and more into it." Kanyā also attends courses at the Barre Center for Buddhist Studies and the Insight Meditation Society (organizations where the majority of practitioners are white) and is starting a meditation class in the small grocery store she owns in western Pennsylvania.

A few people at Wat Phila fall into a third group of people, who completely reject the authenticity of ascribed Buddhism after constructing achieved Buddhist identities. Two people in this group had the time and the resources to return to Thailand after realizing they were not "real Buddhists" to study at temples and monasteries there. Although he was born into a Buddhist family, Kop now believes there is no such thing as a born Buddhist. He came to the United States in 1971 and several years later had this revelation:

> To be Thai is not necessarily to be Buddhist. In fact, many Thais like to think they are Buddhists, but from my observations many of them are not really Buddhists. To me it isn't just what they say, but rather from their actions, which are driven by their true understanding of what Buddhism is. From my own personal experience, I used to think that I was a Buddhist, since I was a Thai. Then one day it hit me. I asked myself these questions: What is Buddhism? What do I know about it? What does it look like to be a Buddhist? I could not answer these questions. That's when I decided to go back to Thailand to learn about Buddhism by becoming a monk. It's really through vipassana meditation that I learned about Buddhism. . . . Going to the Buddhist temples doesn't make a person a Buddhist. People are not really Buddhists until they really understand the Buddha's teachings and use them in their everyday lives.[26]

Sam, a Thai layman, went through a similar experience about five years ago, and the story he tells about his experience has many components of a conversion narrative. At that time, he did not feel he was Buddhist. "I didn't go to the temple or believe all that stuff," he told me. "From what I understand, we were born with Buddhism. Sometimes people don't realize, they don't study, because they were born with it. They just ignore it. It's like me. I was there before and I understand it. I said to myself, 'Before I say I don't believe, why don't I at least go in there and learn.' I am lucky because I had a chance to go back to Thailand, to become a monk, and to study. That's when I started to understand a lot of things." His experiences during those few weeks as a monk led him to change some of his behaviors after he returned to the States. "It doesn't mean that I totally changed, but I slowly try to follow through the Eightfold Path and try to see that if something is good we do it and if something is not good we don't." He has stopped fishing and eating seafood and meat, and tries to carry out the Eight Precepts, especially on Buddha days. "I try to change my behavior. . . . It takes a long time before you can see the result." People like Kop and Sam, who describe themselves now only in terms of achieved identities, are generally people who have been in the States for a number of years and have gone to school here or worked in business or other professions.

This movement from ascribed religious or spiritual identities alone to ascribed and achieved or just achieved identities is not confined to the first generation or to Thai practitioners. Chāt, a second-generation Thai in his late twenties, was raised at Wat Phila and considered himself only minimally a Buddhist when he was growing up. "When I was a kid, I didn't believe any of that stuff they said at the temple. I heard that this happened or that happened in the Buddha's life and I said, 'That's a lie; I didn't see that.'" In college he studied religions, which led him to try meditation. Now he is a serious meditation practitioner and has taught some of his friends how to meditate based on the dhammakaya method taught at Wat Phila. He still considers himself a Buddhist based on his ascribed or birth identity but, like many CIMC practitioners, he does not find much meaning in the Buddhist label: "You don't need to be a Buddhist. Lets say I'm teaching [meditation]. I don't care about that. I don't want you to become Buddhist. Who cares? I don't care." Saṅg, a twenty-nine-year-old student from Indonesia, has been regularly involved with Wat Phila for five years, although he speaks no Thai. His parents were Chinese Buddhists, though in talking with me he dismissed his ascribed Buddhist identity, quickly saying that "my parents went to many temples to ask many Chinese gods for luck and for things. . . . I learned about Buddhism from them but I was not serious about it. I learned more about Buddhism in the past several years." While Dr. Nūaṅg, a college professor, identifies as a Buddhist, her story shows that not all Thais who develop achieved religious identities do so exclusively in the Buddhist tradition. "My whole family is Buddhist," she told me. "My grandparents are religious. My grandmother was very good. She would make food and then the family would go to the temple almost every weekend. I come to Wat Phila, but I have also been going to the Unitarian Universalist church. Now they meet at the same time, so I had to make a choice. I chose the temple, though sometimes I go to the church if they are having a program that interests me."

The distinction between practitioners with ascribed and achieved religious identities is also evident in two different attitudes parents at the temple have about their children's upbringing and religious identification. Parents who consider themselves Buddhist by birth but who have not developed achieved religious identities assume that their children were also born as Buddhists and should therefore act as Buddhists and should come to the temple. Some of their children came to the temple when they were younger, but now almost all come only for festivals and holidays, frustrating their parents. Parents like Dr. Malin who constructed achieved Buddhist identities during their time in the United States are generally much less concerned with their children's religious identity. Dr. Malin said she and her husband do not expect their daughter to be a Buddhist. "She must decide for herself," she told me. While they certainly encourage her to come to the temple and give her Buddhist books to read, they realize that just as they developed Buddhist identities for themselves, so must their daughter.[27]

The changes in practitioners' religious or spiritual identities at Wat Phila are revealing on a number of levels. First, these changes suggests that immigrants, particularly those who have been in the United States for a number of years, speak English well, and do not live in ethnic enclaves, develop new ways of thinking about religious identity that may not have existed in their home countries, particularly if those home countries like Thailand were not very religiously diverse. Second, they clearly show that what it means for people to say they are Buddhist at two different points in their lives is not necessarily the same. And third, they speak to the range of religious identities and approaches to tradition that may coexist within individual Thai temples.

The reasons that practitioners' identities change are primarily related to their exposure to a range of religious traditions in the United States. Many went to Christian schools or colleges where they engaged in conversations with people from other religious traditions, and a few tell stories of people trying to convert them. Most have attended friends' and coworkers' weddings, bar mitzvahs, or other celebrations in non-Buddhist religious traditions that have led them to reflect on their own religious identity. While there are certainly more opportunities for this kind of exposure in the States than in Thailand, it is interesting to note that exposure to non-Buddhist religions in Thailand seems to have been insufficient to lead people to construct achieved Buddhist identities there. Mai, for example, was born as a Buddhist but grew up in a Christian environment in Bangkok, where her father worked for a Baptist church. She went to Sunday school, joined the choir, and was "into it" for a few years, although she still considered herself a Buddhist. It was not until she came to the United States, got involved with Wat Phila, and observed many other religious traditions in her life in suburban Philadelphia that she developed an achieved Buddhist identity.

These shifts in religious and spiritual identity are particularly evident among first-generation Thai practitioners in the United States because many have lived in the States for many years. As a group they are somewhat geographically dispersed; many have good English-language skills, and many experience religious diversity within their families and workplaces. Unlike Cambodian and Lao Theravada Buddhist practitioners, who live mainly in ethnic centers and have limited English-language skills, Thais are scattered in urban and subur-

ban neighborhoods in the States, and less than one-third are linguistically isolated.[28] Many are exposed to other religious traditions, not only in their neighborhoods but also in their own families. About half of married Thai women are
married to non-Thai men, few of whom are Buddhist by birth, and many have
children who are therefore raised in interreligious households.[29] One woman
at the temple told me about problems that developed in her family because her
daughter is a Christian and wants to go to Thailand to convert people. Many
first-generation Thai immigrants also encounter people of other religions in
their workplaces. Dr. Malin told me about one of her coworkers: "I think he
wants me to be a Christian. He taught about the Bible. . . . I think there is a
meeting there one time per month and he invited me to go. One time he came
back from watching a movie and I asked him what it was and he said 'The Life
of Christ' or something. . . . Later I got into an argument with him because I
was questioning some things about Christianity and I don't think he liked it."
It is by encountering people with so many different religious identities, beliefs,
and practices, in some cases over many years, and developing their own identities in relation to them that many practitioners at Wat Phila have come to
achieved rather than just ascribed Buddhist identities in the United States.

In addition to describing themselves as Buddhists in many ways, practitioners at Wat Phila view the relationship between their religious identities as
Buddhists and their ethnic identities as Thais differently. Some equate these
two identities, saying that being Buddhist is equivalent to being Thai.[30] They
often mention the saying "To be Thai is to be Buddhist." These practitioners
tend to have ascribed Buddhist identities and to come to the temple, with their
families, in more traditional ways. They normally dress in Thai clothing, for
example, and offer food from formal silver dishes to the monks. Many are particularly interested in rituals and often conceive of the Buddha as a protector.
When asked what Buddhism means to them, people in this group talk about
their families and Thai people as a group as much as they talk about what
Buddhism means for them as individuals.

A second, larger group of people at Wat Phila do not equate their religious
and ethnic identities. When they talk about what it means to be Buddhist,
they rarely, if ever, talk about being Thai. These are generally people who have
constructed achieved Buddhist identities, in the process learning more about
Buddhism than whatever knowledge they inherited from their parents. Most
emphasize what the tradition teaches them about how to behave in the world.
Dr. Nūa*ng*, for example, told me that to be a Buddhist means to learn "how
to lead a good life." As a Buddhist, she said, "I feel at peace with myself. I
feel good, like I did something good. Buddhism teaches you to be kind and

generous to other people." Mai also explained what it means to be a Buddhist in individual terms, that is, "Trying to do the best you can to be a better person." Mai added that trying to be a better person is "kind of modern actually" and that it has changed her approach to things. Sam said that to be a Buddhist means "to look upon yourself. You don't look outside and then complain that's no good. . . . I just try to improve myself from what I learn and take in." Emphasizing that nothing is forever, he says this inward looking is not easy but can improve one's life.

As they talked about what it means to be Buddhist, largely in terms of their own lives, some of the people in this second group simultaneously emphasized the ultimate hollowness of the phrase or identity "Buddhist." When I asked her what it means to be a Buddhist, Som told me that it is a way to "make you feel better, to make you grow, to make you see things more clearly." The identity, though, she added, is not important. It was the teachings, especially about suffering, that she emphasized: "You can still have pain," she told me, "but you can eliminate your suffering. Like if you're sick, that is nature. You're born and you grow older and then you have some disease and your body deteriorates. That is the nature of your life. But you don't suffer if you understand the process and you accept it." Kop concurred: "To me Buddhism is about understanding the suffering and how to set oneself free from it. To be free from it, one must know what suffering is, its root causes, how to get rid of it, and the paths that lead to such freedom." Buddhists are people, he continued, "who practice being Buddha, which means being awake, knowing, and free." It is the practice of "being Buddha" that Kop says ultimately matters rather than any connection to a word or description of himself as Buddhist. Buddhist "is just a name," Kop told me, and while it can be a helpful descriptor, he does not place much meaning in it as an identity category for himself.

Despite their different understandings of Buddhist identity, all of the practitioners quoted here coexist at Wat Phila, participating in the same ceremonies and rituals. The diversity and presence of all of these practitioners point to the fact that Wat Phila as an organization is relatively porous and loosely bounded. The barriers to entry are relatively low; people need to share more practices than beliefs to participate; and there is little pressure to adopt a particular identity to be involved with the temple.

## RELIGIOUS AND SPIRITUAL IDENTITIES AT CIMC

As at Wat Phila, the issue of people's identities is not a central organizational concern at CIMC. Their practice is seen as much more important.[31] In the Way of Awareness meditation course I took with Larry Rosenberg, he told the class, "You don't have to be a Buddhist to follow your breath. I don't care what you believe. I care about your practice." A few months later when I asked him in an interview about the issue of Buddhist identity, he told me a story. "Four or five years ago at the end of a Wednesday night talk, someone raised their hand and asked me a question: 'Are you a Buddhist?' I was stunned. I know a lot of people told me I got very quiet for four or five minutes. I didn't say anything. I just went inside. And my answer was no, if you mean trying to spread an -ism, trying to proselytize, being identified with institutional development, or with the idea that the world would be a better place if there were more Buddhists. I don't have much interest in that. I don't even know when the Buddhist holidays come up. So it forced me to get very precise with myself," he continued. "It wasn't confusing because this has been clear all along, and it's even more clear over the years. The only thing I could honestly say that is truly sincere is, I'm a student of the teachings of the Buddha. I have done my best and continue to study them, put them into practice, and to share what comes out of that with anyone who wants to know it. That part is authentic. If it means I'm a Buddhist, fine. But I said no. And half the room seemed to get depressed and the other half were elated. And a few good friends said 'Oh, don't confuse people. Just say yes for God's sake. For all these years, this is what you study, you do—you've been practicing at Buddhist centers.' And I realized there was some wisdom in what they were saying. That for most people it was confusing. . . . Recently I had to get a medical thing done and they asked me my religion and I said Buddhist."[32]

In a dharma talk, Larry explained, "Real Buddhism is not an institutional thing. You can be born in a Buddhist country and have a Buddhist birth certificate and it can be meaningless. You can be called an atheist and be a Buddhist, because it has to do with how you actually live."[33] Practices, which may or may not lead to identities, are at the center of Larry's approach to the issue of Buddhist identity. Ascribed Buddhist identities not based in practice are not very meaningful from his perspective, and achieved identities may also get in the way of the practice because of the possibility of attachment they create. On the surface, in a doctor's office, when speaking casually, Larry can say he is Buddhist, though he views the identity, like other attachments, as ultimately something to let go of.

Michael, another teacher at CIMC, shares Larry's contention that practice rather than beliefs is at the core of questions about Buddhist identity, but he sees in the identity a marker of membership in a community or institution that Larry does not emphasize. Michael explains, "I would say that it doesn't really mean that much to say that you're a Buddhist. So I can't see why NOT say it. I'm involved in a Buddhist world, I teach the stuff. So why not just say it? I guess that's what it means. It doesn't feel particularly charged for me. It doesn't have a lot of inherent meaning in that sense. To say you're a Buddhist, it just means that I'm part of the community that has Buddhism really at its core."[34] These two themes, a focus on practice and a relationship to community, are two of many that emerged from discussions about religious and spiritual identity with practitioners at CIMC, though generally, practitioners emphasize practices, like Larry, rather than community, like Michael, when talking about Buddhist identity.

Practitioners at CIMC have four main approaches to their religious or spiritual identities, all of which are based in Buddhist practices, specifically meditation. One group identify themselves through both ascribed and achieved components of religious identity. This is particularly true among the one-third of people I interviewed who were born in the Jewish tradition, some of whom continue to practice Judaism. Sara was born as a Jew and has been practicing Buddhism for six years. She describes herself as both Jewish and Buddhist: "I am Jewish and that is how people identify me first, from my name and my appearance. I joined a synagogue two years ago and I go home for the holidays. I don't do any kind of Jewish practices in my home, but Judaism moves me emotionally. And I consider myself a Buddhist." Another woman spoke, after a Wednesday night talk, about how she combines Jewish and Buddhist practices and identities, saying that she was frustrated because a Jewish chant kept running through her head as she was trying to be quiet and meditate. Larry responded by encouraging her to combine the practices, and implicitly to combine the identities: "If the chant is regular," he said, "you might be able to combine it with the breaths in some regular fashion." Nick who told me he was born a Christian, played with the language of "Budd-istian" in thinking about his religious identity during graduate school. He has practiced meditation regularly for twenty years and explains, "There are beliefs I hold independent of Buddhism that some monks and teachers would be concerned about. I'm developing a hybrid practice. I sit daily, do retreats, and have been having conversations with Christian leaders. I think in the end I will end up being a Christian with a Buddhist practice." At retreats, though, he says the question of religious or spiritual identification totally falls away: "I'm not sitting there aspiring to be a Buddhist—I'm aspiring to the essence," which he defines as experiences that come through the meditation practice.

Others at CIMC identify using ascribed and achieved categories but do not actually practice their ascribed religion. For the Jewish people in this group, calling themselves Jewish is part of their cultural or family identities. Katie, an artist, told me she was raised as a Reform Jew and identifies as Buddhist and Jewish. She has practiced Buddhism for twelve years and says she is not going to reject her Jewish or her Buddhist identity, though she points out that she has never felt a spiritual connection with Judaism. Jon does not go to a synagogue or practice Judaism privately, but says, "I think my religion is Judaism and I practice Buddhism meditation." He doesn't identify as Buddhist, however, because that label suggests to him a belief system, and he is explicitly not looking for a belief system. "I'm looking for real concrete stuff to make me a better person and to help me understand more what this life is about." Christine has been practicing meditation at CIMC for twelve years and also describes herself as Jewish, even though she says, "I'm not a practicing Jew and I feel less and less even a cultural Jew, but that's who I am. And sometimes I'll identify as a meditator." She continues, "I have never said I was a Buddhist. . . . I would never call myself a Buddhist. I also dislike -isms as much here as in other religions so I sometimes identify as somebody who practices Buddhist meditation and if somebody wants to give a full sentence that's what I'd say. I'm Jewish but I practice Buddhist meditation. That feels better." Christine does not call herself Buddhist because she feels the phrase applies only to those born into the tradition or who have gone to great lengths to change their lives, which she feels she has not done.

A second group of people at CIMC describe themselves only through the language of achieved religious identity. Some of the people in this group were not raised in religious traditions, while others have rejected the traditions they were raised in. While some people in this group identify clearly as Buddhists, others voice ambivalence, preferring instead to see themselves as students of Buddhist meditation. Dawn, a forty-two-year-old woman who has been meditating for eight years, says, "I do call myself a Buddhist now. . . . I think just that I do hew to that worldview." Rick came to CIMC several years ago after learning to meditate as part of a drug rehabilitation program and describes himself as a "budding Buddhist." "I am inclined to become a Buddhist because the teachings speak to me at an 'ah ha' level and make me curious to go after more." Art, a long-term practitioner, identifies as Buddhist only when he speaks in a casual or informal way. He prefers to think about himself as a "follower of Buddha's teachings."

A third group of people at CIMC describe themselves in terms of multiple achieved religious and spiritual identities. These are generally people who have spent considerable time and energy investigating different religious traditions one at a time, but now combine them. Timothy describes himself as a follower of the Iyengar school of yoga, Taoism, Sufism and Buddhism. Catherine says she is a Buddhist, but that she doesn't like being labeled because that is not all she is: "I could say that I'm a Sufi," she told me. Carol describes herself as a pagan-Buddhist. Everyone in this third group talks about Buddhism as a philosophy, rather than a religion, and when they make this distinction, I hear them prioritizing practice over belief systems and doctrines. Almost everyone at CIMC privileges practices over beliefs, but people in this group do even more so because they are combining Buddhist practices with those gained from other religious traditions. Robert spoke for everyone in this group when he told me that "religion is what you believe. That doesn't reflect how you lead your own life." A philosophy or way of life is how you actually live, people in this group say, and Buddhist practices are one part of these people's philosophies.

A fourth group of people at CIMC rejected their ascribed religious identities and have not constructed achieved identities, viewing the terms available as ultimately so hollow as to be meaningless. People who describe themselves as growing up in strict religious environments are particularly likely to fall into this group. These people are so resistant to what they often call "religious dogmas" that they are not comfortable identifying themselves even in terms of Buddhist practice. Kevin, a Mormon by birth, says it is not accurate for him to say "I am a Buddhist or I am not a Buddhist." "I do not see the purpose of calling myself a Buddhist, because it feels like another layer. I'm not putting on layers, I'm taking them off." Michelle, a Catholic by birth, agrees: "Buddhism is, can be, another label. And the whole point of the meditation sometimes and the freeing ourselves from identifying to things is ridding ourselves of those labels. . . . If anyone asks, I've had great advantages in my life from studying Buddhism and practicing meditation, but to say I am a Buddhist, no."

Some people in each of these four groups at CIMC expressed considerable ambivalence about actually using the term "Buddhist" to describe themselves. Some, like Art, will use it casually but prefer to emphasize the teachings in their self-descriptions. This emphasis on practice is telling, because it is in contrast to dominant Christian ideas of religious identity based on beliefs, which many practitioners have rejected. Around CIMC, people are referred to as "meditators," "practitioners," or "yogis," descriptions that focus on practice and avoid the issue of Buddhist identification altogether. Other people at CIMC are uncomfortable with the term "Buddhist" because they feel it is culturally loaded. Helen, for example, has been practicing Buddhism for more than ten years and is happy to say she follows Buddhist practices but thinks that to call herself Buddhist is a bit of a misnomer. Like Christine, she feels there is a sense in which it "implies a whole cultural background and upbringing and various specific cultural experiences" that are not in her experience. Other people are concerned about the stigma some listeners might attach to the term "Buddhist" in the American context. Greg, a twenty-three-year-old graduate student, told me that he tries to follow Buddhism "to a T" and is considering becoming a monk. He finds questions about religious identity difficult, however, and is wary of saying he is a Buddhist because of the connotation he feels it carries in the West: "A lot of people I've talked with equate it with the New Age movement, with the Hare Krishnas." Buddhism is very different from these other movements, he believes, and he is uncomfortable with any kind of self-identification that might have such connotations.

As at Wat Phila, the issue of ethnic identity is important for some practitioners at CIMC, specifically for those who were born as Jews and continue to describe themselves in terms of the Jewish tradition. The question of why so many people born Jewish are attracted to Buddhism, to be Jew-Bus or Bu-Jews as they are sometimes called in the popular press, has not been thoroughly answered, although the reasons are likely related to similarities between the two traditions, the networks of early Buddhist teachers, and how Jewish people have been received in the United States.[35] Some commentators also argue that for non-Asian Buddhists, there is a relationship between how practitioners think about their religious or spiritual identities and how they think about their national identities, though I did not find this to be the case at CIMC. While in the 1960s and 1970s some people who were attracted to Buddhism were also rejecting parts of what it meant to be an American, this is not the case now at CIMC.[36]

Practitioners at CIMC currently fall into one of the four identity groupings described here as a result of their Buddhist practices, their present interest in the religious tradition in which they were raised, and the extent to which what they have learned at CIMC or from the Buddhist tradition more generally is satisfying to them apart from other teachings or traditions. Regardless of which identity grouping practitioners fall into, their experiences in total point to the fact that religious or spiritual conversion is not always a complete process.[37] Some of the practitioners completely left the tradition of their birth, while others developed, and maintained, blended identities and practices.[38] Regardless of their specific identities, all of these practitioners gather at CIMC and, as at Wat Phila, their presence points to the organization's relatively simple prerequisites for entry (an interest in meditation practice alone) and its relative flexibility and adaptability in including a range of different people. As at Wat Phila, identity is not a central organizational issue at CIMC (remember Larry Rosenberg was "stunned" when someone asked him about it following a dharma talk) and there is little pressure to conform to particular ways of thinking about oneself and one's practice in relation to the Buddhist tradition.

## Conclusions

Practitioners at Wat Phila and CIMC emphasize the Buddha's teaching to "come and see" in their conversations about their personal identities. Regardless of what they draw from the tradition, most of them do develop some kind of identity in relation to the Buddha's teachings, rather than to Wat Phila or CIMC as organizations. Some practitioners at both centers, and especially at CIMC, express ambivalence about calling themselves Buddhists, with some pointing to the hollowness of any identification and others to uncomfortable cultural implications the term holds for them. At both Wat Phila and CIMC, however, many practitioners describe themselves through achieved religious or spiritual identities that they have chosen in the United States. This emphasis on choice is expected at CIMC based on what sociologists have documented about how people born in the United States construct religious and spiritual identities.[39] The language of choice used by practitioners at Wat Phila, however, is somewhat of a surprise and points to how practitioners there are adapting and assimilating in the United States. Equally surprising is the fact that many practitioners at CIMC hold onto their ascribed or birth identities while also choosing to develop identities through their involvement in the Buddhist tradition.

The fact that Wat Phila and CIMC include practitioners with such a range of religious and spiritual identities shows that identity is not a central organizational concern at either center. While Buddhist practice is a concern at both organizations, the identities people develop as a result of that practice are, in most cases not talked about, even among friends. The range of identities constructed by practitioners at each organization also speaks to the overall porousness and loosely bounded nature of these two centers. It is because of these loose boundaries that Christian Smith's subcultural identity theory does not account for the religious growth and strength of these two organizations or of Buddhism in America more broadly. While his theory may accurately describe evangelicals, Christian fundamentalists, or other groups that occupy subcultures and build walls to distinguish themselves from others in the religious marketplace, Asian and white Buddhist individuals and organizations do not build the boundaries that Smith argues would lead them to thrive.[40] Rather than thriving because the subculture is strong, Wat Phila and particularly CIMC seem to be striving precisely of their weak subcultures. While each group has a core of committed practitioners without whom the organization would not continue, people identify with the Buddha's teachings in a wide range of ways, and that range of identifications is not a problem. While most of the people at Wat Phila are Thai, and the center does have some boundaries because all of the services are conducted in Thai, CIMC has very porous boundaries that make Buddhism accessible to a range of people and as a result actually encourage people to come and learn more.

Rather than a subcultural identity theory, Wat Phila and CIMC point to the need for more of a cohesive particle theory of minority religious identity. Like iron filings attracted to a magnet, individuals at Wat Phila and CIMC are individually attracted to whatever they define the core ideas of Buddhism to be or, for some practitioners at Wat Phila, the ethnic component of the gathering. They quietly construct personal identities around those ideas and physically come together into loosely bounded centers where identity is not a central theme. Because the Buddha taught people to "come and see," the centers, particularly CIMC, maintain porous boundaries, and this loosely bounded nature is understood by practitioners to be part of the very message the Buddha and the centers are teaching.

*Chapter 7*

# OBSERVATIONS THROUGH
# A GENDERED LENS

It is mostly women at Wat Phila. It's rare to see a man.
DR. NŪANG, FEMALE PRACTITIONER AT WAT PHILA

I guess CIMC does seem a little matriarchal in some ways.
I mean there certainly is a heavily female presence.
DAWN, FEMALE PRACTITIONER AT CIMC

At the *Kathin* festival in October 2000, lay people lined up outside Wat Phila to offer cooked rice, fruit, bottles of water, and even toothpaste to the monks on this day that marked the end of the Buddhist Lent. A well-dressed Thai man in his fifties held a wicker basket filled with apples and bananas and tried to quiet his teenage children. "How long will we stay here?" his fifteen-year-old son whined. "If mom is going to stay as long as she wants, I should have brought my pajamas." The man shot his son a warning look just as his wife rushed by, giving him instructions as she passed. "Put everything in the basket in the monks' bowls. You have to do it, I don't have time." At CIMC, women are just as central to the organization's operations. Two-thirds of the people who lead the morning and evening meditation sessions are women, and women are the ones who often help with the center's weekly housecleaning and gardening.[1] Two-thirds of the people who regularly attend Wat Phila and CIMC are women, and gender is central to how each organization is structured and operates.[2]

While women's and men's voices have been central to the discussions of Buddhist community and personal identity in previous chapters, I directly address the issue of gender in this chapter by first asking how practitioners at Wat Phila and CIMC interpret the Buddha's teachings about gender and the importance of gender in the Buddhist tradition more generally. Practitioners at Wat Phila and CIMC both believe that the Buddha taught the same thing about and to laywomen and men.[3] Despite these common teachings, however, men and women at Wat Phila occupy more distinct roles than at CIMC. At Wat Phila, the monks and temple treasurer are men, while women do much of the volunteer work at the temple. In their volunteer work, however, women have responsibilities they would not have in Thailand and, as a result, are carving out new ideas about women's central role in Buddhism in the United States.[4] At CIMC, there are some differences in the formal teaching and leadership roles held by women and men and fewer in their voluntary roles. These differences persist even though the teachers and practitioners strive to create a truly egalitarian organization. I understand the differences between women and men observed at Wat Phila to result from historical, cultural, and demographic factors, and those observed at CIMC to result from cultural factors. As in most religious organizations in the United States, women are involved in Wat Phila and CIMC in greater numbers than their proportions in the Thai and American populations in the United States would predict.[5] I explore the organizational and personal implications of women's greater participation in Wat Phila and CIMC in this chapter's conclusion.

This chapter contributes a gendered perspective to discussions of the history and practice of Buddhism at Wat Phila, CIMC, and the United States more generally.[6] It also contributes more broadly to existing research about the gendered nature of organizations.[7] I defined gender in this chapter on two levels. At the individual level, I understand sex or sex category as the description of an individual based on generally agreed upon biological criteria, and gender as the socially constructed expectations and behaviors for individuals based on their sex definitions.[8] Organizationally, I define gender as a characteristic of an organization that is based on the sex of its leaders and practitioners, the ways women and men are structured inside the organization, and the organizations' teachings and policies about women and men.[9] The purpose of this organizational definition is to think analytically about how gender structures and informs organizational cultures and activities, and provides insight about more general social processes occurring within the organization and society more generally.[10]

## History

The Buddha taught male and female lay people and monastics during his lifetime, and what the Buddha actually thought and taught about the differences between women and men is the subject of significant scholarly discussion.[11] At Wat Phila, differences in the Buddha's teachings about women and men or the ability of laywomen and men to practice Buddhism or attain enlightenment are rarely mentioned directly in dhamma talks. Talks do occasionally focus on the roles of monks and nuns. Maha Nom gave a talk one Sunday about Mahapajapati Gotami, the Buddha's stepmother and aunt who wanted to become a female monk, or *bhikkhuni*. She decided to leave her royal social position to live as a monastic. She shaved her head, put on a white robe and no shoes and walked many miles to see the Buddha. When she arrived, Ananda, the Buddha's cousin and attendant, spoke to the Buddha on her behalf. At first the Buddha refused to allow women to become monks, saying that a homeless life is more dangerous for women than for men and that if women became monks, Buddhism would only continue for half as many years. Ananda pleaded with the Buddha, saying that Mahapajapati Gotami had raised the Buddha for many years and should have an opportunity to realize *nibbana*. Eventually, the Buddha allowed his stepmother and other women to become nuns, and he created eight additional guidelines for their lives. Shortly after she became a female monk, Mahapajapati Gotami became an *arahant*, or enlightened being, Maha Nom explained.[12] Practitioners at Wat Phila occasionally mention female nuns, generally stating that the Buddha did not want women to become nuns because he feared for their physical safety. Most people agree with the Buddha's logic. In the Theravada tradition, the order of nuns ended in the eleventh century and some people are working in Sri Lanka and Thailand today to support and restart the order.[13] Practitioners at Wat Phila generally do not have strong opinions about these efforts.

Differences in the Buddha's teachings about women and men apart from the subject of women as monastics are not often discussed in casual conversation at Wat Phila. When asked about gender directly in interviews, practitioners are nearly unanimous that the Buddha and Buddhism teach the same things about women and men, saying things like "Buddhism does not state any differences between women and men," "It's the same—the teachings for women and men," and "Like the Five Precepts. There's isn't one set of Five Precepts for women and another set for men." While the dhamma is the same, a number of people pointed out differences in the sangha. "The teachings don't differentiate," Dr. Malin told me. "The dhamma is the same; the sangha is different." Noo, a Thai engineer, says that the only difference in the Buddha's teachings about women and men right now is that women are no longer allowed to become monks or to touch monks because of the *vinaya* rules that guide monks' conduct.

Women and men are equally able to access and practice the dhamma, the teachers at CIMC argue, though, as at Wat Phila, gender is not often mentioned directly in their teachings. The teachers rarely speak about women or men as groups, focusing instead on the commonalties that underlie all human beings. "Under our conditioning, we are all the same," Larry taught in a meditation class I attended. "Our conditioning is part of our biography and individual story, but under that we are all the same." Numerous practitioners remarked on how all of the teachers, but Narayan in particular, create environments through the inclusive nature of their teachings, in which women and men feel equally welcome and comfortable. While there were gatherings just for women at CIMC in the past, these ended in the early 1990s and all of the teachings there, as at Wat Phila, are provided in mixed-sex groups.

CIMC differs from Wat Phila, however, in that gender, specifically the ways Buddhism has been practiced by women and men historically, is often a subject of casual conversation, and practitioners are particularly concerned with the gender component of Buddhism historically. The Buddha's historical and cultural context is often mentioned in these discussions, particularly in discussions about nuns and the additional rules the Buddha gave to the nuns.[14] Practitioners often describe Buddhism, as practiced historically, as a largely patriarchal religion and emphasize changes as Buddhism has moved west. "In the Theravada tradition in the West there's a really strong core of women teachers and a really conscious effort not to create or replicate any kind of hierarchical, male-dominated structure," Helen, a longtime practitioner, told me. Narayan believes that male teachers in the West have been extremely supportive rather than sexist. She explains, "There are a lot of women teachers and at this point there are a lot of strong women teachers."[15] Female practitioners, in particular, often refer to the importance of female teachers in the development of Buddhism as a more gender-egalitarian practice in the West. One practitioner referred to Christina Feldman, one of the first female teachers, saying, "I like how she and others were trying to bring some balance into a system that is really quite male and patriarchal." Narayan told me she was surprised recently to hear a female practitioner say there were too many female teachers. "I thought, why wasn't this said when there were many more men than women teaching? Anyway, it does point to the fact that things have changed and that there are enough women teaching these days. I do think it is a good situation for both men and women."[16] Many commentators also point to the gender-egalitarian undertones of Buddhism in the United States as one of the core ways Buddhism is changing and being changed by white American-born practitioners in the United States.[17]

## Gendered Organizations?

Although practitioners at Wat Phila and CIMC generally agree that the Buddha taught the same dhamma to women and to men, the ways the dhamma is enacted at Wat Phila and CIMC as organizations are very different. At Wat Phila, people say that since only men can become monks, gender influences the sangha but little else about the organization. The sangha, however, influences all aspects of the organization, and women and men are consistently involved with Wat Phila in different ways. CIMC was designed to be an organization in which women and men would be involved in the same ways. Although this has partially happened, there are more men than women in formal leadership and teaching roles at CIMC. Overall, women and men are generally involved in CIMC in less patterned ways than Wat Phila.

### WAT PHILA

Male images and men themselves are central to the formal organizational structure of Wat Phila. The Buddha is male, as is Luāngphō Sot and, with one exception, the images of the Buddha, Luāngphō Sot, and other monks displayed around the temple are men. The temple is formally led by five monks and a temple treasurer who are male. Taan Ajahn, the abbot, is president of the temple and Man, a layman, is the treasurer. Unlike other Thai temples in the United States, Wat Phila does not have a lay committee or other formal committees that help to carry out the work, though at many other temples these committees are largely male.[18]

While men are central to the formal leadership of Wat Phila, women are involved in most aspects of temple life, although in ways different from the men. Women prepare most of the meals for the monks. Nim, a hairdresser who lives a few blocks from the temple, prepares rice soup for breakfast for the monks on Wednesday mornings. "No one wants to do that," she told me, "because you have to get up so early. I get up at 4:30, a.m., but then I go home and take a nap." Sometimes women prepare the food alone and sometimes in groups, like the New Jersey group described in chapter 5. On Sundays, women are involved in all aspects of the service and often lead and direct activities. Women comprise about three-quarters of the morning meditation class. When the class ends, everyone normally goes into the kitchen to greet one another, have coffee, and talk informally. Women move around the kitchen talking and preparing food to offer to the monks for lunch, while the men normally stand along one counter in front of the coffee machine drinking coffee and chatting. In addition to leading the food preparations and later offerings, women often lead the lay chanting service on Sunday mornings, a role they would not necessarily occupy in Thailand. While both women and men can lead this service, one of several women took turns leading it during most of this research at Wat Phila.

In addition to their daily and weekly involvement in Wat Phila, women are also integrally involved in festival planning and preparations at the temple. On the Thursday before a big *Kathin* festival, the abbot discussed arrangements for the celebration with twelve people who had come to the temple that day, ten women and two men. The couple officially making the *Kathin* offering and responsible for seeing that things ran smoothly was there. No*ng*yao, the woman in this couple, sat directly under the abbot and took detailed notes during the hour-long conversation about how to set up the temple and organize the celebration, while her husband sat at some distance from the abbot and rarely participated in the conversation. At festivals, women prepare all of the food in the kitchen and largely control the speed at which activities take place by regulating when to make food available to the monks and lay people. Three women collect all of the financial donations from the people gathered during the festival, and women sell the flowers, candles, and sticks of incense that are often a part of the festivities. While men help at festivals by helping the monks receive rice and other material goods and by doing dishes in the kitchen and helping to prepare and clean up the temple, women are at the center of the organization, preparation, and leadership of the occasions.

Outside of formal or scheduled activities at Wat Phila, women and men are involved informally in Wat Phila in different ways. Women often take care of the monks, seeing that they have food, medicine, and other items that they need. In January 2001, I accompanied three laywomen and three monks on a trip to a nearby mall to purchase snow boots for the monks responsible for shoveling the snow and long underwear for one of the monks who was often cold. The abbot was ill through much of my fieldwork and it was largely women who brought him Ensure and other special food products and who often drove him to doctor's appointments in the area.[19] Men, on the other hand, tend to take care of the physical property around the temple. A group of men recently designed and constructed a new garden in front of the temple and worked on repairing a wall in the basement.

Women's high levels of involvement in Wat Phila must be understood in the context of the rules that govern interaction between women and monks, rules that require constant negotiations in day-to-day activities around gender. The five resident monks are guided in all of their behaviors by the *vinaya* rules outlined by the Buddha, including rules about how monks can interact with women.[20] These rules are quite detailed but generally stipulate that a monk may not be alone with a woman, may not touch a woman, and may not engage in private relations with a woman. Different monks and lay people interpret this rule differently, often based on the situation and how well respected the people involved are.[21] Ideally at Wat Phila one monk is not alone with a woman without another monk or preferably another monk and laywoman present. This rule is occasionally bent, however, such as when a monk needs to go somewhere and a woman is the only person available to drive him.[22] Monks and women also may not touch each other in any way. If a woman wants to hand an item to a monk or vice versa the item must rest on a neutral surface in the exchange. Monks carry small pieces of orange cloth with them. If a laywoman wants to hand a monk something, he places the piece of cloth in front of him and the woman places the item on the piece of cloth. When she removes her hands, the monk picks up the item. If a monk does not have the piece of cloth with him, he may improvise by using a table or piece of paper as the neutral area. This rule is rarely bent at Wat Phila. Monks and women never touch, but occasionally a monk will pass an item to a woman without a neutral surface area or by dropping it and letting the air serve as the neutral area. Finally, monks may not have sexual relations with women.[23] While it is expected and encouraged that laywomen and men will seek advice from the monks, preferably from the head monk, these conversations always take place in the main meditation hall with other people around. Women are allowed in the building where the monks live only with another person as chaperone and are discouraged from entering the monks' personal areas inside the house. Women's significant involvement in Wat Phila, and specifically in the care of the monks, must be understood against the backdrop of structures that outline the pragmatic ways this care may be provided.

## CIMC

Women are more involved in the formal leadership of CIMC than Wat Phila and there are fewer differences in how women and men are involved with the organization more generally. While differences in how women and men are involved in Wat Phila are part of the structure of the organization through the leadership and particularly the *vinaya* rules that govern the lives of the monks, CIMC was designed to minimize differences in how men and women are involved in the organization. Efforts to be gender-equitable at CIMC begin with male images of the Buddha around the center that are joined by several images of Kuan-yin, a female *bodhisatta* of compassion.[24] While she is not seated on the altar next to the Buddha, her images hang in several rooms around the center and she is often mentioned by American-born Buddhist practitioners largely because of her femaleness. Instead of an all-male monastic leadership, two male and one female teacher provide teaching and leadership of the center. While Larry, the founder, is a man, Narayan was centrally involved with CIMC from the start and currently serves as the president of the board of directors. At present there are four men and three women on the board. When the three teachers are not counted, there are two men and two women on the board. Based on the proportion of women and men involved with CIMC, however, men are more represented on the board of directors and among the teachers than they are in the center's population.

Men are also more represented in the gender composition of people who provide teachings at CIMC at the Wednesday night talks, often the largest gathering of the week. Excluding the three teachers, six women (30 percent of the total) and thirteen men (70 percent of the total) gave talks on Wednesday nights in 2001. Maddy Klyne, the center director, is aware of this imbalance and has tried hard during her tenure to bring more women speakers to CIMC. She mentioned to me that it is more difficult to get women to come to CIMC to speak on Wednesday nights, but the reasons why this may be the case are not clear.

Women and men are generally involved in the operation of CIMC in similar ways, though women are slightly more involved in some kinds of volunteering at the center. About two-thirds of the people in classes tend to be women, although this varies by teacher, with more women attending courses with Narayan and more men attending courses with Michael. Approximately two-thirds of the practice leaders (people who lead the daily morning and evening sittings) are female, a proportion that matches the proportion of women in the population at CIMC. Both women and men introduce the speaker on Wednesday nights, collect donations at the door, and clean up afterward. Men and women both volunteer at the center in other ways, though women generally cook for retreats, help with the weekly cleaning, and attend spring cleaning and gardening days in numbers greater than their numbers in the population.[25]

In addition to considering how women and men are involved in CIMC, it is important to briefly note that some evidence suggests that women and men approach the teachings presented at CIMC in very different ways. A range of books written by female practitioners for other female practitioners makes this argument theoretically, and Narayan began to make the argument empirically in an interview.[26] In talking about how women and men approach the practice, Narayan explained, "One generalization . . . sometimes with men there is this sense that they think they should already be enlightened and if they are not it is going to be a next day kind of thing. As in, why aren't I in the fourth *jhana* after three months of sitting? In contrast, women seem to be more *kilesa* oriented. They are more painfully aware of their limitations and insecurities and start their practice from there." Narayan does not judge either of these approaches, but rather points out their strengths: "You could say the first is that the aspirations are very strong, so that is wonderful. With women sometimes you can say the insecurities are very strong and there's more reality about what their true situation is."[27]

## Explanations

To understand why women and men are involved in Wat Phila and CIMC as they are, I raised the issue in casual conversation as well as in interviews at both centers. While some people, like those quoted at the beginning of the chapter, recognize the differences I observed, others rarely think about the gender dimension of their centers. At Wat Phila, I find that the differences in how women and men are involved with the center are related to the way Buddhism is passed along in Thai families, the ambivalent role of traditional Thai culture in the construction of Wat Phila, and a number of demographic factors. While not immediately recognizable to practitioners at Wat Phila, the demographic factors are essential to understanding the ways Thai people practice Buddhism there and across the United States. At CIMC, the ways in which women and men are involved with the center are directly a result of teachers and practitioners who value gender equity and are attempting to integrate Buddhism into American culture in a way that places gender equity at the core. The differences in the ways women and men are involved at CIMC point to some arguments about why women are disproportionately involved in most religious organizations in the United States and also reveal some of the difficulties of constructing truly gender-egalitarian organizations.

### WAT PHILA

Practitioners at Wat Phila learned about Buddhism from their families, and they describe this teaching as coming largely from their mothers and largely related to food. Many emphasized the fact that it was their mothers and grandmothers rather than male relatives who both went to the temple regularly and taught them about Buddhism as children. Mai spoke about how she and her mom would take food outside to the monks on alms rounds early in the morning. Dr. Malin said her mother went to the temple and cooked for the monks regularly and Dr. Nūang said her grandmother would cook every week and three generations of relatives would go to the temple to offer the food. "It united the family," Dr. Nūang and others remember. When she looks at Wat Phila now, Dr. Nūang sees that the majority of practitioners are women and thinks that women may be more interested in coming because they bring the food. "Thai men don't like to make food," she explains. "Women initiate by making food."

Women and men both describe learning about Buddhism from their mothers, and this learning partially explains why more women than men are involved in Wat Phila. Like their mothers, women at Wat Phila often view bringing food to the temple as a continuation of family traditions, almost a part of their domestic responsibilities. "In Thailand," Mai explained, "traditionally men work. They go out in the field and they work all day and the women are home preparing food and taking care of children. They have time and they can visit the temple. In the evening, men come home and have supper and they are tired and don't want to go to the temple. But the women make time to go to the temple. That's why women played and continue to play important roles in Buddhism." As Mai describes it, serving the monks and the temple is part of women's domestic work because of the necessity of food preparation and women's traditional daily routines in the home. Dr. Chan, a male practitioner, agrees, saying that to go to the temple you must prepare food, and that in Thailand men go away from the house early in the morning and it is women who stay home, take care of the kids, and have an opportunity to go to the temple. Serving the monks and the temple continues as women's work in the United States, in part because of the ways their mothers passed it along to them. [28]

While many Thai men learned about Buddhism from their mothers, these teachings often suggested that it is women's work to prepare food and take it to the temple. Men's connections to Buddhism result less from food preparation and offering than from the experiences many of them had as monks earlier in their lives. Temporary ordination is common in Thailand and most of the men who are regularly involved with Wat Phila spent between three weeks and a few months as monks in Thailand. Plā lived as a monk for three weeks at Wat Po just before he came to the United States as a student in 1973. Dr. Chan also spent three weeks as a monk at the temple in the village where he was born in central Thailand and he continues to feel a special connection with that temple. "Usually the community doesn't accept the males as a potential in-law," he explained, "unless you have been a monk. So in order to complete the requirement you have to be a monk a complete *phansa* [3 months]. I was not, because I was in school. That was an exception in the so-called modern society." Mū became a monk twice, first before he finished school and second after he finished school and had worked for the government for two years. When describing how they learned about Buddhism, men at Wat Phila mention their mothers, but focus on the time they spent as monks. Now that they are adults, their descriptions of their fathers as rarely coming to the temple except on holidays shed light on their lower attendance and men's lower attendance at Wat Phila generally.

In addition to acknowledging the ways Buddhism is passed along in Thai families, practitioners explain the different tasks performed by women and men at Wat Phila with reference to Thai culture and tradition. "Actually," Som told me, "we can all do the same jobs, but traditionally men do more with heavy lifting and things like that and women do more of the cooking." In talking about the gender differences at Wat Phila, Sam said they are all because of "custom that is embedded inside Buddhism; that is what makes it different." While some people see the reproduction of Thai culture along gender lines as a good or inevitable thing, quite a number of people think Thai culture is reproduced at Wat Phila in a slightly amended way that favors or supports the greater responsibilities women have there.

The amended or changing role of Thai culture is particularly evident in how practitioners talk about women leading the chanting services on Sunday mornings.[29] "It's mostly women; it's rare to see a man," Dr. Nūang observed. With a sly smile, Nū told me that if you go to Thailand, you never see women leading chanting sessions, only men. "But over here," she says, "the women are better than the men . . . you have to use the people who are skilled at being leaders." Her husband agreed, saying, "Women practice constantly and can lead. . . . Men are also too busy and they don't want to make the food [required to come to the temple]." Mai explained why women lead the chanting and have additional new responsibilities at the temple more generally, saying, "The culture says men are superior to women, but if you look at it in the opposite way you see that it's really women who control things. Without the women, nothing would happen." Without the women, there would be no food on Sundays, planning at the festivals, and care taken of the monks.[30] Without this underlying support, Wat Phila would be a very different kind of organization. While Wat Phila seeks, in part, to look like a temple in Thailand, these changing gender divisions of labor are a central way the tradition has adapted and changed in the United States.

Women also have more responsibilities at Wat Phila than at many temples in Thailand because of their numbers and the positions they occupy in several different communities in the United States. While personal history and cultural factors explain some of the differences in how women and men are involved in Wat Phila, demographic and structural characteristics are also a large part of the explanation. Women outnumber men in the Thai population in the United States. According to 2000 census data, close to 60 percent of all Thai people in the United States are women (see table 7.1). While many Thai women came to the United States in the 1970s to work as nurses and other professionals, between 1969 and 1977 approximately 20,000 also entered the country as the brides of American servicemen.[31] Among foreign-born Thai women in the United States, about half were married to non-Thai men according to the 1990 census.[32] More recently some Thai women have come to the United States as the mail-order brides of American men, though the exact number of these women and their prevalence in the population is difficult to determine.[33]

Women outnumber men at Wat Phila and therefore have more responsibilities there, both because there are not many men available to serve and because many of the women are university administrators, business owners, nurses, and other professionals accustomed to leadership roles[34]

Thai women's family relations in the United States also explain why they are more involved in Wat Phila than men. Women at Wat Phila fall into one of three groups. The largest group are women who come to the temple alone, generally because they are either widows or married to white or African American men who are not interested in attending or who are not invited. Most of their husbands do not speak Thai and cannot follow events at Wat Phila. Dæng, a Thai woman in her forties, told me that her husband has occasionally come to the temple, but that he thinks "Thai church is too long." Some women report that their husbands feel excluded from temple events, while the majority say that they like it that way. When I asked one Thai woman whether her American-born husband and son ever come to the temple, she answered yes. "They come to pick me up and to drop me off. I like that they don't come in. That way I can do whatever I want without worrying about them." Most of the widows at Wat Phila are between the ages of forty and sixty and became more involved with the temple following the death of their husbands.

The second largest group of practitioners at Wat Phila is Thai couples. Some regularly come to the temple as a couple, while in other cases the woman attends more than the man. Dr. Malin comes to Wat Phila more than her Thai husband and says she thinks community expectations are different for women and men. "If I go alone to the temple, no one says anything," she told me. "If my husband goes alone, everyone is surprised." The third group of people at Wat Phila are Thai women who come with their white or African American husbands. Two or three such couples are regularly involved in the temple. Thip, her white husband Philip, and their daughter come almost weekly. Philip speaks some Thai and is well integrated into temple activities. Other couples

TABLE 7.1. U.S. Residents Born in Theravada Buddhist countries or identifying racially or ethnically in terms of one by sex

| Country | 1980 | | 1990 | | 2000 | |
|---|---|---|---|---|---|---|
| | Men | Women (%) | Men | Women (%) | Men | Women (%) |
| Burma | — | — | — | — | — | — |
| Cambodia | 8665 | 7,379 (46) | 71,797 | 77,250 (52) | 100,511 | 105,541 (51) |
| Laos | 25,268 | 22,415 (47) | 76,361 | 71,014 (48) | 101,254 | 96,949 (49) |
| Sri Lanka | — | — | — | — | 12,872 | 11,715 (48) |
| Thailand | 18,023 | 27,256 (60) | 36,956 | 54,404 (60) | 62,604 | 87,679 (58) |

*Note:* Census data from 1990 and 2000 include people who were born in one of these five countries as well as people born in the United States who identify racially or ethnically in terms of one of these five countries. Census data from 1980 include only those people who were born in one of these five countries. Detailed data about race, ethnicity or ancestry were not collected about people from these five countries in the 1980 census. Information about people born in Burma or identifying racially or ethnically as Burmese was not available broken down by sex. This data was also not available for Sri Lanka, except in 2000 as indicated.

*Sources:* Numbers from 2000 represent people who listed an Asian group alone or in any combination. U.S. Bureau of the Census, *1980 Census of Population,* vol. 2, *Subject reports,* PC80-2-1E, *Asian and Pacific Islander Population in the United States,* issued January 1988. U.S. Bureau of the Census, *1990 Census of Population, Asian and Pacific Islanders in the United States,* issued August 1993, table 1: General characteristics of selected Asian and Pacific Islander groups by nativity, citizenship, and year of entry, 1990. U.S. Bureau of the Census, *2000 Census of Population and Housing,* Summary File 2, *Advanced National.*

come more sporadically. Kanyā occasionally brings her white husband to the temple, but, she says, "he just falls asleep. He tells me he is meditating but I hear him snoring."

For all of the women, but especially for the women married to non-Thai men, coming to Wat Phila is the one opportunity they have during the week to be with Thai people, speak Thai, and eat Thai food. Many of these women rarely cook Thai food because their husbands and children do not like it, and few live in areas or neighborhoods with high concentrations of Thai people. While the lack of men available to take on responsibilities at Wat Phila is one reason why there are so many women involved, another reason is that the temple gives them a unique opportunity to be with other Thai people in an American environment in which there are few such opportunities. This incentive is especially strong for women who are widowed or who are married to non-Thai men. For some of these women, the temple is a place where they can have some freedom and autonomy from their families. It is important to note that most Thai women at Wat Phila work, so free time does not explain why they are more involved than men. Some of the women do not drive, so they carpool to the temple with friends, a fact that makes their high levels of involvement particularly significant.

CIMC

Practitioners' histories do not explain why there are more women than men involved in CIMC. As the first generation of convert Theravada Buddhists in America, practitioners at CIMC do not have any specifically Buddhist history. There is no reason demographically why women outnumber men two to one at CIMC.[35] Between 61 and 67 percent of practitioners at CIMC are women according to sample membership lists, a June 1998 survey, and observation at classes and center events. While population data about white Buddhists in the United States do not exist, this observation parallels James Coleman's finding that there were more women than men in seven Buddhist groups he studied (overall, 57 percent of practitioners were women). Differences in the numbers of women and men were even more pronounced in the Theravada or vipassana meditation groups he studied.[36] Coleman argues that more women than men are attracted to Theravada or vipassana groups because the groups have heavily psychological undertones and are organized in nonhierarchical ways. Other commentators argue that the lack of male gods and patriarchal religious "furniture" to bump up against or the emphasis on interconnection attracts women to vipassana meditation groups in greater numbers than men.[37] It is important to note that women do not dominate numerically at Theravada Buddhist groups in the United States overall. Numrich found that more men than women attended the meditation groups of white American-born people at the Thai and Sri Lankan temples he studied, and there is evidence that more men than women attend events at the Washington Buddhist Vihara and the Bhavana Society, two monastic centers.[38] While American-born men seem to attend groups led by male monastics in greater numbers than women, women seem to attend lay-led groups in greater numbers, as evident in Coleman's findings, at CIMC, and in data about the gender distribution of practitioners at meditation retreats at the Insight Meditation Society and the Dhamma Dhara center in the Goenka tradition in Shelburne Falls, Massachusetts.[39]

The greater number of women than men involved in CIMC also reflects broader national trends in voluntary groups and religious groups specifically. In his study of small groups, Robert Wuthnow found that women were more likely to belong to a small group (44 percent of women in comparison to 36 percent of men). In studies about religious participation generally, women are consistently more likely than men to belong to religious organizations and to participate regularly.[40] Among Christians, women are regularly found to be more involved with churches and to be more spiritual than are men.[41]

Researchers argue that women are more involved in religious groups in the United States than men because they are more closely involved in the processes of birth and death, because they value community in different ways than men, and because they may be more risk-averse than men.[42] While several practitioners themselves hypothesized that women are more involved in CIMC and religious groups in the United States because they are closer to birth, death, and emotional issues generally, I was not able to test this possibility in this study.[43] At CIMC there is some evidence for the community argument, as more women than men say they came to CIMC not just in search of teachings but in search of connections with other people.[44] Anissa, the woman mentioned above who formed her own small groups when she was not able to attend CIMC, and several other people who tried to start smaller meditation groups in their communities were all women. It was the men in chapter 5 who relied on CIMC primarily as a silent community. While the women came in search of silence, they also actively sought out and were involved in speaking communities. "Look at our conditions," one longtime female practitioner told me. "I just want to say, women are taught to connect. I'm not saying guys are not, some guys are, but more of our conditioning is relational. Everything is relational. So it's not a shock that we want a connection to others and maybe to some higher or greater good." Women's desire for small communities and people with whom to practice in silence and speech is likely related to women's greater attendance at CIMC generally and in classes specifically.[45]

Women's involvement in CIMC's leadership results not from a lack of men, but from design, though the design is not flawless or fully equitable in terms of who holds positions, as the gender distribution of teachers, board members, and Wednesday night speakers reflects. The movement toward gender equity at CIMC, however, is a conscious effort that the vast majority of practitioners feel has been effective. Christine, the owner of a feminist bookstore, told me, "I'm a feminist, I mean, I just see everything in terms of gender. . . . I have never had a problem at the center with gender issues and that was actually very important to me. It is one of the first . . . spiritual institutions that I participated in where I felt gender issues were not relevant. And why? I think because of the teachers." While convinced that there is sexism everywhere, Christine added that at CIMC "it was not registering on my radar screen and that was enough

for me. . . . I've never felt that air. I've always felt that it was a healthy place."
Carol described her problems with the gender dimensions of other Buddhist
teachers and teachings before concluding that CIMC is really very good as far as
gender issues go. "I heard the Dalai Lama talk once and that was very difficult
for me," she explained. "He said that according to his reading and his teaching
there is only one way in this particular lifetime that a woman can reach enlightenment. . . . There were three or four ways and women could only make
it one way. So I do have certain struggles around that . . . but CIMC is really
very good so I don't have a problem there." While the male majority among
the teachers, board members, and Wednesday night speakers makes it appear
that CIMC is not as gender equitable as it could be, the practitioners largely do
not have that sense.

While practitioners at Wat Phila and CIMC agree that the dhamma teaches
the same thing about women and men, that teaching translates into the gender
distribution in each organization in very different ways. At Wat Phila, women
and men generally have different jobs and responsibilities at the temple, with
men in the formal leadership and women in all aspects of voluntary and informal leadership, although women do have more responsibilities at Wat Phila
than they would in a temple in Thailand. At CIMC practitioners are aware of
the ways Buddhism has been interpreted and practiced by women and men
historically and as a result they aim to create a community in which there are
no gender distinctions or divisions. Despite their awareness and efforts, however, men do hold more leadership positions and women are more involved in
some voluntary activities at CIMC. This points to how difficult it is to create
truly gender-egalitarian organizations.

## Effects

The gender dimension of Wat Phila and CIMC does not lead women and men
at either center to practice Buddhism differently in their homes or to construct
different personal identities. The gender component of these organizations
does influence how the organizations function. While there are no female-led
temples or all-male or -female meditation centers to compare Wat Phila and
CIMC to, it is helpful to point out some of the ways that gender shapes and is
shaped by organizations.

At Wat Phila, men who occupy the leadership positions clearly influence
how the organization is structured and functions. Women and men practice
Buddhism differently at Wat Phila, in large part in response to the all-male
sangha. For historical and cultural reasons, as argued above, women tend to

prepare the food and take care of the monks, and men tend to take more care of the buildings and grounds. The most significant outcome of the gender distribution of responsibilities at Wat Phila is the opportunities this distribution creates for women to have responsibilities that they likely would not have in Thailand. These increasing responsibilities show Thai women carving out new roles for themselves in Buddhism as practiced in the United States. A second important outcome of the gender distribution of Wat Phila is the unique gendered spaces it creates, particularly for women. Especially on weekdays, the kitchen at Wat Phila is often a women-only space, where women meet, like the New Jersey group does on Thursdays, to make merit through their donations to the monks as well as to spend time with other Thai women. Only two of the eight women who usually attend on Thursdays are married to Thai men, and for these women, as noted above, Wat Phila is an important religious and cultural space that has a clear gender dimension. In the kitchen at Wat Phila women talk about husbands, health, and other topics often not discussed in more gender or racially mixed company. Similar single-sex groups for men may occur with the monks inside the *kuti,* or monastic residence.[46] The informal leadership opportunities and the small communities that Wat Phila allows for women are two of the most important outcomes of its gendered nature.

Organizationally, the gendered effects of CIMC as an organization are largely about the lack of gender distinctions practitioners experience there. Practitioners do not generally experience CIMC as a gendered space, and the majority of people do not seem to recognize that there are more women there than men. There are no spaces at CIMC where only women or men gather. While the greater number of men than women in leadership positions undoubtedly influences how the organization operates, it is important to recognize that a person's sex does not necessarily predict his or her position on issues related to gender. The high degree of sensitivity to gender and other issues at CIMC has led to an organization that is moving toward being genderless, by which I mean an organization in which gender differences have few personal or organizational effects.

## Conclusion

The monks, teachers, and practitioners at Wat Phila and CIMC generally understand the dhamma to teach the same things about male and female lay people. From these teachings, for a range of historical, cultural, and demographic reasons, these two organizations have developed in very different directions along gender lines. Like the majority of religious organizations in America, men lead at Wat Phila and women are the majority of practitioners, though women at Wat Phila have more responsibilities than women in Thailand and are developing new understandings of the woman's place in Buddhism as practiced in the United States. At CIMC, gender is viewed, in large part, as something to be transcended rather than embraced. Differences between women and men are rarely mentioned, even though they do exist at the center, as the teachers and organization strive to help people move beyond many of the ways they have been conditioned to behave.

As an analytic lens, gender at Wat Phila and CIMC points to how the organizations are differently structured and provide places for women and men to be involved in different ways. It also points to women's greater involvement in religious organizations in the United States and to the importance of recognizing those differences when examining how organizations function and operate, and how people influence those organizations and are influenced by them in their daily lives.

*Chapter 8*

## TAKING STOCK,
## LOOKING FORWARD

Much has changed in the United States since 1966 when Ven. Bope Vinitha flew from Sri Lanka to Washington, D.C., with a Buddha statue and relic of the Buddha on his lap to start the Washington Buddhist Vihara. Since then, hundreds of temples, monasteries, and meditation centers in the Theravada Buddhist tradition have started across the United States, and hundreds of thousands of people have learned about Buddhism from the monks and lay teachers who lead these groups. Unlike in Thailand, Sri Lanka, and other countries in Southeast Asia where Theravada Buddhist teachings and organizations are often taken for granted, the first generation of immigrant and convert Theravada Buddhist practitioners in the United States had to make deliberate decisions to learn about and practice the tradition. With intent and great effort, they have supported and constructed new organizations in the United States through which they hear and practice the dhamma.[1]

Over the past thirty-five years, aspects of the Theravada Buddhist tradition came to the States from South and Southeast Asia with immigrants in search of work, returning Peace Corps volunteers holding onto pieces of their experiences, traveling monks and teachers intent on keeping the tradition alive, and through books and audiotapes that explain how to meditate and take refuge in the Buddha. These carriers have interacted with the American context of reception in multiple ways, leading Theravada Buddhism to take many forms.[2] Immigrants like those at Wat Phila generally started temples much like those in their home countries, bringing the monks, the Buddha images, the religious practices, and often the architects and blueprints needed to construct buildings that physically resemble temples in Thailand, Sri Lanka, and other countries in Southeast Asia. Despite the physical similarities of their centers, however, the immigrant Theravada Buddhists made many adaptations, ranging from the building materials to the monks' dress to the responsibilities of women.

Among convert practitioners these adaptations took different forms, as the teachers and practitioners at CIMC and many other organizations moved away from monastic-led organizations toward centers led by male and female lay teachers based firmly on the practice of meditation. While consciously moving away from monks, temples, rituals, and others aspects of what some call the cultural trappings of Buddhism in Southeast Asia, many convert Theravada Buddhist practitioners nevertheless worked over the past thirty-five years to preserve and pass along the essence of the Buddha's teachings in the United States.

## Religious Adaptation

### COMMON PATTERNS

Increased immigration, particularly from Asia and Latin America, has led Buddhist practitioners as well as practitioners in many other religious traditions in the United States to change and adapt their traditions over the past thirty-five years. Research points to a number of commonalities in how post-1965 immigrants adapted their religions in the American context of reception. First, and perhaps most important, many new immigrants, Christian and non-Christian alike, created religious organizations with congregational forms in which people gather once a week, normally on Saturday or Sunday.[3] This is described by R. Stephen Warner as "de facto congregationalism," and as Fenggang Yang and Helen Rose Ebaugh point out, is one way immigrants adapt their religions in the United States.[4] The development of congregational-type gatherings results directly from the structure of American life, in which weekends are when many people are free and able to come to religious centers, and from underlying Protestant religious traditions in America that lead congregations to be an unofficial norm. Unlike in many immigrants' home countries, where membership in particular religious groups is assumed, membership in these new religious "congregations" is not automatic, but voluntary, and requires concerted, continuous, effort on the part of practitioners.

As at Wat Phila, many other post-1965 immigrant practitioners adapted their traditions in ways that allowed people to come for both religious and non-religious ceremonies particular to their home countries.[5] At Wat Phila this is evident in people gathering for Buddhist holidays as well as other holidays, like the king of Thailand's birthday, that do not have any direct Buddhist significance. Wat Phila and most other religious organizations started by recent immigrants are also ethnic centers where people go to speak traditional languages, eat traditional foods, meet with others from their home countries, and obtain assistance from others involved with the organization. Korean churches, for example, maintain cultural traditions, provide social services, and offer status and fellowship in addition to religious services.[6] When I visited a Thai temple in Washington, D.C., one weekday afternoon, several Thai women were there folding newsletters for the temple while watching a Thai television program, eating Thai food, and chatting with each other in Thai. Informal opportunities for socializing like these exist in most religious organizations started by immigrants to the United States in the last thirty-five years and point to the importance of temples and churches not only as religious organizations but also as social stages where the challenges of economic, political, and cultural adaptation are eased.

In addition to these structural adaptations, Fenggang Yang and Helen Rose Ebaugh point to adaptations in internal organization shared by many new immigrants' religious organizations. Many have more structured schedules and patterns of worship than in their home countries, changed roles for women and clergy, and more use of the vernacular than formal languages for worship, among other things. Many new immigrant religious organizations also tend to include more lay people, often more laywomen, among their leaders in the United States than they do in their home countries.[7] There is evidence of each of these adaptations at Wat Phila. Although it is impossible to fully assess all of the adaptive strategies utilized by post-1965 immigrants who form religious groups without more comprehensive data than are currently available, existing research clearly shows that many of the ways that the leaders and practitioners at Wat Phila created their organization resemble the ways other post-1965 immigrant religious groups have been constructed in the United States.

Similarly, many of the ways the Cambridge Insight Meditation Center has adapted the Buddhist tradition in the United States resemble the ways other non-Asian, primarily white, Buddhist practitioners and converts to several other Asian religions, particularly South and Southeast Asian religions, have adapted those religious traditions in the United States in recent years. Rather than forming a congregation, for example, CIMC and other groups began from people's interest in a specific *practice*, like meditation, mantras, or yoga.[8] Just as Larry Rosenberg's early teachings were based almost exclusively on the practice of meditation, some early white Zen, Soka Gakkai, and yoga teachers met their students not because of their common interest in the tradition or their own personal histories but around shared interest in the practices these traditions offered.[9] These practices were often taught in groups and then practiced individually, appealing primarily to baby boomers interested in religious or spiritual practices with a largely individualistic ethos.[10] The communal components that are very much a part of people's experiences at CIMC developed only through people's commitment to meditation and their changed perspectives through that practice.

Similarly, as in many other convert Buddhist centers and groups started by white people interested in other Asian religions, the practice of meditation at CIMC is initially presented largely outside its historic and religious context. People who come to the center generally learn little, if anything, directly in their first visit about the history of Buddhism, the ways it developed, or the various countries where it is currently practiced. Like some forms of transcendental meditation and yoga, for example, meditation at CIMC is initially presented almost like aerobics or an exercise that can be done without regard for the tradition's context.[11] In the same way that many people approached transcendental meditation, many people initially approach CIMC, and the meditation practice specifically, not because they want to understand Buddhism or find a religious tradition, but because they are seeking a way out of their own suffering and struggles and a way to have more peace and understanding in their lives. People who remain involved with CIMC generally do develop more interest in and understanding of the Buddhist tradition, but only after some time.

And finally, as at many other Buddhist and convert Asian religious centers, visiting CIMC and learning about Buddhism and meditation does not require membership in the organization or belief in any particular set of religious doctrines or traditions. Like Christians who take yoga classes and Jews who visit Zen centers, visitors to CIMC initially practice meditation devoid of particular beliefs or requirements of organizational memberships. For some practitioners, as Stephen Batchelor argues, the ideas presented at CIMC are "Buddhism without beliefs."[12]

## DISTINCTLY THERAVADA BUDDHIST ADAPTATIONS

Practitioners at Wat Phila and CIMC share several strategies of adaptation in their first generation, suggesting several unique ways Theravada Buddhist organizations more generally may be adapting in the United States.[13] First, as both centers adapted Theravada Buddhism in the States, the monks and teachers at both centers emphasized that the Buddha taught people to "come and see," and practitioners often repeat this teaching to visitors. The Buddha taught, they say, that people should hear his teachings, try out what he teaches, and then take what makes sense to them, leaving the rest behind. People at both centers are encouraged not to believe most, or even any, of what they see but to try the practices the Buddha taught and see if they are helpful in their lives.

In teaching people to "come and see," both centers encourage and support some variation in the teachings and practices offered and welcomed at each center. At Wat Phila, this means that dhamma talks are often broad, combining a teaching of the Buddha, a story of the Buddha in a previous life, and a Thai folktale in ways that allow for multiple interpretations. Dhamma talks almost always take place in the context of chanting, meditation, and other rituals in which everyone present participates. While some practices, like fortune-telling, are not welcome at Wat Phila, many others are, and people with a range of approaches to the Buddhist tradition regularly participate. Kop, a layman, and Nū, a laywoman, often sit side by side at Wat Phila and participate in the same chanting, meditation, and merit-making ceremonies, despite their very different approaches to the Buddhist tradition. One Sunday, Kop explained to me that the purpose of chanting is to remind us about the Buddha and his teachings, teachings that we then accept or reject based on our own meditation practice and study. Later that morning, Nū told me that she likes the morning chanting because it allows her to make merit for a better rebirth, to show respect to Luāngphō Sot, and to thank Luāngphō Sot for help he provided in her life that week. People at Wat Phila who know Kop and Nū are not bothered by their differing approaches to the Buddhist tradition, and the monks are aware and supportive of both approaches within Wat Phila as an organization.

At CIMC the breadth of teachings and practices welcomed and supported is evident in the list of people that Larry, Narayan, and Michael consider their own teachers, the range of influences evident in the center's physical space, and the range of people who give talks on Wednesday nights. As at Wat Phila, practitioners with very different approaches to the Buddha's teachings share the same space. Jean and Helen, for example, have taken several classes together and both occasionally attend a Wednesday evening talk or Thursday morning retreat. Jean came to CIMC on the advice of her therapist and uses meditation mostly for stress relief in combination with a few other practices her therapist recommended. Helen, on the other hand, has studied Pali and Buddhism for many years. She describes meditation as the core of her approach to Buddhism and Buddhism as the guiding system in her life and is clear in talking about her practice that before she includes a piece of the Buddha's teaching in her way of seeing the world she spends time trying to judge for herself whether or not it is true. Despite their different approaches to the Buddha's teachings and the Theravada Buddhist tradition more generally, both Jean and Helen are involved with CIMC and learn and benefit from the teachings and talks there. Boundaries around what is and is not welcome at CIMC are maintained directly by the board and teachers in their decisions about who can teach at the center and indirectly by the practitioners, as was evident in the experiences of the visitor described in chapter 4, who left CIMC disappointed because people there did not share his interest in light and energy movements between people.

The "come and see" attitude and relative flexibility in the teachings and practices present and welcome at Wat Phila and CIMC lead each to a second adaptive strategy that favors loosely bounded organizations that enable a range of people to be involved in different ways. It is the Buddhist emphasis on practices, rather than beliefs, as in Christianity and other religions of the book, that allow Wat Phila and CIMC to comfortably maintain degrees of internal diversity in their organizations as they adapt to new places, not only in the United States, but around the world.[14] Regardless of what they believe, almost everyone at Wat Phila chants, meditates, or participates in the rituals and ceremonies done as a large group. And everyone at CIMC meditates, often in smaller groups at the center. It is these practices that are at the core of both organizations and because practitioners share the practices, they coexist despite their different beliefs and interpretations. Most notably, this emphasis on practice is different from the approach taken at many evangelical Christian churches where sets of beliefs, about the Bible and Jesus Christ, are the core ideas around which the organizations are structured.

The third adaptive strategy evident at both Wat Phila and CIMC, and resulting from the centers' emphases on practice and loosely bounded organization, is the deemphasis of organizational identity, membership, and personal identity. Neither center emphasizes its organizational identity with markers like large signs, items bearing the center's name, or lengthy discussion about how their center is different from others. Similarly, people at Wat Phila and CIMC are committed to their centers, but few people at either place spoke about membership as having any particular significance. At Wat Phila the concept of membership does not exist, and the temple maintains a mailing list rather than a membership list. People do join CIMC as members, but there is no formal ceremony, people who are members do not differ in any significant ways from people who are not members, and individual practitioners do not know or care who is or is not a member of the organization. People at Wat Phila and CIMC are proud of their centers, but do not identify themselves in terms of them. Rather, practitioners at both centers identify in terms of the Buddha's teachings, with some simultaneously deemphasizing the importance of such personal identification. While some practitioners easily identify as Buddhist, often describing changes in their lives that have led to this identity, others are ambivalent about the word "Buddhist," saying that the Buddha himself was not a "Buddhist," so there is no reason for them to be. A few practitioners at both centers point out the ultimate hollowness of any particular religious identity, saying that the point is not the identity but the practice.

These three adaptive strategies, (1) the "come and see" attitude and flexibility in teachings and practices, (2) loosely bounded organizations based on practices, and (3) the deemphasis of organizational and personal identities present at Wat Phila and CIMC, result in large part from how the monks, teachers, and practitioners at both centers understand the Theravada Buddhist tradition and view the heartwood in the Buddha's teaching as told to me by Bhante Gunaratana and outlined in chapter 1. As each of the people in the sutta returned with a piece of the tree, the others told them it was not the heartwood. It was only the last person in the sutta, Bhante Gunaratana said, who got the core, "the very solid heartwood of the tree." The true heartwood that the people in this sutta seek is the perpetual, timeless emancipation from suffering. Bhante Gunaratana sees the non-Asians that he teaches in retreats across the country as the ones really seeking the heartwood, while other teachers and monks see it differently. The monks, teachers, and practitioners at Wat Phila and CIMC agree that the heartwood is the complete end of suffering, best accessed through the meditation practice taught and nurtured at both centers.

Practitioners at Wat Phila see the tree this sutta describes as one with many branches, all of which can lead practitioners to less suffering. Meditation is the best path, most agree, though it is only the monks, the majority believe, who can achieve the depths of meditation that lead to enlightenment, or nibbana, the complete end of suffering in this lifetime. The lay people support the monks in their meditation practice, through the exchange of material and spiritual goods, and they also meditate, chant, and participate in merit-making ceremonies and other rituals, all of which can been seen as the inner bark, outer bark, sapwood, and other parts of the tree. These other activities will not lead to nibbana in this life, most lay practitioners believe, but they can decrease suffering in this life and lead to better rebirth in the next. All of these parts of the tree are necessary in order for Theravada Buddhism, which they generally view as a religion, to take root in the States.

While practitioners at CIMC believe that the complete end of suffering is the heartwood of the tree, they also believe that lay people and monastics are equally able to access the heartwood and that it is possible to achieve the complete end of suffering or enlightenment in this lifetime. In the early days, the teachers and lay practitioners at CIMC focused only on the meditation practice, believing that any other branches of the Theravada Buddhist tree were just the sapwood and would only get in the way. Over the years, however, the teachers and practitioners have come to realize that the tree cannot survive with only the heartwood and they have gradually introduced other branches through rituals and ceremonies, regular gatherings to take the precepts, and holiday gatherings. These branches, they increasingly believe, support the meditation practice, and combined with meditation can lead to the complete end of suffering in this lifetime. Practitioners at CIMC fall along a continuum in response to questions about whether the teachings they hear at the center are "Buddhist," "Theravada Buddhist," or "religious." Some prefer the word "spiritual," and others would like to beg the whole question in order to focus more narrowly on the teachings and meditation practice.

## IN SUMMARY

American society has generally been supportive of Buddhism and Buddhist groups, and both Wat Phila and CIMC were started in this broadly supportive context.[15] The monks, teachers, and practitioners started each group from scratch, working within the institutional and structural spaces available in the United States for new religious and nonprofit organizations. Wat Phila and CIMC, as a result, resemble other new groups started in different religious traditions in the United States in the past ten to twenty years. Understanding how these groups developed within the existing American context of reception, however, tells only part of the story of how Theravada Buddhism adapted in the United States. To fully understand the story, the history, organizational patterns, and specific teachings, beliefs, and practices that are a part of Theravada Buddhism must also be considered, and it is this history that leads to the distinct adaptive strategies evident at Wat Phila and CIMC. It is the combination of factors present in the American context of reception and Theravada Buddhism's history and practice that explains what Max Weber would describe as the "elective affinity" between aspects of Theravada Buddhism and American society that led Wat Phila, CIMC, and other Theravada Buddhist organizations across the country to develop and adapt in distinctive ways in the past thirty-five years, and particularly the past ten years.[16]

More generally, the history and development of Wat Phila, CIMC, and Theravada Buddhism in America point to the importance of examining all of the global paths and networks along which a religious tradition arrives in the United States to understand how it adapts and changes in a new environment. Many studies of religion and globalization have been largely historical and focused only on immigrants in the contemporary United States. The current study shows what is gained conceptually and theoretically by considering all of the ways a given religious tradition arrives in the United States and takes shape in its first generation, not just in the abstract, but in the lives of individual practitioners. Rather than looking only at immigrants, taking this approach broadens the question to consider the movement of a religious system and charts a conceptual approach to empirically based studies of religion and globalization that may also be used more broadly to examine how other sets of ideas travel and are diffused and adapted structurally and culturally in new places.

Globalization has been both a homogenizing and distinguishing factor for Theravada Buddhism in the United States in its first generation and this study points to factors to consider in future research about how globalization influences the migration, development, and adaptation of religions in the United States and other geographic locations. These factors include the societal conditions of exit and reception, the particularities of the religious tradition, the ways in which the tradition arrives in the United States, the resources practitioners have, the practitioners' goals, and the practitioners' ties with their home countries.

## Looking Forward

This book paints a detailed picture of Wat Phila, CIMC, and Theravada Buddhism in its first generation in the United States, but says little about the future which is, of course, unknown. Since I concluded this research, several important changes have taken place at both centers. In March 2002, an important part of the first generation at Wat Phila passed with the death of Taan Chaokuhn Rattanamēthē (Taan Ajahn), the abbot and founding monk of the temple, from the cancer he battled for years. A viewing was held at the temple, as is the custom in Thailand, and monks from other Thai temples in the States chanted over a seven-day period in the presence of the body. At the end of that time, two Thai laymen accompanied Taan Ajahn's body to Thailand, where it was cremated at Wat Pāknām, surrounded by flowers and wreaths sent from practitioners in the States. Some of Taan Ajahn's ashes remain at Wat Pāknām and others were brought back to the States and now sit on the altar at Wat Phila. After Taan Ajahn's passing, Maha Nom was appointed abbot. Maha Supit and Maha Laothong continue to assist with the running of the temple and two new monks recently arrived from Thailand. Sunday gatherings and festivals continue, and the lay people are currently collecting funds and breaking ground for a new building on the property.[17] In the fall of 2003, the temple also began to offer meditation classes in English for people who live in the area.

More than fifty people attended the first session, on a Saturday morning in September, and the monks and lay people plan to make these classes a weekly occurrence.

Less has changed at CIMC as Larry Rosenberg, Narayan Liebenson Grady, and Michael Liebenson Grady continue to teach a growing number of practitioners. An additional administrative position was recently added to help the existing staff at the center. Director Maddy Klyne recently began to teach occasional beginners' classes at the center, and Matthew Daniell, a longtime meditation and hatha yoga practitioner, began to teach yoga classes for meditation practitioners at CIMC. Wednesday night talks, classes, retreats, and community activities continue and the number of people attending most of these events continues to increase.

As time passes and the monks, teachers, and practitioners in the first generation age, Wat Phila, CIMC, and other Theravada Buddhist organizations across the country will likely face a number of challenges. First, demographically the children of practitioners at such organizations do not automatically become Buddhist practitioners themselves. Newly arrived immigrants from Thailand continue to expand the number of first-generation practitioners at Wat Phila, but only a few children of first-generation immigrants attend regularly . Members of this second generation do occasionally come to the temple for festivals, but they normally spend their time as far away from their parents and the activities going on inside the temple as possible. As the second generation gets older and begins to form families, it is possible that they will come back to Wat Phila, though the second generation in many immigrant groups in the United States has traditionally stayed away from religious centers.[18] As the abbot of the New York Thai temple Wat Vajiradhammapadip argues, fewer people will probably come to Thai temples in the future because the second generation understands little of what takes place there.[19] As the number of Thai and other Asian Buddhist temples in the United States has continued to increase, competition between them for first- and second-generation practitioners' time and financial support has also increased. U.S. immigration laws, patterns in Thai immigration, and the decisions made by second-generation Thais as they age will all influence the future demographic challenges faced by Thai temples in the United States.

CIMC and other convert Theravada Buddhist centers will likely face demographic challenges in the United States as well. Although these centers have continued to attract new practitioners, many are in the same age range as current practitioners. Very few members of the second generation are involved with CIMC, and as at many other convert Theravada Buddhist centers, many do not have children, or the children they do have are grown and not interested in Buddhism. Even if the few second-generation children involved with CIMC and other convert Buddhist centers stay involved, there are not enough of them to replace the baby boomers, who are currently the demographic center of these organizations.[20] In part as a response to this fact, the Insight Meditation Society is continuing its retreat for people aged fourteen to nineteen and has recently initiated an outreach program to assist young people financially who want to attend longer retreats at the center.[21]

A second challenge many immigrant Theravada Buddhist organizations in the United States will face is that as the monastic and lay founders of immigrant centers age, temples will need to decide how to pass along the responsibilities of leadership. Thus far, Thai temples have continued to import monks born and trained in Thailand, and this practice will probably continue as long as first-generation Thai immigrants are in the majority at the temples. Some temples have made motions to broaden their support base, for financial reasons as well as because they see so many non-Thais in the States interested in Buddhism.[22] Language is an issue in doing so, however. The English language training that monks receive at missionary monk school before coming to the States has improved, but many monks at Thai temples in the United States are not comfortable speaking English or interacting with non-Thai speakers. If temples do want to reach out to non-Thais or to the non-Thai-speaking children of first-generation parents, language will be a challenge. There is also a cultural gap between the monks at many Thai temples and non-Thai speakers and second-generation Thais who were raised in the United States. Without an indigenous sangha or extensive language and cultural training, this gap will be difficult to bridge.[23]

CIMC and other convert Theravada Buddhist organizations will also face challenges in leadership, especially in selecting and training new teachers. Like Larry Rosenberg, the first generation of teachers generally went to Thailand and other parts of Asia and returned and began to teach. They were not selected or trained to teach in a particular way, but adapted the dhamma in content and form to the American context as they saw fit. Selecting future teachers is now more deliberate, and creating a process to do that is proving difficult in many organizations. First, without a monastic order and training curriculum, there is no obvious model to use when training teachers. Second, there are no clear requirements about who can become a teacher and how people who want to become teachers should express that desire and prepare themselves. At the Insight Meditation Society, practitioners interested in teaching have generally spent time at the center on the staff or in other capacities waiting to be recognized by one of the senior teachers and trained through long periods of silent practice. Some of this may change with the opening of a teacher training program at IMS in conjunction with the start of the Forest Refuge center, a new organization located next door to IMS. Joseph Goldstein and others created the Forest Refuge center as an "environment where people can devote themselves to the cultivation of insight and compassion for extended periods of time." He explains that "because the interest [in meditation] in our country is so strong and the demand for teachers so strong, the tendency is to rush the process . . . but it's not an instant process. It really takes a long time of maturation."[24] Jack Kornfield also started a teacher training program of his own at Spirit Rock several years ago. The programs at IMS and Spirit Rock exist independently of one another, however, and there are currently no shared model, standards, or credentials in how these teachers are being trained.

Immigrant and convert Theravada Buddhist organizations will also likely face challenges in maintaining their physical structures and securing resources. While the first generation constructed the buildings, the second generation, if there is to be one, will need to maintain and possibly expand them. In some cases, attempts to do so have tapped into broader tensions about what kinds of new buildings should be constructed and how resources should be allocated. Many newer Thai temples are in debt, a factor which influences all of these discussions.[25] Similarly, many convert centers struggle every year to make ends meet while trying to decide whether the teachings should be offered for free following the system of *dana* or whether membership and class fees should be charged. Issues related to centers' physical structures and resources will only increase with time as buildings and other infrastructure age.

Finally, the most important challenge facing immigrant and convert Theravada Buddhist organizations alike is how to preserve the heartwood or essence of the Buddha's teachings in the United States. At some immigrant centers, this is a question about how to keep the dhamma from being crowded out by ethnic and cultural events like the summer schools that some temples run to teach children about Buddhism, Thai culture, and Thai language. At CIMC and other convert centers the relevant question is how to make sure the dhamma does not become just another trend or form of stress relief. "Dharma is getting expressed now in terms of stress reduction, the school system, the medical system" Larry Rosenberg explains, "Awareness can enrich our culture; I'm all for that. But if in the process we lose touch with the roots of where this came from, I think it could be a big loss. . . . I have a healthy respect for something that survived 2600 years through thick and thin. . . . No matter what other things happen . . . study should continue. Long-term practice should continue." The danger at CIMC and other convert centers is that without clear ways to preserve and pass the dhamma along, it may end up coopted into just another aspect of contemporary therapeutic and health and fitness teachings.

Underlying all of these challenges is the question of what shape Theravada Buddhism will take in the United States in future generations. On one hand, the Theravada Buddhist map described in chapter 2 may remain largely as is— a group of loosely connected organizations best understood in terms of where the founders of the centers were born, where the people who attend the centers were born, or the lineage of the organization. On the other hand, the category "Theravada" might also become so fluid as to become useless, particularly as Buddhist centers founded by non-Asians include many other teachings and practices.[26] Or perhaps the map will be reconfigured. As Thai and other Asians become increasingly assimilated to the United States, perhaps their approach to the Theravada Buddhist tradition will change and come to resemble native-born Americans' visions. Or perhaps organizations founded by immigrants and those founded by converts will begin to work together more. Many of the non-Asian monks at monastic centers like Metta Forest Monastery and Abhayagiri Monastery have connections with second-generation Thai practitioners that might facilitate such reconfigurations, particularly if these second-generation Thais move into the leadership of different temples.

Regardless of how Theravada Buddhism develops in the future in America, it will in some ways reflect the commitment, dedication, and hard work of the practitioners in the first generation described here. These people donated their time, money, and labor to create organizations where they could practice in the diverse ways they understand the tradition. As Wat Phila, CIMC, and the many other Theravada Buddhist organizations in the United States continue to grow, change, and adapt, the monks, teachers, and practitioners will continue, as they have thus far, in their own ways to seek the heart.

*Appendix A*

# RESEARCH METHODS

This research developed directly from time I spent in Kandy, Sri Lanka, between January and August 1999 with the support of a Fulbright fellowship. My host family in Sri Lanka held meditation classes in their home. It was by attending a few of these classes and visiting many Buddhist temples around the island that I began to wonder how Buddhism is understood and practiced by different people in their day-to-day lives. Thinking about what I knew of Buddhism in America, I wondered how Buddhism changed when it moved from Sri Lanka to the United States and how Sri Lankans and non-Asians in the United States understood and practiced it.

When I returned to the United States in the fall of 1999, I continued to think about these questions and more broadly about the relationship between how religions or ideas travel and how they are constructed and understood by people in new locations. Out of these questions, exploratory visits to Buddhist centers, and conversations with Asian and white Buddhist practitioners, the present project took shape. Early in my explorations, Donald Swearer, who is the Charles and Harriet Cox McDowell Professor of Religion at Swarthmore College, invited me to visit Wat Mongkoltepmunee (Wat Phila), a Thai temple in the suburbs of Philadelphia, with his undergraduate class. This visit, combined with the opportunity to study Thai language at the University of Pennsylvania, the fact that many more Thai than Sri Lankan-born people live in the United States, and the little research that has been completed about Thai Buddhism in the United States, led me to examine a Thai rather than a Sri Lankan temple in this study.

Taan Čhaokuhn Rattanamēthē, the abbot of Wat Phila, gave me permission to do research at the temple in January 2000. Between January and August, I attended the temple occasionally and began to meet people. I completed one year of Thai language study in the summer of 2000 with Nongpoth Sternstein at the University of Pennsylvania and a second year during the 2000–2001 academic year. From September 2000 through March 2001, I attended Wat Phila every Sunday and conducted participant observation at Thai language classes, meditation classes, and morning services that normally lasted from nine to three. While I washed dishes, helped to prepare food, and ate lunch, I spoke with people informally about the temple and about their lives. I also spent many Thursdays at the temple during this time with a group of twelve women who were responsible for preparing and serving lunch to the monks. I accompanied these women and several of the monks to restaurants and on shopping expeditions. I taught English to three of the monks for several months, and generally tried to be around the temple as often and in as many different settings as possible, introducing myself as a graduate student at Princeton University doing research about their temple to understand how people practice Buddhism in America.

After several months of participant observation, I began to interview lay people at Wat Phila to learn about how they came to the United States, how they came to the temple, and how they practice Buddhism, among other things. My interview guide (included here) lists the kinds of questions I asked. The interviews themselves were semistructured around these issues because I found that was the most effective way to gather information from respondents. I first interviewed a laywoman suggested by the abbot and then gathered a "snowball sample" by interviewing people she suggested and others I had met during my time at the temple that far. These interviews took place at the temple as well as in people's homes, workplaces, and restaurants and generally lasted from one to three hours. The interviews were conducted primarily in English with bits of Thai included now and then, and were taped and transcribed. Many of the people I met in the course of this research were not comfortable with this formal interviewing style, so I supplemented these twenty-five formal interviews with thirty informal interviews. The latter were not scheduled in advance and generally took place over lunch or while washing dishes at the temple. I asked respondents the same questions, but the approach was more relaxed and conversational. These informal interviews were not taped, but I wrote detailed notes immediately following each conversation and was able to reproduce most of the conversations almost verbatim. These formal and informal interviews were, in many cases, the beginnings of conversations between me and individuals at the temple that have continued to the present time. Combining interviews with participant observation over many months at Wat Phila was particularly valuable because it allowed me to observe people in the temple context and then try to understand, through interviews, how they view themselves in that context.

I continued participant observation and interviews at Wat Phila from July through September 2001. I started to write this book in September 2001 and continued to go to the temple a few times each month for Sunday services. I attended almost all of the festivals the temple sponsored between September 2000 and September 2002. In addition to interviewing lay people at the temple, I spoke with each of the five monks who lived at the temple during that year. I also reviewed historic documents and newsletters related to the history and founding of the temple.

While it is impossible for me to know how people at Wat Phila viewed me, I felt that I was gradually welcomed as a kind of strange child. In the kitchen I was often referred to as *lūk-farang*, or non-Thai child, and was taught how to do everything from slicing pears the Thai way to selecting ripe pineapples, preparing food to present to the Buddha image, and washing the huge pots used during festivals. I learned the manners and norms that guide how people relate to one another at Wat Phila in the early months of research, often with a certain amount of embarrassment and laughter. Several months into the research, for example, I went to Nim's house on a Thursday afternoon with some of the women for makeovers after preparing lunch for the monks. As I sat in the living room watching Thai DVDs and chatting with a few of the women, Maha Supit, one of the monks at the temple, arrived with another woman after doing an errand. He came into the living room and sat on a chair, and I followed the women as they quickly moved to sit on the floor so their heads would be lower than his head, a convention when in the company of a Thai monk. After some time, my legs got stiff, and as I tried to quietly adjust my position the bottom of my foot pointed directly at Maha Supit. One of my Thai "mothers" slapped my leg, seemingly by instinct, and I pulled it back immediately. Amid a lot of laughter and my own red face, I learned that it is considered extremely rude to point your foot at a monk.

After several months of fieldwork, I began to exchange small gifts and favors with many of the people I met at Wat Phila and now consider many of them my friends. Before his death in March 2002, Taan Čhaokuhn Rattanamēthē, the abbot of Wat Phila, described me as "kohn thai," or a Thai person, to a visitor to the temple, and a laywoman paid me a high compliment one day by asking, despite my light hair and skin, if my mother was Thai. I have continued to visit Wat Phila and am regularly in touch with several people I met there. On numerous occasions, I helped individuals and the temple generally with different tasks, mostly related to college admissions, proofreading documents in English, and talking with non-Thai speaking visitors to the temple about Buddhism.

After beginning research at Wat Phila, I spoke with academics, Buddhist teachers, and practitioners about which Buddhist organization founded by non-Asians in the Theravada Buddhist tradition would allow for the best comparison with the temple. Everyone I spoke with agreed that the Cambridge Insight Meditation Center (CIMC) would be the ideal comparison and I wrote to Larry Rosenberg, the founding teacher there, in October 2000, inquiring about doing research at the center. He responded saying I could come if I agreed not to write during classes or conduct interviews inside the buildings at CIMC. Between April and June 2001, I lived in Watertown, Massachusetts, with Ruth Nelson and Margo McLoughlin, two women who are regularly involved with CIMC, while I conducted intensive research at CIMC. With the teacher's permission, I participated in two formal classes in addition to conducting participant observation at weekday morning and evening meditation sessions, Monday chanting sessions, Wednesday evening cleaning sessions and talks, Thursday retreats, cleaning and gardening days, and every other activity possible. I conducted participant observation at all of these activities, writing detailed field notes as soon as possible after each event.

After several weeks of participant observation at CIMC, I posted a sign on a bulletin board introducing myself and asked whether people would be willing to talk with me. The sign read "Greetings. I am a graduate student at Princeton University working on a dissertation about Buddhism in America. I am visiting CIMC for the next few months (April through June 2001) and am looking to talk with people about their experiences with insight meditation. I would like to talk to people with all levels of experience. If you are interested in being interviewed, I would be delighted to hear from you (and lunch or coffee is on me)." A few people I had not met contacted me after reading the sign, and many more I had already met mentioned the next time we talked that they would be willing to speak with me. Over the next two months I formally interviewed thirty-seven practitioners. I aimed to interview both women and men, people who have been involved with CIMC for longer and shorter periods of time, and people who are involved in different ways. I sought to ensure diversity by interviewing people who came to the center at different times, used the center in different ways, and seemed friendly with different groups of people. Among the thirty-seven people I interviewed, I made initial contact with them by means of the following: referral of another practitioner (8), Thursday retreats (7), suggestion of director Maddy Klyne (7), notice on bulletin board

(6), staff or resident at the center (5), Wednesday night talks (3), social event (1). Before completing the interviews, I asked Maddy Klyne to look over the list of people I had spoken with and suggest others who might bring different perspectives. She suggested seven additional people whom I interviewed shortly before completing this research. While much of the information I gathered at Wat Phila came through participant observation and informal interviews, much of the information I gathered at CIMC came through these thirty-seven formal interviews. As at Wat Phila, the interviews were based on a guide (included here) that listed the topics I wanted to cover. Interviews took place in parks, restaurants, coffee shops, and at people's homes and workplaces. Each interview lasted between thirty minutes and two hours, and there were several people I interviewed over several meetings. Each interview was taped and transcribed. I also interviewed the three teachers at the center.

In addition to conducting participant observation and interviewing practitioners at CIMC, I gathered information about the history of the center from old schedules, minutes from board meetings, and the tape library that includes more than 1,500 audiotapes. These tapes were made at almost every ceremony and talk from the time the center opened to the present. Tapes of Larry Rosenberg's visions of the center when it first opened, of Opening Day, and of the center's anniversaries since that time were extremely valuable, as were tapes of the talks the teachers gave at different points in the center's history. Magazines, newspapers, and newsletters from many other Buddhist organizations as well as hundreds of books in the library at CIMC were also valuable as I worked to piece together the history and development of Theravada Buddhism in America.

Practitioners at CIMC were extremely generous and willing to talk with me, and several specifically mentioned wanting to be part of how people understand Buddhist practice in America. Because I was participating in classes and meditation sessions, most assumed I was a meditator. Larry Rosenberg, himself a former field researcher, approached me early in this research to say that meditation is like participant observation: "It teaches you to pay attention to your own reactions and use your body like an instrument." Believing that ethnographic research is ultimately about relationships, I built relationships throughout my fieldwork at CIMC by listening as well as speaking and answering questions about my own history and interest in Buddhism and meditation as appropriate. For example, when people asked if I was a Buddhist, I said no and explained how my interest in Buddhism developed in Sri Lanka. I have returned to CIMC numerous times since completing the formal research for this study and have developed friendships with several of the people I met there.

Besides Wat Phila and the Cambridge Insight Meditation Center, I visited many other Theravada Buddhist centers across the country and talked with monks, teachers, and lay people in order to understand the history and breadth of Theravada Buddhism in America. The centers I visited, several of them more than once, include the Barre Center for Buddhist Studies in Barre, Massachusetts; Bhavana Society in High View, West Virginia; the Burmese Mahasatipatthana Meditation Center in Malden, Massachusetts; the Cambodian Triratanaram Temple in North Chelmsford, Massachusetts; Insight Meditation Society in Barre, Massachusetts; the Philadelphia Meditation Center in Haverford, Pennsylvania; Vajiradhammapadip Temple in Mount Vernon, New York; Vipassana Meditation Center Dhamma Dhara in Shelburne Falls, Massachusetts; Washington Buddhist Vihara in Washington, D.C.; Wat Boston Buddha Temple in Bedford, Massachusetts; Wat Thai Washington, D.C., in Silver Spring, Maryland; and meditation classes in Reading Pennsylvania, led by monks from Wat Thai Washington, D.C.

Monks, teachers, and lay leaders I interviewed or corresponded with include Ajahn Amaro, Gloria Ambrosia (Taraniya), James Baraz, Ron Browning, Ven. Thubten Chodron, Ven. Maharagama Dhammasiri, Christina Feldman, Joseph Goldstein, Ven. Henepola Gunaratana Mahathera, Philip Jones, Joseph Kappel, Edwin Kelly, Frank Kilmer, Luke Matthews, Wes Nisker, Andrew Olendzki, Phra Ratchakittiwēthī, Mary Reinhard, Bart Sensening, Phra Arry Akincano Sriburatham, Thanissaro Bhikkhu, Santikaro Bhikkhu, Phra Withētthammarangsī (Surasak Chīwīnanthō), and the monks at Wat Boston Buddha Temple and the Mahasatipatthana Meditation Center. With the assistance of Sidhorn Sangdhanoo, I also gathered information from all of the Thai temples in the United States (eighty-seven total). Sidhorn Sangdhanoo conducted telephone interviews lasting approximately one hour with the abbots of sixty of these temples to gather information about their history, programs, attendees, and future plans.[1] The interview guide is included below. I also conducted a thorough review and content analysis of Buddhist publications, including *Insight* magazine published by the Insight Meditation Society; *Tricycle: the Buddhist Review*; *Inquiring Mind*; and newsletters from other organizations across the United States.

I defended my dissertation in July 2002 and gave several copies of the dissertation to the monks at Wat Phila and the teachers at CIMC. The monks and lay people at Wat Phila had a small celebration for me and, after I formally presented my dissertation to the monks, they asked me to make a speech. In addition to thanking all of the practitioners at the temple for their generosity, I encouraged them to read the dissertation, saying I was anxious to hear what they thought and to incorporate their comments and suggestions into future versions of the manuscript. Similarly, I contacted all of the practitioners I interviewed at CIMC, made the dissertation available to them, and welcomed feedback. I was pleased to receive many helpful suggestions from the teachers, monks, and practitioners at both centers (as well as many other readers) and believe their responses to the dissertation made this a stronger book.

This research was approved by the Institutional Review Panel for Human Subjects of the University Research Board at Princeton University.

## Wat Mongkoltepmunee Interview Guide

### BACKGROUND

Where do you live?
How long have you lived there?
Where did you live before that? Where were you born?
Are you married? Do you have any children?
Where were you educated? Are you employed? Where?
Do you have other family members here in the States? Where are they?
How did you learn about this temple?
How long have you been coming to the temple?
How often do you come?
When do you come? Sundays? Weekdays?
Have you been to Buddhist temples other than Wat Mongkoltepmunee in the
    United States? Which ones?

### CHILDHOOD

Were you born as a Buddhist?
How did you learn about religion as a child?
How did your mother practice Buddhism?
How did your father practice Buddhism?
Did you have a *to būchā* (puja shelf/table) in your home?
If male, did you go to the temple as a young man to be a novice (*buat nēn*)?
    What temple? Why or why not?

### ADULTHOOD

Did your view on Buddhism change as you became an adult?

What does being a Buddhist mean to you now?

How have you learned about Buddhism as an adult? Monks? Classes? Retreats? Books? Internet?

How would you summarize your religious beliefs, in a few sentences?

What do you do at home to practice Buddhism? Pray? Meditate?

Do you have any special religious objects in your house?

Do you ever read Buddhist texts? Suttas? Books in Thai? Books in English?

What would you say you get out of practicing Buddhism?

If meditates, what would you say you get out of meditation? What is the point of doing it?

How have you taught your children about Buddhism?

Have you learned about other religions?

### OUTSIDE THE TEMPLE

In what ways, if any, does Buddhism enter into your daily life?

How do Buddhist teachings influence your work?

Have you ever talked about Buddhism at work?

How, if at all, has Buddhism influenced the way you handle your money?

Do you think about Buddhist teachings when you hear the news or learn about politics?

### GENDER

Do you think Buddhism teaches different things about women and men?

At the temple, do women and men practice Buddhism differently?

### COMPARISONS

How do you practice Buddhism differently from relatives and friends in Thailand?

Do you think more *farangs* (non-Thais) in the United States are interested in Buddhism these days than in the past?

If yes, why do you think so many *farangs* are interested?

### CONCLUSIONS

Is there anything we talked about that you would like to say more about?

If you were doing this research, are there questions you would want to ask?

Do you have friends who might be willing to talk to me about some of the things we have been discussing?

Questions about kamma, merit, nibbana, precepts, and rebirth were asked throughout the interview.

## Cambridge Insight Meditation Center Interview Guide

### HISTORY

How did you come to the Cambridge area?

How did you come to CIMC?

How did you come to your practice of insight meditation?

How is your practice related to Buddhism? (Who introduced you to both? Who was the first meditator you met? First Buddhist? Why did you came to this practice?)

What was your religious or spiritual upbringing as a child and young adult?

Since you were introduced to meditation, how have you learned? (Classes, retreats, teachers, books, Internet, suttas, other centers—what people have been influential?)

Since you were introduced to Buddhism, how have you learned? (Classes, retreats, teachers, books, Internet, suttas, other centers—what people have been influential?)

### PRACTICE

How do you practice at home? (What kind of meditation do you do? Do you practice privately at home or with other people?)

Can you describe the area where you practice? (Is there an altar or other objects?)

How are you involved with CIMC? (Classes, retreats, other tasks—cleaning, cooking, etc.)

What would you say you get out of insight meditation/Buddhism? Why?

What would you say you get out of your involvement with CIMC? Why not just practice at home?

How do you identify religiously now? If Buddhist: What does it mean to identify as Buddhist? Did something happen to signify this change? If not Buddhist: Why do you not identify as Buddhist? How are you different from people who identify as Buddhist? Do you think at some point in the future you will identify as Buddhist?

Do you practice other religions? Are you involved with other religious organizations?

## RESULTS OF PRACTICE

How have you changed or what seems different in your life since starting your practice? In your daily life? In your work (e.g., choice of career, practice at work, talk about at work)? Regarding money (e.g., what you buy, attitudes toward money, give money to charities)? Around politics (e.g., involvement in public life, current events, voting)?

What about your family—how do they respond to your practice?

If you have children, have you taught your children about Buddhism or meditation?

## GENDER

What does Buddhism teach about gender?

How is gender an issue at the center?

Have you come to think differently about yourself as a woman or a man through your practice?

## THEME

Can you tell me about your thoughts and feelings about:
Buddha
Precepts
Kamma
Merit
Nibbana
Rebirth

## CONCLUSIONS

What other centers have you been to in the United States? Abroad?

Have you been to Asia? If yes, did that trip influence your practice?

Have you had any contact with Asian Buddhists in the United States?

What do you think about Tina Turner, Richard Gere, and others saying they are Buddhist?

Did any of the things we talked about today make you think of something you
would like to talk about further?

### DEMOGRAPHICS

Where do you live?
How old are you?
Are you married or partnered?
Do you have children?
Are you employed? Where?
What is your education?
Do you socialize with people from CIMC?
Are there other people at CIMC whom it might be helpful for me to talk with?

## Thai Buddhist Temples/Organizations in the United States

### CONTACT INFORMATION

Name:
Address:
Phone:
E-mail:
Website(s):
What language are the Web sites in:
1. Leadership at present
    How many monks?
    Name of head monk?
    How long has head monk been at the temple?
    Name of monk spoken to:
    Language interview is conducted in:
    Date of phone call:

### HISTORY

2. Year Started:
3. How started:

## ACTIVITIES

Weekly and Monthly schedule:

4. Do you have chanting or meditation services every day at your temple? (If yes, when? what is chanted or what kind of meditation? How many people come on average? What language is the service in?)

5. Do people come to the temple on Sundays for a service? (If yes, when? What happens in that service? How many people come on average? What language is the service in?)

6. Do people come to the temple on Saturdays for a service? (If yes, when? What happens in that service? How many people come on average? What language is the service in?)

7. Do you have Thai language classes at your temple?

8. Do you have English language classes at your temple?

9. Do you have Thai music or dance classes at your temple?

10. Do you have a Sunday school or Buddhist school for children at your temple? (If yes, what language is it in?)

11. Do you have a dhamma school or Buddhist school for adults at your temple? (If yes, what language is it in?)

12. Do you have meditation classes at your temple? (If yes, when? What kind of meditation? How many people come on average? What language are they taught in?)

13. Is your temple involved with other programs in your community? (If yes, what sorts of programs?)

14. At your temple, do monks perform services for people who died?

15. At your temple, do monks perform services for newborn babies?

16. Do monks at your temple perform or attend weddings?

17. What festivals are held each year at your temple?

## PUBLICATIONS

18. Do you have any weekly or monthly publications?

19. If yes, what language are they in? How many people are on the mailing list?

## ATTENDANCE

20. What kind of building is your temple?

21. Do Asian people who are not Thai come to your temple? (If yes, what countries are these people from?)

22. Do non-Asian people come to your temple? Do these people come with Asians or by themselves?
23. How many people would you estimate came to your temple last week?
24. How is your temple supported financially? Is it in debt?

### RELATIONSHIP WITH OTHER BUDDHIST GROUPS

25. Do you belong to the Council of Thai Bhikkhus or the Dhammayut Order?
26. Are you involved with any Buddhist groups in your area?
27. Do you have a special relationship with certain temples in Thailand?

### FUTURE

28. What do you have in mind for the future of the temple?

# REFUGES AND PRECEPTS

## Three Refuges

### ENGLISH

I go to the Buddha for refuge.
I go to the dhamma for refuge.
I go to the sangha for refuge.
For the second time, I go to the Buddha for refuge.
For the second time, I go to the dhamma for refuge.
For the second time, I go to the sangha for refuge.
For the third time, I go to the Buddha for refuge.
For the third time, I go to the dhamma for refuge.
For the third time, I go to the sangha for refuge.

### PALI

Buddham saranam gacchami.
Dhammam saranam gacchami.
Sangham saranam gacchami.
Dutiyampi buddham saranam gacchami.
Dutiyampi dhammam saranam gacchami.
Dutiyampi sangham saranam gacchami.
Tatiyampi buddham saranam gacchami.
Tatiyampi dhammam saranam gacchami.
Tatiyampi sangham saranam gacchami.

## The Five Precepts

### ENGLISH

1. I undertake the precept to refrain from destroying living creatures.
2. I undertake the precept to refrain from taking that which is not given.

3. I undertake the precept to refrain from sexual activity.
4. I undertake the precept to refrain from incorrect speech.
5. I undertake the precept to refrain from intoxicating drink and drugs which lead to carelessness.

### PALI

1. Panatipata veramani sikkhapadam samadiyami.
2. Adinnadana veramani sikkhapadam samadiyami.
3. Abrahmacariya veramani sikkhapadam samadiyami.
4. Musavada veramani sikkhapadam samadiyami.
5. Surameraya-majja-pamadatthana veramani sikkhapadam samadiyami.

## The Eight Precepts

The above Five Precepts plus:

### ENGLISH

6. I undertake the precept to refrain from eating at the forbidden times.
7. I undertake the precept to refrain from dancing, singing, music, going to see entertainments, wearing garlands, using perfumes, and beautifying the body with cosmetics.
8. I undertake the precept to refrain from lying on a high or luxurious sleeping place.

### PALI

6. Vikalabhojana veramani sikkhapadam samadiyami
7. Nacca-gita-vadita-visukadassana-mala-gandha-vilepana-dharana-mandana-vibhusanatthana veramani sikkhapadam samadiyami.
8. Uccasayana-Mahasayana vermani sikkhapadam samadiyami.
*Source:* Access to Insight, www.accesstoinsight.org.

# NOTES

## Chapter One

1. The names of the places described in this book, Wat Mongkoltepmunee (also called Wat Phila) and the Cambridge Insight Meditation Center (also called CIMC), are real, and I use their formal and informal names interchangeably. The names of the teachers, monks, and staff members at each center are also real. The names of the people involved with these centers who are not teachers, monks, or staff members have been changed to protect people's privacy. Most Thai people have nicknames and people at the temple go by their nicknames. For this reason, I refer to the Thai practitioners here by pseudonyms that are common Thai nicknames. Nōi, for example, translates from Thai as "little"; Mū as "piggy"; and Plā as "fishy."

2. Si*ng* went to college in the United States and then returned to Thailand, where he met Mai and they were married. Two of his brothers were in the United States as American citizens, and they sponsored him to return in 1987. He started an import flower business which became a florist shop after several years. Mai joined Si*ng* in the United States in 1989.

3. I use quotation marks throughout this book to indicate people's exact words. Many of these phrases come from tape-recorded interviews. Others come from field notes I constructed during or immediately following periods of participant observation. When there was no ambiguity about the meaning, I changed verb tenses inside quotation marks to make quotations easier to read in the flow of the text. Participant observation and interviews at Wat Phila were conducted in Thai and in English. Translations from Thai to English are mine unless otherwise noted.

4. "Sāthu" means "It is well" and is said to show appreciation for the teachings.

5. Becky and the majority of practitioners at CIMC and other convert Theravada Buddhist centers in the United States are white or Asian, and I refer to them as such. Some centers are working to change that with retreats and programs specifically oriented toward non-Asian people of color, especially African Americans.

6. Most frequently, Becky practices a form of meditation based on the Buddha's Anapanasati Sutta that she learned from Larry Rosenberg. For a description of this kind of meditation, see Rosenberg with Guy 1998.

7. Estimates about how many Buddhists there are in the United States vary. In the 1991 City University of New York National Survey of Religious Identification (N = 113,000), researchers argued that between .2 and .4 percent of the U.S. population (between 500,000 and one million people) were Buddhists. These data, however, were collected only in English

(Kosmin and Lachman 1993). Martin Baumann estimated in 1997 that there were between three and four million Buddhists in the United States (Baumann 1997, 16). Responding to frequent overestimates of the number of non-Western religious practitioners in the United States, Tom Smith recently estimated that based on data from the General Social Survey and a survey of high-school seniors called Monitoring the Future, there are between 1.4 and 2.8 million Buddhists in the United States, probably closer to 1.4 million (Smith 2002). I estimate that the number of Buddhists is closer to 2.8 million because the number of non-English-speaking Buddhists is likely underestimated in these surveys.

8. Tweed (1992) describes the late nineteenth century as another period when interest in Buddhism increased in America.

9. An electronic search of "Buddhism" and "Buddhist" in the subject line at WorldCat (the Online Computer Library Center Union database), for example, shows that the number of books published in English increased from 138 in 1965 to 505 in 1995. Similar patterns are evident in other databases.

10. Adler 1994; Van Biema 1997; DeMont 1999; Fraser 1997; Helm 1996; Kamenetz 1996; Young 1989.

11. http://www.adherents.com/movies/buddhist_box.html.

12. Comprehensive data about changes in the number of Buddhist centers in the United States do not exist. The most systematic data collected show that the number of Buddhist meditation centers increased from 429 in 1987 to 1,062 in 1997, but these data are based only on information about centers where meditation is taught or encouraged (Morreale 1998, xvii). The number of Asian temples also increased during this period. For example, the number of Thai temples in the United States increased from 0 to approximately 87 between 1965 and 2000, based on data I collected. For information about markets in Buddhist objects and art see Padgett 2000.

13. Wuthnow and Cadge, forthcoming.

14. I use the words "convert" and "conversion" loosely to describe a group of mostly white people who were born in the United States, not Asia, and learned about Buddhism outside their families.

15. See Warner and Wittner 1998. While post-1965 immigrants have contributed to ethnic and religious diversification in the United States, it is essential to point out that the majority of these immigrants are Christians (Warner 2000; Jasso et al., 2003).

16. See Coleman 2001; Prebish 1999b; Prebish 1999a; Queen 2000; Seager 1999; Williams and Queen 1999; Tanaka 1998; Tweed 1992. Earlier research includes Fields 1981; Layman 1976; Prebish 1979.

17. Despite the lack of a specific empirical comparison, there is a great deal of discussion among scholars and researchers about how to name and conceptualize the relationship between immigrant and convert Buddhists. See Prebish 1999b; Williams and Queen 1999; Prebish and Tanaka 1998; Tweed 1999; Nattier 1998.

18. I refer to the country as Burma rather than Myanmar throughout this book. Theravada Buddhism also influenced the development of Buddhism in Vietnam and is still practiced in some regions. Vietnam is excluded from this list and Vietnamese Buddhist temples in the United States are excluded from chapter 2 because most Vietnamese practice forms of Mahayana Buddhism that are heavily influenced by Chinese Buddhism.

19. Numrich 1996. Other studies that examine aspects of Theravada Buddhism include Bankston 1997; Cheah 2001, 2002; Davis 2002; Douglas 2003; Fitzpatrick 2000; Fronsdal 1998a, 1999, 2002; Fung 1999; Johnston and Siegel 1987; Mortland 1994; Numrich 1994,

1998; Padgett 2002; Perreira 2002, forthcoming; Shattuck 1996; Smith- Hefner 1999; VanEsterik 1992, 1999; and Warren 2002.

20. Studies of Mahayana Buddhism include Asai and Williams 1999; Chandler 1999; Farber 1987; Finney 1991; Hori 1998; Kashima 1977; Lin 1996; Metcalf 1997; Nguyen and Barber 1998; Soeng 1998; Tanaka 1999; and Tuck 1987. Studies of Vajrayana or Tibetan Buddhism include Lavine 1998; Lopez 1998; and Mullen 1999.

21. Richard Seager's arguments about the likely long-term influence of Theravada Buddhism are made in Seager 1999, 136–57.

22. For example, modern capitalism (Arrighi 1994; Wallerstein 1988, 1980; Braudel 1977, 1972–1973; Wallerstein 1974).

23. Rogers 1995.

24. By "practice" here I refer to something that someone does. Practices, like those described here, are the ways new ideas and objects are enacted. The examples listed here are quoted in Rogers 1995. See also Strang and Soule 1998.

25. For two reviews of recent research about globalization, see Guillen 2001; and Held et al., 1999.

26. Berger and Huntington 2002; Berger 2002.

27. I define religion institutionally as sets of interlocking organizations or institutions constructed around the worship or reverence of a particular sacred idea or object. A cultural definition of religion, provided by Clifford Geertz, defines a religion as "a system of symbols which acts to establish powerful, pervasive, and long-lasting moods and motivations in men by formulating conceptions of a general order of existence and clothing these conceptions with such an aura of factuality that the moods and motivations seem uniquely realistic" (Geertz 1973, 90). These definitions are not mutually exclusive and are often combined operationally. Recent research about religion and globalization includes Beyer 2001; Levitt 2000; Hopkins et al. 2001; and Jenkins 2002.

28. For a recent review, see Levitt, forthcoming.

29. Waters 1995, 125–33; Berger and Huntington 2002, 12–16.

30. Hallisey and Reynolds 1995, 336.

31. For a description of how Buddhism has moved to different parts of the West see Prebish and Baumann 2002.

32. As Catherine Albanese argues, the story of religion in America is one of meeting and change (Albanese 1997).

33. Handlin 1951; Herberg 1955.

34. For example, see Ebaugh and Chafetz 2000; Warner and Wittner 1998; Yang and Ebaugh 2001b; Eck 2001; and the Pew Gateway projects currently underway in New York, Miami, Los Angeles, Washington, D.C., Chicago, and San Francisco.

35. Helen Rose Ebaugh and Janet Saltzman Chafetz, for example, compared how first-generation Buddhist, Protestant, Hindu, Muslim, Greek Orthodox, Catholic, and Zoroastrian immigrants in Houston, Texas, created new religious organizations (Ebaugh and Chafetz 2000).

36. Levitt 1998.

37. Levitt 2001a, 2001b.

38. Fenton 1988; Fields 1981.

39. Finney 1991.

40. These centers include the Dhammakaya International Meditation Center of California, Seattle Meditation Center, Atlanta Meditation Center, (Dhammakaya) Medita-

tion Center of Chicago, and Dhammakaya International Meditation Center of New Jersey. These centers are closely affiliated with the Dhammakaya movement in Thailand. See Swearer 1991 and Heikkila-Horn 1996 for details about the growth of this movement in Thailand.

41. I borrow the concepts of "context of exit" and "context of reception" from Portes and Rumbaut 1996, 84–92, 168–75.

42. For general histories of Buddhism in America see Prebish 1999b; Seager 1999; Fields 1981; Prebish 1979; Layman 1976.

43. The ways these elements are drawn together has everything to do with who is doing the gathering and defining. I explain national and individual approaches to this process, though the process of gathering and defining happens at all levels of analysis. At the national and other levels these definitions and the meanings given to them are often contested, as explained by DiMaggio 1997; Swidler 1986.

44. Swidler 1986, 273; Wuthnow 1996.

45. I recognize that Thailand is not monolithic and that it is more appropriate, in this example and in many cases, to talk about the different definitions of Theravada Buddhism in different regions of Thailand or among different people in the same time period. I outline the national description or definition of Theravada Buddhism here in a monolithic way for ease of explanation. I believe that the national definition described here reflects the definitions and conceptualizations of individuals within the nation, although individual contributions to the national definition vary depending on the person's power and status.

46. For example Tiyavanich 1997; Tambiah 1976, 1970.

47. Berger 1967; Geertz 1973.

48. See Hall 1997; Orsi 1996; Ammerman 2002. Other empirical examples are found in Griffith 1997; Gould 1997; Klassen 2001; Davie 1995; Bender 2003; Frederick 2003; Orsi 1997, 1996.

49. Orsi 1997, 16.

50. I recognize that in studying organizations I am necessarily overlooking many "nightstand Buddhists" (people who have "some sympathy" for the religion but "do not embrace it exclusively or fully"), Asians who consider themselves Buddhists but who are not involved in Buddhist organizations, and others (Tweed 1999).

51. The first generation of immigrant Theravada Buddhists in the United States are historically, financially, and culturally quite diverse, and I do not intend this study to speak for all immigrant Theravada Buddhist individuals or groups in the United States.

52. I would have preferred to study an immigrant and a convert group in the same city, but the Thai temple in Boston is quite small and the convert Theravada Buddhist group in the Philadelphia area is new and also quite small.

53. The abbot or head monk of Wat Phila was ill during the time I conducted this research and died in March 2002.

54. Interview with Ven. Henepola Gunaratana Mahathera, August 29, 2001.

## Chapter Two

1. Visit to the Washington Buddhist Vihara, Washington, D.C., and interview with Ven. Maharagama Dhammasiri, January 30, 2001.

2. Theravada Buddhist monks from different countries spend the rain retreats in different ways, normally staying close to their temples, studying, meditating, and teaching.

Some temples in the United States plan special teaching or meditation retreats for lay people during the rain retreats, and some lay people spend more time at the temple during these months than they do during the rest of the year. The three-month retreat at the Insight Meditation Society runs from mid-September through December of every year.

3. The current Thai-style temple and multipurpose building at Wat Thai Washington, D.C., for example, was completed in 1994 at a cost of more than 1.2 million dollars (pamphlet, *History of Wat Thai Washington, D.C.*, 1997).

4. Richard Seager argues that Theravada Buddhism is being reshaped through immigration and conversion more than the other two branches of Buddhism (Seager 1999, xiv).

5. See Charney 1997; Lewis 1997; Proschan 1997; Rumbaut 1997; Seneviratne 1997; Hein 1995; Gordon 1987; Minocha 1987.

6. There is no way to count the number of Theravada Buddhists in America who were born in the countries where Theravada has traditionally been practiced, or the number raised as children of immigrants from these countries. Data from the Immigration and Naturalization Service and the U.S. Census allow for general estimations, but as Paul Numrich points out, this data is not entirely reliable (Numrich 2000b). H. L. Seneviratne estimates that half of the immigrants to the United States from Sri Lanka are Sinhala Buddhists and the other half are Hindu Tamils and others (Seneviratne 1997). Burmese is a broad category that includes many different ethnic and religious identities, and only some of these groups are Theravada Buddhist (Charney 1997). The majority of Thais are probably Buddhist, though there is a network of Thai Christian churches in the United States (Lewis 1997; Codman-Wilson 1992). Many Lao people are Buddhists; others are Christian (Proschan 1997). The movie *Blue Collar and Buddha* about Wat Phothikaram in Rockford, Illinois, provides an excellent example of the tensions faced by people born as Lao Buddhists who were sponsored in their immigration by Christian churches in the United States (Johnston and Siegel 1987). Many Cambodians are likely Theravada Buddhist (Rumbaut 1997).

7. Information about the number of Sri Lankan temples in the United States was provided by Ven. Maharagama Dhammasiri at the Washington Buddhist Vihara. The number of Thai temples is based on data I collected (Cadge and Sangdhanoo 2002). The number of Burmese monasteries in the United States is based on http://web.ukonline.co.uk/buddhism /viharabr.htm#USA and confirmed by Joseph Cheah. I personally confirmed the existence of twelve of these twenty-four temples. The estimate of the number of Lao temples in the United States comes from the secretary of Wat Lao Buddhavong of Washington, D.C. Many are listed at http://members.dancris.com/ byblos/watlao.htm. The estimate of the number of Cambodian temples comes from Sovan Tun, vice president of the Cambodian Buddhist Society in Silver Spring, Maryland. All of these estimates are based on the number of temples that existed in January 2001 and exclude information about temples that disbanded before 2001.

8. These centers include "only those where meditation is taught, or at least encouraged." These numbers are best taken as impressionistic because aspects of this data collection were admittedly unscientific (Morreale 1998, xviii).

9. Data about the number of people attending retreats at the Insight Meditation Society were provided by Edwin Kelly, executive director. The mailing list of IMS also grew consistently over the years, as evident from their archives.

10. Few people I met in the course of this research actually identified themselves as Theravada Buddhists. Most identified just as Buddhists or, for Asians, occasionally as Sri Lankan Buddhists or Thai Buddhists.

11. Movements around stress relief are often based directly or indirectly on vipassana meditation. See for example Kabat-Zinn 1995.

12. The data presented in this chapter were collected in 2001 through reviews of all existing paper and electronic literature about Theravada Buddhist groups in the United States. The data about Thai temples and white meditation centers were collected through a combination of telephone interviews and analysis of Web pages. I also visited the majority of the organizations described and gathered information from their archives and interviewed monks and teachers across the country. Information about the history and development of Lao and Cambodian temples was particularly difficult to gather, primarily for language reasons, and as a result these branches of Theravada Buddhism in the United States are touched on but not described in detail.

13. Coleman 2001; Eck 2001; Gregory 2001; *Religion and Ethics Newsweekly* 2001; Fields 1998.

14. Numrich 1996.

15. For most of the twentieth century, scholars estimated that the Buddha was born in 563 BCE and died in 483 BCE. In recent years scholars have argued that the exact date of the Buddha's birth is closer to 400 BCE than 500 BCE (Robinson and Johnson 1997; Gethin 1998; Mitchell 2002; Harvey 1990).

16. Bareau 1987.

17. For a detailed historical discussion, see Gethin 1998; Mitchell 2002; Harvey 1990.

18. For details, see Bond 1988; Swearer 1995; Fronsdal 1998a, 1999; Baumann 2002; King 1980, 1976; Mitchell 2002. Western contact with Theravada Buddhism dates back to Christian missionaries in Sri Lanka in the sixteenth century. For more information, see Fronsdal 1999.

19. Morreale 1998, xv–xviii.

20. For more information, see Fronsdal 1998a.

21. Transcript of panel conversation at Theravada in the West conference at the Barre Center for Buddhist Studies, June 1995. Salzberg went on to say that she sometimes hears people identify themselves as part of the "IMS tradition." While she and I see people who are involved with the Insight Meditation Society as part of Theravada Buddhism in the United States, these people would not necessarily identify themselves that way.

22. For a more detailed discussion of S. N. Goenka's history and teaching, see www.dhamma.org.

23. Fronsdal 1999, 484.

24. Quoted in Verhoeven 1997, 311. See also Seager 1995.

25. Tweed 1992.

26. Several groups of Burmese monks visited in the United States in the 1950s (see U Myat Htoo, "Happy 20th Anniversary Theravada Buddhist Society of America," http://www.tbsa.org/articles/; last accessed April 25, 2002). The late Sri Lankan monk Ven. Havanpola Ratanasara enrolled in graduate school at Columbia University in 1957 and simultaneously represented Sri Lanka at the United Nations (Shanti and Senanayake 1999).

27. "Most Venerable" is a term of respect often given to monks from Sri Lanka, Thailand, and other countries in Southeast Asia. Other honorific titles, like Ajahn and Bhante, are also used throughout this book.

28. The celebration was organized by Kurt F. Leidecker, president of the Washington Friends of Buddhism, and Nimalasiri Silva of the Embassy of Ceylon. Roehm 1991.

29. Interview with Ven. Maharagama Dhammasiri, January 30, 2001; Madihe Pannasiha Mahanayaka Thera 1991, 1–2.

30. Roehm 1991, 9–22.

31. The Vihara recently purchased seven acres of land in Silver Spring, Maryland, where they plan to build a new temple. When I visited in January 2001, drawings of the new temple hung on the wall inside of the main front door.

32. Interview with Ven. Maharagama Dhammasiri, January 30, 2001. Fitzpatrick 2000; Blackburn 1987.

33. Fitzpatrick 2000; Blackburn 1987.

34. The Buddhist Study Center was granted legal status in 1965, and at the end of 1973 invited a monk from the Thai Buddhist Temple in London to advise them about starting a Thai temple in New York. Two monks came in 1974 to organize cultural ceremonies and services for the temple, and in 1975 two nonprofit organizations were formally started and conflict ensued. Wat Vajiradhammapadip was formally established in July 1975 (Payutto 1999, 206–10).

35. Piyananda 1990, 4–10.

36. Numrich 1996.

37. Piyananda 2001, 13.

38. For a complete history of Dharma Vijaya Buddhist Vihara, see Numrich 1996. For a description of the different ways that Sri Lankan Buddhist temples have adapted in the United States, see Blackburn 1987.

39. www.watthaila.org. Accessed February 16, 2001. No longer available.

40. Payutto 1999, 198–204.

41. Ibid.

42. *History of Wat Thai Washington, D.C.*, 1997.

43. Payutto 1999, 219–20.

44. At least one smaller Theravada Buddhist organization was started by non-Asians before IMS. In the early 1970s, Ven. Anagarika Sujata, who was trained in the Theravada Buddhist tradition, established a meditation center in Florida that later became Stillpoint Institute in San Jose, California (Prebish 1979, 13; Layman 1976, 180).

45. Kornfield 1993.

46. Goldstein 1999.

47. Moraine 1995–1996.

48. Kornfield 1998, xxvi.

49. Hudson 1996. Fronsdal (1998a) also makes this argument.

50. Fields 1981; Kornfield 1996.

51. A one-page orange flyer mailed in 1976 outlines the purpose of IMS. Early in its history, the Insight Meditation Society was confused, by some, with the Insight Meditation Center in Rangoon, Burma. IMS sent a letter to their supporters on March 25, 1976, clearly stating that there was not and had never been any formal relationship between the center in Burma and this center in Barre, Massachusetts. In an interview on June 19, 2001, Joseph Goldstein did not remember there being any discussion at the time the center was named about whether or not to include "Buddhism" in the name.

52. According to a letter dated November 10, 1975, sent under the heading "Insight Meditation Society" from Anicca Farm in Conway, Massachusetts, the purchase price was $175,000. At the time the letter was mailed, the society had $37,000 and needed another $13,000 by January in order to buy the building.

53. Ho 1975.

54. "Insight Meditation Society" 1996, 8.

55. Interview with Joseph Goldstein, June 19, 2001.

56. 1977 brochure.

57. See Ling 1981; "Intensive Meditation" 1975.

58. Salzberg 2001, 2.

59. Flyers in IMS archives. Kelly 1979.

60. Buddha Sasana Nuggaha Organization, Mahasi newsletter, April 1994.

61. Information about Taungpulu Kaba-Aye Sayadaw and Mahasi Sayadaw visiting IMS in 1978 and 1979 is from individual announcements of their visits in the IMS archives. For information about the development of early Burmese temples, see: See U Myat Htoo, "Happy 20th Anniversary Theravada Buddhist Society of America." http://www.tbsa.org/articles/Happy20thAnniversay.html [sic]; and http://www.myanmar.com/ACOCI/CULTURE/2000/3buddhism.htm.

62. An academic history of Burmese Buddhism in the United States has not yet been written. See Cheah 2001.

63. See table 2.1.

64. Some Cambodians established a small, cramped temple in Providence before 1975 (Smith-Hefner 1999). For a discussion of how one early Cambodian temple was started in Revere, Massachusetts, see Smith-Hefner 1999; for a temple in Long Beach, see Zhou, Bankston, and Kim 2001.

65. Eck 1997.

66. http://www.watlao.org. For more information about Lao temples in the United States see Bankston and Zhou 2000; White 2000; VanEsterik 1999; Bankston 1997; VanEsterik 1992; Muecke 1987.

67. This is documented in an exchange between Thera Mahinda and King Devaanampiya-Tissa of Ceylon about the establishment of Buddhism in Ceylon. See Numrich 1994; Gombrich 1988. Strictly speaking, this is a dynastic chronicle and not a Buddhist text.

68. Piyananda 1990. Personal communication with Bhante Yogavacara Rahula, May 7, 2003.

69. See Cadge and Sangdhanoo 2002.

70. The first Dhammayut Thai temples opened in the United States in the 1980s, though the organization that oversees these temples, the Dhammayut Order in the USA, was not registered until 1993.

71. For information about Thai immigration, see Desbarats 1979.

72. This is the usual pattern. Some Thai temples, like those in the Chicago and Los Angeles areas, were formed by schism from one main temple. See Numrich 1996 for an example. Some monks, like Ven. Mongkolthepmolin, started more than one temple, as described in Padgett 2002.

73. Although her article is not about a Theravada Buddhist temple, see Breyer 1993.

74. For more about Cambodian Buddhists in the United States see Kuoch 2000; Smith-Hefner 1999; Mortland 1994.

75. Melton 1993.

76. Interview with Ajahn Santikaro, August 1, 2001.

77. The purpose of *Inquiring Mind* was to "gather articles and both present the philosophy and tips on practice and interviews with teachers . . . and to print the schedule for retreats." The *Inquiring Mind* newsletter shared a mailing list for many years with Insight

Meditation West, a group in California that later became Spirit Rock. Like Insight Meditation West, *Inquiring Mind* was initially focused on vipassana meditation and later included materials about Zen Buddhism and Tibetan practice. Interview with Wes Nisker, September 6, 2001.

78. http://www.vipassanahawaii.org.

79. *Insight Meditation Society Newsletter*, September 1986.

80. Interview with Joseph Goldstein and Sharon Salzberg, *IMS: A Twice Yearly Publication of the Insight Meditation Society* (Barre, MA: IMS, 1990).

81. Spirit Rock History, compiled at first strategic planning meeting, November 1999.

82. Goenka, n.d.

83. Goenka 2000, 46.

84. Ibid., 49–50.

85. Interview with Luke Matthews, manager, Vipassana Meditation Center, Dhamma Dhara, Shelburne Falls, MA, July 2, 2001.

86. Ibid.

87. Tworkov 1995.

88. Gunaratana 1998. See also www.bhavanasociety.org/history.htm and the archives at the Bhavana Society.

89. Tworkov 1995, 40.

90. The financial support of Asians and Americans continued into the 1990s when Thai people in Thailand and the United States donated more than $70,000 for the construction of the main meditation hall at the Bhavana Society.

91. Gunaratana 1998.

92. Interview with Ven. Henepola Gunaratana Mahathera, August 29, 2001.

93. Prior to 1989, there are numerous examples of people being ordained for short periods of time, generally by visiting Burmese monks. Frank Kilmer, for example, was ordained by Taungpulu Sayadaw in the fall of 1979 at a monastery outside of Boulder Creek, California, as was Ron Browning. Both remained monks for several days. Interview with Frank Kilmer, April 28, 2003; Interview with Ron Browning, May 6, 2003.

94. Bhavana Society archives, maroon binders 5, no 3, July–September 1989.

95. Press release, "Buddhist Meditation Center Ordains Three North Americans" (copy in the Bhavana Society archives).

96. Gunaratana interview.

97. These councils included all Buddhists, though Theravada Buddhists were often in the lead. For example, the late Ven. Havanpola Ratanasara, a Sri Lankan monk, pioneered many of these education and ecumenical initiatives (Seager 1999, 216–31). These councils and other forms of inter-Buddhist dialogue and conversation continued into the 1990s. See Numrich 2000a.

98. Numrich 1996.

99. For a discussion of how spouses are involved at Wat Thai L.A. see Perreira, forthcoming.

100. Numrich 1996, 185–200.

101. Numrich 1996.

102. Roether 1995.

103. http://www.here-and-now.org/watmetta.html;Thanissaro Bhikkhu 2000.

104. Thanissaro Bhikkhu 2000, 3.

105. Numerous white Americans were ordained as monastics at Wat Pah Nanachat in

northeast Thailand under Ajahn Chah in the 1970s and 1980s. Led by Ajahn Sumedho, several of these monks started Amaravati Buddhist Monastery and other monasteries in England. For more information see Bell 2000; Amaro 1998. In England, Theravada Buddhism has taken a much more monastic form among converts than in the United States (Bell 2000; Batchelor 1994; Sucitto and Amaravati Sangha 1993).

106. Interview with Ajahn Amaro, May 24, 2001; *Fearless Mountain Newspaper* 2541, Spring 1998; *Forest Sangha Newsletter*, Amaravati, January 2000.

107. Amaro 1998.

108. Amaro interview.

109. Swearer 1995.

110. Camerini 1993.

111. Written comment from Ajahn Amaro, fall 2002.

112. Letter from Thanissaro Bhikkhu, September 30, 2000; Gunaratana interview.

113. Perreira 2002.

114. The number of sitting groups advertised in *Inquiring Mind* increased from 110 in the fall of 1990 to 232 in the fall of 2000. The number of practitioners at IMS increased during the decade from 1,000 per year to more than 1,400. For descriptions of retreats in the 1990s, see Cox 1995; Malmgren 1991; Suskind 1984; Bombardieri 2000. Theravada Buddhist groups that teach meditation, a vague category that includes both Asian temples and groups attended primarily by whites, also more than doubled between 1987 and 1997 (Morreale 1998).

115. *IMS Newsletter*, Spring 1993.

116. John Bullitt, ed., *Access to Insight*, http://www.accesstoinsight.org.

117. Philips 2000; Van Dusen 2002.

118. Spirit Rock History.

119. Kelly 2000.

120. For the past several years, Buddhist monks with overseas assignments from Thailand have been required to go through a training program for several months before receiving their passports. For monks coming to the States through the (Mahanikaya) Council of Thai Bhikkhus, this training lasts for about eighty days and includes chanting and English language and culture. For monks coming to the States through the Dhammayut Order of the USA, training lasts for two months and includes, among other things, computer classes.

121. Cadge and Sangdhanoo 2002.

122. Ibid.

123. One question that emerges immediately is why some white people go to Asian temples and others to insight meditation centers or sitting groups. The availability of certain organizations in given geographic areas is likely part of the explanation. In Boston, for example, there is a small group of people who used to attend CIMC and now meet together once a month and support Ajahn Amaro and other white monastics from Abhayagiri Monastery when they visit the Boston area. These people clearly prefer the Buddhism of white monastics to that taught at CIMC, and the question of why this is the case, while beyond the scope of this book, needs to be explored.

124. See Numrich 2000a, 1999.

125. Now, 60 percent of funds come from course fees, 20 percent from the endowment, 15 percent from the annual membership appeal, and 5 percent from miscellaneous sources. Interview with Edwin Kelly, executive director IMS, June 14, 2001.

126. Goldstein interview.

## Chapter Three

1. See Casanova 1997; Menjivar 1999; Levitt 2001b. Wat Phila and CIMC are examples of what Peggy Levitt calls "recreated transnational religious organizations," or religious groups that started themselves when they arrived in the United States because there were no established religious organizations to receive them (Levitt, forthcoming).

2. The presence of Kuan-yin is interesting because she is a Mahayana *bodhisatta* in a Theravada Buddhist temple. Her presence reflects the influence of Chinese Buddhism at Wat Phila and in Thailand, where she has also been quite popular in recent years.

3. Lao and Cambodian people attended some of the early meetings and were marginally involved before starting their own temples in other parts of the Philadelphia area.

4. This history is based on conversations with lay people and the abbot who were involved with the founding of Wat Phila and on a book written in Thai titled "Commemorative Volume Published for Distribution on the Birthday of Phra Maha Phainōt Phatthakō, upon his promotion to Phra Rattanamēthē, by the followers of Luāngphō Wat Pāknām, December 5, 2538 [1995]," 334.

5. *Luāngphō* is a respectful term used in Thai for a very senior, well respected person. It translates literally as "venerable father."

6. Magness 1988. This book was given to me by the monks at Wat Phila.

7. "Commemorative Volume."

8. The history of Luāngphō Sot (Luāngphō Wat Pāknām) is the subject of another book. In short, after his death in 1959 one of his female students, Mæ Chī Jan, continued to teach at Wat Pāknām and eventually broke off to start Wat Phra Dhammakāya with a group of wealthy young students. At present Wat Phra Dhammakāya has become one of the wealthiest temples in Thailand, with centers in many countries, including five in the United States. Wat Phra Dhammakāya also runs the Dhammakaya Foundation, and has gotten into considerable trouble with the authorities over financial matters. The leaders of Wat Pāknām also asked monk Ajahn Sermchai to start a temple called Wat Luāngphō Sot to continue the teachings. Wat Luāngphō Sot continues to operate in Thailand in cooperation with the Dhammakaya Buddhist Meditation Institute, which is not connected to Wat Phra Dhammakāya. Wat Pāknām also continues to teach Luāngphō Sot's methods of meditation and has founded Wat Phila as well as temples in Germany and Japan (Swearer 1991).

9. For important holidays, like the *Kathin* ceremony in 2000, monks from Wat Pāknām visit Wat Phila.

10. When Taan Rattanamēthē arrived in the United States, his name was Phra Maha Phainōt Phatthakō. He received the new name, Rattanamēthē, in 1995 to signify a step up in his ecclesiastical status. *Taan* is a respectful term of address used for a monk.

11. Swearer 1999.

12. "Commemorative Volume."

13. Interview with Boonchuay and Nantipha Ieamniramit, August 15, 2001.

14. Starting in 1994, all Thai monks who come to the United States have been required to complete three months of missionary monk training, organized by the Council of Thai Bhikkhus and the Dhammayut Order, which focuses on English language skills and chanting. The Council of Thai Bhikkhus and the Dhammayut Order arrange visas for the monks, who are normally admitted to the United States as religious workers. After a number of years, some apply for and receive green cards. Interview with Phra Arry, January 30, 2001.

15. Language remains one of the biggest challenges for the monks. Maha Charin went

to an ESL class for one semester, but the distance to the class and the teaching style made it difficult for him to continue.

16. Lay participation in decisions at temples in Thailand varies greatly. At some temples lay people have little influence and at other temples lay committees are completely in charge. Systematic data need to be collected from temples in Thailand and the United States to completely substantiate the assertion that American temples allow lay people more decision-making power.

17. The word "congregation" comes from the Latin root meaning an assembling (herding, gathering) together of people. It is defined generally as a group of people who gather regularly in a particular place to worship. See Warner 1994; Wind and Lewis 1994; Hopewell and Wheeler 1987. This is one of the primary ways first-generation immigrants are understood to adapt religiously to life in the United States. See Ebaugh and Chafetz 2000; Warner and Wittner 1998; Warner 1994. Wat Phila differs, however, from the congregational structure outlined in Ebaugh and Chafetz 2000 because it does not have a formal roster of members who elect leaders and there is no formal local governing body.

18. Some practitioners at Wat Phila mark *wan phra* at home by chanting, meditating, wearing white, and not eating after noon.

19. These children are second-generation Thai children as well as several children born in Thailand and adopted by white American-born parents. The adopted children come to Thai class with their parents but normally do not stay for other activities at the temple on Sundays.

20. These festivals include New Year's Festival (January), *Mākhabūchā* (February), *Songkrān* (April), *Wisākhābūchā* (May), *Āsālahabūchā* (July), *Wan Chāt* (June), and *Kathin* (October).

21. Wat Phila coordinates the dates of its festivals with the large Thai temples in New York and Washington, D.C., so that large festivals are not held on the same day. See VanEsterik 1992 for more on changes in how time is conceived in Laos/Southeast Asia and the United States around Buddhist rituals and gatherings.

22. See Appendix B for a list of the precepts.

23. This laicization has been observed elsewhere (Numrich 1996; Yang and Ebaugh 2001b).

24. There are presently six different versions of the rules. The Pali canon contains the only complete *Vinaya Pitaka* in an Indic language. See Robinson and Johnson 1997.

25. See Thanissaro Bhikkhu 1996b, 2001.

26. Different lay people at Wat Phila hold the monks to different standards of behavior. Some supply movies and entertainment, while others think this is bad. Some censor their conversations around the monks, while others do not.

27. Another important adaptation to the *vinaya* relates to what monks can wear. The cotton robes they wear in Thailand do not keep the monks warm in Philadelphia, so at Wat Phila in the winter, the monks wear yellow or orange socks and hats and put towels around their shoulders. For information about the adaptation of *vinaya* rules in the States, see Numrich 1994; Prebish 2003.

28. At present there are about 2,200 people on the mailing list who receive newsletters from the temple several times a year and announcements about upcoming festivals.

29. About five members of the second generation come regularly. Many more come to festivals occasionally with their parents.

30. U.S. Census data for 1990 show that among Thai people born abroad who live in the United States and are over the age of fifteen, 13,876 men and 27,479 women are married. Even if every Thai man listed is married to a Thai woman, that still leaves about half of the Thai women not married to other Thais. U.S. Bureau of the Census, *1990 Census of Population, Asian and Pacific Islanders in the United States*, issued August 1993, table 1: General characteristics of selected Asian and Pacific Islander groups by nativity, citizenship, and year of entry, 1990.

31. In one of his first public talks about the center, Larry Rosenberg explained the purpose of the fence: "The fence was an attempt to enclose us in some way. . . . It is a very delicate thing. If you put up a fence with sharp spiky things, it says don't come . . . this is a very benign gentle fence that anyone can get into. But it's trying . . . to suggest, that from wherever you have been there is something to walk into. You can leave some of your cares and responsibilities behind." Larry Rosenberg, *Visions of the Center*, tape 2, October 9, 1985, CIMC library.

32. Larry Rosenberg, *Opening Day at CIMC*, audiotape, July 21, 1985, CIMC library.

33. Most notably the curved wall behind the altar.

34. Interface was a center that taught meditation, tai chi, yoga, and other mind-body practices.

35. This history is constructed primarily from interviews with Sarah Doering (June 20, 2001), Larry Rosenberg (June 18, 2001), and Narayan Liebenson Grady (June 29, 2001).

36. Rosenberg interview.

37. The house was built in 1890 and mainly occupied by a doctor who lived and practiced medicine there. It became the only birthing center in Cambridge in the early 1900s. When the doctor's wife died, he married his nurse, and when he died, his nurse turned the house into a shelter for homeless, poor, and elderly people. It had been in disrepair for fifteen to twenty years before it was purchased and renovated to become CIMC (Rosenberg, *Visions of the Center*, audiotape 2).

38. In outlining his vision for the center, Larry described all of the reasons why 331 Broadway was not ideal: "I picked up an old book about this practice from medieval times and read a chapter about what the ancients thought about a suitable place for meditation. . . . It says the yogi goes to a dwelling—a forest, the foot of a tree, a mountain, hillside. . . . 'But you are to avoid a large monastery. . . . [At] a new monastery, there may be much work to be done by the inmates. . . . [Instead find] a dilapidated place . . . a place that is well used by the public. . . .' In the last sentence there is a ray of hope for us . . . : 'But the earnest seeker, the ardent yogi, wherever he happens to live, will find a place suitable for his practice.' " (Ibid.).

39. Narayan Liebenson Grady, one of the teachers at CIMC, explained to me that the center was an educational organization for the first five years or so before its leaders decided that it was really a religious organization. She told me, "I was just so happy when we turned into a religious organization. I just felt it was more accurate and appropriate, and I guess the tax thing changed at that point . . . , but we weren't thinking of it in terms of the taxes" (Narayan Liebenson Grady interview).

40. Rosenberg interview.

41. Ibid.

42. Rosenberg, *Visions of the Center*, audiotape 2.

43. Rosenberg interview.

44. Larry explained, "I prefer the term 'vipassana' myself because it has a narrow and

much more specific meaning. . . . People feel comfortable with the word 'insight,' but you have to winnow away all the other meanings." Rosenberg interview.

45. Larry continues to encourage practitioners at CIMC to do retreats at IMS. CIMC, IMS, the Barre Center for Buddhist Studies, and the Forest Refuge center in Barre are loosely related to one another as a kind of "floating campus."

46. Larry Rosenberg, *Thai Forest Tradition*, audiotape, September 28, 1988, CIMC Library.

47. Personal communication from Narayan Liebenson Grady to author, April 2002.

48. Larry told a story in one of his early talks about his vision for the center about Anagarika Munindra, an Indian who had taught some of the people gathered. "And someone asked him how many Buddhists are there in the world?" Larry said in telling the story. "And he said, I don't know . . . because many people who are not called Buddhist, are. In other words they are living a life that is directed towards wisdom and compassion. And many people who are called Buddhists, aren't. I don't know how to count it up. I don't know how many Buddhists there are in the world." Larry went on to say that the emphasis of the center was not on being a missionary. He said, "Atheists are welcome here. Christians are welcome here. Jews, Zoroastrians, Marxists, Communists, noisy people, quiet people, gentle people . . ." (Rosenberg, *Visions of the Center*, audiotape 2).

49. Rosenberg interview.

50. The purpose of the board was outlined for me in interviews with two nonteacher members of the board of directors.

51. Rosenberg 1996, 1961.

52. Larry Rosenberg, *Self Knowing: A Quiet Passion*, audiotape, December 13, 2000, CIMC library.

53. Ibid.

54. Rosenberg interview; Larry Rosenberg, interview with the Pluralism Project, Harvard University, audiotape titled *Buddhism in Boston Interview*, September 17, 1991, CIMC library; Rosenberg with Guy 1998.

55. Larry also became more interested in Theravada meditation after reading a book of Ajahn Buddhadasa's teachings that he found in a used bookstore in Minneapolis that Donald K. Swearer translated from Thai into English.

56. Rosenberg interview; Rosenberg 1998, 1999.

57. Pluralism Project interview.

58. Rosenberg 1996, 9.

59. The best explanation, he says, is that on his father's side there are fourteen generations of rabbis. The Jewish tradition is the complete reverse of Buddhism, Larry has said. "All rabbis can marry. Not only that, they have esoteric teachings that you're not eligible to receive until you're something like forty-two years old and have at least two children. They say, 'Unless you've bounced around in the world a little bit, how can we trust these teachings to you?' That makes a lot of sense" (Rosenberg 1996, 8).

60. Narayan Liebenson Grady interview.

61. Grady 1995.

62. Personal communication from Narayan Liebenson Grady to author, April 2002.

63. Narayan Liebenson Grady interview.

64. Personal communication, April 2002.

65. Narayan Liebenson Grady interview.

66. Personal letter from Narayan Liebenson Grady to author, July 2001.

67. Interview with Michael Liebenson Grady, June 28, 2001.

68. Personal communication from Michael Liebenson Grady to author, April 2002.

69. Michael Liebenson Grady interview.

70. Personal communication, April 2002.

71. Narayan Liebenson Grady interview.

72. See Coleman 2001, chap. 5, for discussion of these scandals.

73. The responsibilities of the administrative director have increased greatly with the evolution of the center. As of July 2001, Pash Voynow worked thirty-five hours per week and Jef Weisel worked twenty-five hours per week.

74. Interviews take place in the teacher's rooms. The teacher and practitioner sit facing each other on wingback chairs, and a white-noise machine whirs outside the room so privacy is assured. The rooms each have Buddhist art or a small image of a Buddha or a hand of Buddha. Tissues and a small clock often sit on a table between the two chairs. Interviews last between five and thirty minutes.

75. CIMC invites people to join as members for $240 per year, recognizing that for some people this amount is too high and for others too low. Financial aid is provided through work exchanges and scholarships to everyone who requests it. A fundraising letter is sent to everyone on the mailing list each fall and some additional funds come through unsolicited restricted and unrestricted donations. Interview with Maddy Klyne, June 13, 2001.

76. In June 2001, CIMC had 3,368 people on its mailing list.

77. One working-class practitioner I spoke with mentioned feeling somewhat uncomfortable in this largely homogenous environment. In response to similar concerns, the teachers and staff at CIMC will soon be having a training program so they can explore hidden kinds of racism.

78. In the center's history, a few non-English speakers have given talks that were translated.

79. This estimate is based on my observations as well as on a count of the partial membership list dated May 11, 2001. According to this list about 61 percent of members are women.

80. The center does have storytelling once a year, and high school and college students often visit as part of courses.

81. The only information that has been gathered about the population at CIMC comes from a 1998 survey it sent to its 350 members and made available at the center for completion by nonmembers. It was returned by 202 people, 87 percent of whom were members. Of the respondents, 67 percent were women; 55 percent were in their 40s and 50s; 45 percent had more than five years of practice experience; and 41 percent had one to five years practice experience.

82. It is interesting to note how practitioners learned of Wat Phila and CIMC in the first place. People come to Wat Phila through their friends and family members, referrals from Thai restaurants in the area, and referrals from monks and other temples in the United States and Thailand. Most are looking for a Thai temple, a Buddhist temple, or a way to have contact with monks. Wat Phila is the only Thai temple in the area—the next closest are in New York and Washington, D.C.—and people tend to come to Wat Phila specifically because of its location. There are currently Laotian and Cambodian temples in the Philadelphia area and a few Theravada Buddhist or vipassana meditation centers led by white people, but Thai practitioners at Wat Phila tend not to go to these other centers because they are culturally less familiar. A few practitioners at Wat Phila do attend a dhammakaya

meditation center in northern New Jersey that is led by Thai monks and has classes in Thai, but because of differences in the teachings and history of the center, few people at Wat Phila are interested in being regularly involved there.

Practitioners initially come to CIMC on the advice of friends, teachers, or therapists, or through one of many other Buddhist or meditation-oriented organizations in the Cambridge area. While some practitioners come to CIMC because they are specifically interested in Theravada Buddhism or vipassana meditation, many more come because they are interested in Buddhism or meditation generally. (Aside from Thai and Burmese temples that do little teaching in English, there are no other Theravada Buddhist organizations in the immediate vicinity.) Practitioners who come to CIMC interested in Buddhism or meditation more generally often have attended or considered attending classes or retreats at the Cambridge Zen Center, the Boston Shambhala Center, the Cambridge Buddhist Association, the Community of Interbeing, the Cambridge Center for Adult Education, Wellspace, Science of Spirituality, or one of a number of yoga groups in the area. People who get involved with CIMC rather than, or in addition to, one of these other groups tend to describe doing so because of a connection they felt with a particular teacher at CIMC or because of what they describe as the clarity of the teachings they found there.

83. My findings support research by Darren Sherkat, Christopher Ellison, Lynn Davidman, and others who argue that people's motivations for "religious" activities often encompass the sacred (contact with God, otherworldly interventions) and the profane (opportunities to make personal and professional connections, etc.) (Davidman 1991; Sherkat and Ellison 1999).

84. Rosenberg interview.

85. Ibid.

86. These insights build on DiMaggio 1998.

## Chapter Four

1. The dhamma talk quoted here was given on September 24, 2001, and was translated by Sompoppol Jampathom. It is paraphrased here for conciseness and ease of reading.

2. This talk was given on April 18, 2001. What is included here was summarized by Narayan Liebenson Grady for this chapter in April 2002.

3. I describe these centers as containers because I need a way to discuss the teachings and practices present at each without the assumption that they are all explicitly taught. The ideas of merit and kamma at Wat Phila, for example, are not taught by the monks, but are assumed and are central to teachings, ceremonies, and rituals at the temple.

4. This approach draws loosely on the production, selection, and institutionalization approach to culture outlined in Wuthnow 1987.

5. See chap. 2, n. 15, for a discussion of the dates of the Buddha's life. This section draws heavily on Robinson and Johnson 1997; Gethin 1998; Mitchell 2002; Harvey 1990; Hallisey and Reynolds 1995.

6. Quoted in Robinson and Johnson 1997, 12.

7. "Dhamma" is translated as law, teaching, and doctrine. John Ross Carter argues that "salvific truth" is a more adequate translation because "salvific" reminds English speakers of this quality of truth. See Carter 1982a, 1978.

8. The discourses include the Long (*Digha*), Medium (*Majjhima*), Connected (*Samyutta*), Numerical (*Anguttara*), and Little (*Khuddaka*).

9. These sections are the *Sutta Vibhangha, Khandhaka,* and *Parivar*

10. Dhamma talk, December 11, 2001, translated by Sompoppol Jampathom.

11. Dhamma talks, November 5 and December 3, 2001, translated by Sompoppol Jampathom.

12. For a complete description, see Magness 1988.

13. Taan Ajahn teaches practitioners to say mantras like *samma-arahan* and *bud- dho.*

14. See Swearer 1995; Tambiah 1976; Tiyavanich 1997; Numrich 1996; Ishi 1986; Tambiah 1970.

15. Dhamma talk, December 3, 2001, translated by Sompoppol Jampathom.

16. In addition to describing the dhamma in his talk on December 11, 2001, Maha Nom outlined the other components of Buddhism as a religion, which includes rituals and ceremonies, people (such as monks and lay people), materials (such as images, robes, and alms bowls), and places (buildings).

17. See Tiyavanich 1997; Swearer 1995; Ishi 1986; Tambiah 1976, 1970.

18. As in Orsi 1996.

19. This argument about Protestantization is made about Buddhism in parts of Southeast Asia by Gombrich 1988, and about Buddhism in the United States by Wallace 2002.

20. Quoted in Prebish 1999b, 152.

21. Narayan Liebenson Grady, *Dharma as Refuge*, audiotape 1136, February 22, 1995, CIMC library.

22. For examples, see Brus 1996; Grady 2000.

23. Practitioners at CIMC are, in many ways, evidence of the approach to Buddhism articulated by Stephen Batchelor in his book, *Buddhism without Beliefs.* "The four ennobling truths are not propositions to believe," he writes, "they are challenges to act" (Batchelor 1997, 7).

24. Rosenberg with Guy 1998, 3.

25. For a complete discussion, see ibid. For the original sutta, see Majjhima Nikāya 118. A translation by Thanissaro Bhikkhu is available at http://www.accesstoinsight.org/canon/majjhima/mn118.html.

26. Rosenberg with Guy 1998.

27. Grady, n.d.

28. Personal communication from Narayan Liebenson Grady to author, July 2001.

29. Narayan learned metta meditation from Sharon Salzberg at the Insight Meditation Society. For more information about metta meditation see Salzberg 1995.

30. Interview with Michael Liebenson Grady, June 28, 2001.

31. In 2001, invited speakers included Myoshin Kelly, Santikaro Bhikkhu, Mu Soeng, Joseph Kappel, Gregory Kramer, Doug Phillips, Paula Green, Ajahn Amaro, Taraniya, Andrew Olendzki, Issho Fujita, George Mumford, Corrado Pensa, and Thanissaro Bhikkhu.

32. Fronsdal makes a similar argument. He argues that when Asian teachers teach white Americans they tend to emphasize freedom from greed, hatred, and delusion, while white teachers tend to stress the potential found through freedom (Fronsdal 1998a).

33. For this reason and others, Fronsdal argues that Ernst Troeltsch would call vipassana meditation "mysticism" or "religious individualism" rather than a church or a sect, because "personal and inward experience and belief predominate over collective belief and worship" (quoted in Fronsdal 1998a, 169).

34. This relationship is not confined to CIMC or to Buddhism, but is evident more

generally in the United States, particularly among baby boomers in their approaches to religion and spirituality (Roof 1993).

35. Wuthnow 1998a.

36. Interview with Larry Rosenberg, June 18, 2001.

37. See Olendzki 1997. The greater emphasis on psychology in Theravada groups on the West Coast is evident by looking at the *Inquiring Mind* newsletter, published on the West Coast and reflective of thinking there. A great deal has been written in the academic and popular literature, more generally, about the actual and ideal interactions between psychology and Buddhism. For recent examples see Metcalf 2002; Kornfield 2000; Olendzki 1997; Thanissaro Bhikkhu 2002.

38. See Fronsdal 2002 for a broader discussion.

39. The precepts as listed in Appendix B are stated as a list of actions to avoid. In the July 2001 ceremony, practitioners also took the precepts phrased as positive statements, i.e., I undertake the precept to practice compassionate action; I undertake the precept to practice generosity; I undertake the precept to practice responsibility in all my relationships; I undertake the precept to practice kind speech; I undertake the precept to practice caring for my body and my mind.

40. Wuthnow 1998a, 6–8.

41. Ibid., 16–17.

42. I am not implying that the dhamma is some essential set of ideas that are then combined with other ideas and practices and called syncretic. Rather, by pointing to syncretism on two levels, I imply that the dhamma is always interacting with its surroundings and is always in motion, historically and in the present.

43. Rosenberg interview.

44. Fronsdal 1998b.

45. The *Namo Tassa* is translated as "He is the blessed one, freed from all bondage" in the English chanting book at Wat Mongkoltepmunee. Homage to the Buddha is translated as "He who is attained to Truth, far from defilements, Perfectly Enlightened by himself, fully Possessed of wisdom and (excellent) conduct, One who has proceeded by the good way, Knower of worlds, Unexcelled Trainer of tamable men, Teacher of Devas and men, the Awakened One. The One skilled in teaching Dhamma, who in this world with the Devas, Maras and Brahmas, this generation with its Samanas and Brahmins, together with its rulers and mankind, make known, having realized it through higher knowledge, Who pointed out Dhamma; good in the beginning, good in the middle, good at the end. Who explained the Brahmacariya with essential and literal meaning, complete and perfect, of surpassing purity. That Exalted One I worship most highly. To that Exalted One I bow down my head."

46. Dependent origination or dependent coarising (*paticca samuppada*) is an interlocking chain of twelve conditions central to the Buddha's attainment of nibbana (Robinson and Johnson 1997).

47. Cadge and Sangdhanoo 2002.

48. A few people also reported reading books written by Jack Kornfield and other prominent white Buddhists in the United States.

49. By using the terms "rational" and "supernatural," I do not intended to imply that people on the supernatural end of the continuum are somehow irrational. Rather, I need a way to talk about people who believe Buddhism is set of systematic ideas whose understanding requires no reference to otherworldly powers and people, and people who believe Buddhism is a set of ideas that can only be understood with reference to otherworldly be-

ings and influences. Martin Baumann calls these "traditionalist" and "modernist" forms of Buddhism, though his article does not make clear that both forms can and do exist within the same organizations (Baumann 2002, 54–59).

50. Larry Rosenberg himself has practiced yoga for many years. See Rosenberg 2001.

51. Kornfield 1998, xxiv.

52. Fronsdal argues that vipassana meditation practitioners have faith in themselves, the teachings, the practice of liberation, and the community of teachers and students in which they practice (1998b). Sharon Salzberg takes a more expansive view in her recent book (2002).

53. In addition to asking how practitioners' lives are changed, it is also important to ask whether Wat Phila and CIMC as organizations are interested in social change. Neither organization makes formal statements on social or political issues locally, nationally, or internationally or is directly involved with groups advocating social change in their geographic locations. Both centers act in the world primarily by supporting their practitioners in various small ways. The monks at Wat Phila support the lay people on a range of personal issues and regularly welcome visitors who want to learn about Buddhism, especially from nearby universities. CIMC provides space for a discussion group on "Engaged Buddhism" for people who want to apply the Buddha's teachings in a broader social context. For more about engaged Buddhism see Queen 2000. Groups of people who have met through CIMC have also been involved in teaching meditation in prisons and in other social justice efforts.

54. Tipton 1982. Gil Fronsdal (2002) makes a similar argument.

55. See Hall 1997; Orsi 2003.

## Chapter Five

1. The New Jersey group includes about twelve women who live in New Jersey and prepare lunch for the monks at Wat Phila several Thursdays per month.

2. "He [the Buddha] is the blessed one, freed from all bondage" (English Chanting Book: Wat Phila).

3. According to the *vinaya* rules that guide monks' lives, they are not allowed to touch money. At some temples "money" is interpreted as cash (as opposed to checks), so when practitioners make cash offerings they put the cash in an envelope so that the monks do not actually handle it. (A check can be offered without an envelope.) At other temples, "money" is interpreted as cash, checks, or any other form of monetary currency, and monks do not handle it at all.

4. Interviews are private conversations between a teacher and a student about meditation practice that last for five to thirty minutes. At CIMC students sign up for interviews several weeks ahead of time and during Thursday retreats, Narayan tries to see everyone who would like an interview.

5. This point draws on Peter Berger's writings about how humans construct culture through ongoing conversations with significant others (Berger 1967).

6. The religious or spiritual and social components of these groups or communities are not as easily distinguished as I suggest here. For purposes of this discussion, the religious or spiritual components of the community describe those that relate in some direct way to people's understanding of the Buddha's teachings. The social components of community are those that describe people's relations to one another independent of the Buddha's teachings. The overlaps between these definitions are explored later in this chapter.

7. Durkheim 1915.

8. Tocqueville 1945; Wuthnow 1994.

9. Wuthnow 1998b.

10. Carter 1982b.

11. Upasak 1975.

12. Robinson and Johnson 1997, 13. This section also draws on Gethin 1998; Mitchell 2002; Harvey 1990; and Hallisey and Reynolds 1995.

13. Quoted in Robinson and Johnson 1997, 33.

14. Sources say that the Buddha was reluctant to institute the *bhikkhuni-sangha.* In establishing the order, he added rules for women to the *vinaya* followed by the monks. For a detailed discussion see Bartholomeusz 1994.

15. In Sri Lanka the orders of monks and nuns both ended in the eleventh century. The order of monks was started again, but the order of nuns was not, for reasons that are the subject of debate. Ibid.

16. Dhamma talk, December 3, 2001, translated by Sompoppol Jampathom.

17. Dhamma talk, November 11, 2001, translated by Sompoppol Jampathom.

18. *Wat Phila Newsletters,* 2001.

19. For a broader discussion of the changing meaning of the word "sangha" in the United States, see Prebish 2003.

20. The "triple gem" refers to the Buddha, the dhamma, and the sangha.

21. Narayan Liebenson Grady, *Sangha as Refuge,* audiotape 1135, March 1, 1995; slightly revised April 2002, CIMC library.

22. Interview with Joseph Goldstein, June 19, 2001.

23. Remarks by Narayan Liebenson Grady, CIMC *Tenth Anniversary Ceremony,* audiotape 1275, July 22, 1995, CIMC library.

24. Interview with Narayan Liebenson Grady, June 29, 2001.

25. People taking the Eight Precepts come to the temple at nine and take the precepts before participating in the morning meditation service. They are not silent, but move around the temple helping to cook and prepare food and set the table where they will take their meal. Women taking the Eight Precepts refer to themselves as *mæ-chī.*

26. In addition to the groups that gather at CIMC, it is important to note that people form small meditation groups in their neighborhoods or around certain commonalties (like race, or sexuality). People who want to form or join a group advertise on one of the bulletin boards.

27. A few practitioners, however, do not see CIMC as their first Buddhist organizational affiliation. Helen, for example, describes the Insight Meditation Society as her practice home and CIMC as a kind of secondary home while she pursues graduate studies in Boston. Kelly similarly sees the Amaravati Sangha in California as her primary home and CIMC as secondary.

28. Narayan usually officiates at these ceremonies. She received state certification to marry couples several years ago through her affiliation with the Insight Meditation Society. IMS is registered as a religious organization, and at the time, CIMC was not.

29. CIMC brochure, Fall-Winter 2001–2002.

30. Many practitioners at CIMC regularly go on three-to-ten-day silent retreats that could be thought of as a kind of Buddhist festival.

31. *Wat Phila Newsletters,* 2001.

32. Remarks by Larry Rosenberg, CIMC *Tenth Anniversary Ceremony.*

33. Rosenberg, *Visions of the Center*, audiotape 2.

34. Larry Rosenberg, interview with the Pluralism Project, Harvard University, in *Buddhism in Boston Interview*, September 17, 1991, audiotape, CIMC library.

35. Rededication to the Dharma Ceremony, July 20, 2001.

36. Wuthnow 1998b.

37. Interview with Michael Liebenson Grady, June 28, 2001.

38. Robinson and Johnson 1997; Swearer 1995.

39. Tiyavanich 1997.

40. Dhamma talk, December 16, 2001, translated by Sompoppol Jampathom.

41. Practitioners may also make merit by becoming monks or through their meditation. Most of the men at the temple were monks in Thailand for short periods before they came to the States. Young men do occasionally become monks at Wat Phila, and some parents send their sons back to Thailand to become monks. Some, but not all, people at Wat Phila also believe you make merit through meditation, and Buddhist texts support their belief. Mai understands meditation to be the best way of making merit: "I think you make the best merit when you meditate because you become blank. . . . You can donate to build ten temples or one hundred temples but it's not equivalent to meditating," she explained.

42. *Sangha as Refuge*.

43. *Sangha as Refuge*, slightly revised, April 2002.

44. Michael Liebenson Grady interview.

45. Uchiyama 1993, 96.

46. Grady 2001, 203–204.

47. Thanissaro Bhikkhu 2002, 45.

48. *Sangha as Refuge*.

49. Grady 2001, 197–205.

50. Michael Liebenson Grady interview.

51. Most especially see Putnam 2000.


## Chapter Six

1. The ways the Buddha's teachings about the self have been interpreted are discussed extensively among scholars and Buddhist practitioners. For example Collins 1982, 1994; Rahula 1974; Thanissaro Bhikkhu 1996a.

2. Some commentators also follow this line of argument to explain the popularity of Buddhism in America. For example, Coleman 2001; Porterfield 2001.

3. I used the terms "religion" and "spirituality" interchangeably in my fieldwork and do so here as well, even though Wuthnow 1998a convincingly argues that for many people in the United States the two ideas are quite separate.

4. In outlining this theory, Smith argues that "modern pluralism need not undermine religion but can create the conditions in which religion or at least *certain* religions can thrive," specifically those that can embed themselves in subcultures "that offer satisfying morally orienting collective identities which provide adherents meaning and belonging." Religious groups that will be stronger are those that "better possess and employ the cultural tools needed to create both clear distinction from and significant engagement with other relevant outgroups, short of becoming genuinely countercultural" (Smith 1998, 118–19).

5. I focus most specifically on Theravada Buddhist organizations here. Some groups,

such as Tibetan Buddhists, may exist in greater tension with other groups, though this is an empirical question.

6. For a discussion of the construction of the biography of the Buddha, see Reynolds and Capps 1976. For other biographies of the Buddha, see Thomas 2000.

7. This tension between more rational and more supernatural approaches to the Buddhist tradition runs throughout its history (Tambiah 1976, 1970).

8. Dhamma talk, translated by Sompoppol Jampathom, September 9, 2001. For other versions and interpretations of this story see Hallisey and Hansen 1996; Strong 1995.

9. Larry Rosenberg, *Fire Sermon,* audiotape 396, June 3, 1987, CIMC library.

10. Narayan Liebenson Grady, *The Paramis: Summary and Conclusion,* audiotape 1362, August 6, 1997, CIMC library.

11. English Chanting Book: Wat Phila.

12. Swearer 1995.

13. For a description of what it means to go to the Buddha for refuge based on Pali canonical texts, see Bond 1982.

14. Narayan Liebenson Grady, *Buddha as Refuge,* audiotape 1135, February 15, 1995, CIMC library.

15. The word "Buddhist" first appeared in the first edition of Noah Webster's work *An American Dictionary of the English Language*; see *Tricycle: The Buddhist Review* (Fall 2001): 68.

16. See chap. 1, n. 7, above. The arguments made here apply more to people who are involved with Buddhist organizations than to those who are not.

17. Prebish 1979, 43–44.

18. Nattier 1998.

19. Tweed 1999, 74.

20. Tweed 1992.

21. In describing types of statuses, Ralph Linton (1936) was one of the first to use the categories "ascribed" and "achieved." Talcott Parsons later made the same distinction in his discussion of pattern variables (Mayhew 1982, 111).

22. Of course, these identities are themselves constructed (and could be called "achieved" identities), since people are not actually born with specific religious identities.

23. For more detailed discussion of the categories of ascription and achievement, see Cadge and Davidman 2003.

24. This combination of ascribed and achieved identities is evident among other first-generation immigrants; see, for example, Chen, forthcoming.

25. Some researchers would argue that practitioners at Wat Phila are engaging in a kind of conversion called regeneration, in which a belief system is taken seriously that was previously abandoned (Lang and Lang 1961; Nock 1933; Clark 1929).

26. Although he no longer thinks he was born as a Buddhist, Kop is always careful not to make judgments about others who view themselves this way.

27. An interesting side note here is the story of a white American couple who bring their nine-year-old daughter to the temple for Thai language lessons. Their daughter was born in Thailand, and they adopted her and brought her to the United States when she was five. Both mom and dad have told me that their daughter is Buddhist. Being Buddhist to them largely means being Thai—they bring her to the temple for Thai class but not usually for other services and ceremonies.

28. Paisano et al. 1993. To see how Cambodian Buddhists in the States construct religious identities through the Buddhist tradition see Smith-Hefner 1999.

29. These are primarily women who met American men during the Viet Nam war. A few are mail-order brides. Little research has been conducted about Thai women in the United States married to non-Thai men (Footrakoon 1999; Kim et al. 1981).

30. This section builds on research by Gans (1994) and Hammond and Warner (1993). Some research about post-1965 immigrants is also beginning to separate the ethnic and religious components of identity construction by looking at different religious groups within the same ethnic group. See Chen, forthcoming; Yang and Ebaugh 2001a; Jacobson 1997; Hammond and Warner 1993.

31. Described by Batchelor 1997.

32. Interview with Larry Rosenberg, June 18, 2001.

33. Larry Rosenberg, *Taking the Refuges*, audiotape 1303, November 5, 1996, CIMC library.

34. Interview with Michael Liebenson Grady, June 28, 2001.

35. Anecdotal evidence certainly suggests that more Jews are involved with Buddhist practices and groups than their numbers in the population would suggest, though the demographic data needed to support this do not exist. For current thinking about Jewish Buddhists, see Kamenetz 1994; Boorstein 1997; Brodey 1997; Chayes and Solotaroff 1999; Porterfield 2001; Obadia 2002.

36. Prebish 1979; Layman 1976.

37. Snow and Machalek 1984.

38. For similar findings in a study of nine women practicing different forms of Buddhism, see Brodey 1997. For similar findings among vipassana meditators see Fronsdal 1998b. This is also evident in David Preston's study of Zen Buddhism (Preston 1988).

39. For example, see Bellah et al. 1985; Cohen and Eisen 2000; Davidman 1991; Ammerman 1987.

40. It is possible that groups with stronger boundaries, such as black Muslims, grow faster than groups with weaker boundaries, like Buddhists. Regardless of the rate of growth, however, Smith's theory does not account for any growth in weakly bounded groups.

## Chapter Seven

1. Based on the gender distribution of the twenty-five practice leaders at CIMC in June 2001 and my observations of gatherings for housecleaning and gardening.

2. Every Sunday that I attended Wat Phila during my fieldwork, I counted the number of women and men present. Almost every Sunday exactly two-thirds of the people present were women. I made rough estimates of the number of people at festivals and found the gender distribution to be similar. The monks and several lay leaders agree with these estimates. At CIMC, I counted the number of women and men on the "CIMC Partial Membership List, May 11, 2001." This list includes all members except those who specifically asked not to be included. While it is possible that more women than men would want to be excluded from this list, Pash Voynow, the staff member who compiles the list, does not think this is the case. Sixty-one percent of the people on this list are women (N = 296). In June 1998, CIMC mailed a survey to all members and also made it available at the center to be completed by nonmembers. Sixty-seven percent of the people who returned the survey were women. I also counted the number of women and men at all classes, talks, and gatherings I attended at CIMC and tallied the numbers who attended a range of classes and retreats there in 2001

according to the class registrations. Based on these sources and my conversations with Pash Voynow and Narayan Liebenson Grady, I am confident that about two-thirds of the people regularly involved with CIMC are women.

3. This question is the subject of significant debate among scholars. For a recent contribution to the discussion, see Faure 2003.

4. See Rayaprol 1997.

5. According to 2000 census data, nearly 60 percent of the Thai population in the United States is female (see table 7.1) and approximately two-thirds of the Thai people at Wat Phila are female. The fact that more women than men are presently involved with religious organizations in the United States, and have been historically, is well documented (Braude 1997).

6. Existing research about Buddhism in America suggests that Buddhism is being "feminized" as it develops in the United States, particularly among non-Asian practitioners. Some of this research looks historically at how American-born women and men have been differently involved in the development of Buddhism in America and empirically compares how women and men understand and practice Buddhism (Tsomo 1999; Boucher 1997; Friedman and Moon 1997; Batchelor 1996; Dresser 1996; Boucher 1993). Some of this literature is based on historical data but little is based on systematic sociological data or analysis of gender at Buddhist centers in the United States (see Coleman 2001 for an important exception). Much includes feminist critiques of Buddhism (see especially Gross 1993) and, particularly work by Buddologists like Miranda Shaw, Susan Murcott, Tessa Bartholomeusz and others connecting questions about women and Buddhism in the United States to texts and broader Asian history and traditions (Bartholomeusz 1994; Shaw 1994; Murcott 1991). Gender is rarely examined in research about Asian Buddhists in the United States (cf. Ebaugh and Chafetz 2000, however).

7. In thinking about gender in organizations I follow Acker 1990, 1992; Blum 1991; Chaves 1997; Cockburn 1991; Kanter 1977; Kurien 1999. See also Cadge, forthcoming.

8. This definition is based on the definition of gender as the "activity of managing situated conduct in light of normative conceptions of attitudes appropriate for one's sex category" in West and Zimmerman 1987, 127. Although I define sex and gender in binary terms, I recognize that some current scholars do otherwise (Fausto-Sterling 2000).

9. This in part follows Acker 1990.

10. This follows scholars who argue that gender is a useful category of historical analysis and show in their work the kinds of social processes that become evident when gender is considered analytically (Davidman 1991; Scott 1986; Griffith 1997).

11. For example, see Harris 1999; Cabezon 1992; Sponberg 1992.

12. Dhamma talk, December 23, 2001, translated by Sompoppol Jampathom.

13. See Kabilsingh 1991; Wijayasundara 1999; Bartholomeusz 1994; Kabilsingh 1988.

14. Whether or not the order of nuns should be started in Southeast Asia or should exist in the United States is not a topic of much conversation. Some people do not think so, not for reasons related to gender, but because they see no reason for monastic practice, for men or women, especially in the United States. For information about Western Buddhist nuns, see Chodron 2000.

15. Interview with Narayan Liebenson Grady, June 29, 2001.

16. Ibid.

17. Seager 1999; Morreale 1998; Prebish 1999b.

18. Interestingly, Thai women, particularly those who are married to U.S. servicemen, have been centrally involved in starting many of these temples (Padgett 2002).

19. I have also heard practitioners remark on the set of people, mostly women, who are close to the abbot.

20. For a translation of these guidelines, see Thanissaro Bhikkhu 1996b, 2001.

21. A young Thai woman friend scolded me once for speaking with a monk alone in the main meditation hall approximately ten feet from an open door to the kitchen where several other women were talking. On another occasion, an older Thai laywoman who was sitting in on an English lesson I was giving to three monks left to run an errand with two of the monks, leaving me alone with the remaining monk to continue the lesson. These two examples show that practitioners at Wat Phila do not interpret the *vinaya* rules in consistent ways.

22. When I taught English to the monks I was initially asked to bring a friend with me, but when this was not possible I was allowed to be alone with the three monks I was teaching.

23. This rule was even more strictly enforced by the abbot after one of the monks had an affair with a laywoman and subsequently left the temple some years ago.

24. See Reed 1992 for an explanation of how Kuan-yin became female in the assimilation into Chinese culture. See Boucher 1999a for more information about Kuan-yin in the United States.

25. Between April and September of 2000, for example, six of the seven cooks were women.

26. Boucher 1997; Friedman and Moon 1997; Batchelor 1996; Dresser 1996; Boucher 1993.

27. Narayan Liebenson Grady interview. Narayan's observations about the differences in how women and men approach the teachings are reflected in some practitioners' comments. Becky describes men as sometimes seeming to "compete for being spiritual" and Dawn says she has "more of a sense of striving from some of the men" she has come across in retreats, although not so much at CIMC.

28. This argument also explains why women are often more involved than men with Buddhist temples in Thailand (Bartholomeusz 1999; VanEsterik 1982).

29. My understandings of how women are involved in Buddhism in Thailand come primarily from conversations with Don Swearer and from Swearer 1995; Bartholomeusz 1999; Keyes 1984; Kirsch 1982; Lefferts 2000.

30. Although no one at the temple mentioned it, there is a relevant folk saying in Thailand that men are like the front wheels of the car and do all the steering while women are like the back wheels, where all the power comes from.

31. See table titled "Immigrants admitted by classes under the immigration laws and country or region of birth," in INS 1969, 1970, 1971, 1972, 1973, 1974, 1975, 1976, and 1977. In 1971–72, for example 4,102 people from Thailand were admitted. Of those 1,759 were the wives of U.S. citizens, 427 were children of U.S. citizens, 131 were husbands of U.S. citizens, and 2 were parents of U.S. citizens. Many of the wives were married to U.S. servicemen, though the INS does not keep track of these numbers. The only research about these women is found in Footrakoon 1999.

32. Census data from 1990 show that among Thai people born abroad who are over the age of fifteen, 13,876 men and 27,479 women are married. Even if every Thai man listed is married to a Thai woman, that still leaves about half of the Thai women not married to other Thais. U.S. Bureau of the Census, *1990 Census of Population, Asian and Pacific Islanders*

*in the United States*, issued August 1993, table 1: General characteristics of selected Asian and Pacific Islander groups by nativity, citizenship, and year of entry, 1990.

33. For the personal story of one of these women, see Larsen 1989.

34. As Ebaugh and Chafetz argue about women in first-generation immigrant congregations more generally, their leadership positions depend on men's unwillingness to fill them; Ebaugh and Chafetz 1999.

35. According to 2000 census data, women slightly outnumber men in the United States overall.

36. Coleman 2001, 149.

37. Boucher 1999b.

38. Numrich 1996; Fitzpatrick 2000. Conversation with Rev. Yogavacara Rahula, Bhavana Society, August 2001.

39. Data from IMS show that in 1990, women were 57 percent of practitioners there; they were 65 percent in 1995, and 62 percent in 2000. Luke Matthews, manager of Dhamma Dhara Vipassana Meditation Center estimates that 60 percent of the people who attend retreats at the center are women (interview, July 1, 2001).

40. Gallup and Lindsay 1999; Gallup 2001; Gallup and Castelli 1989.

41. According to Kosmin and Lachman 1993, 212–13 (reporting on the 1990 National Survey of Religious Identification), 87 percent of men and 92 percent of women identify themselves as belonging to or believing in religion. Every Christian religious group contains more women than men.

42. De Vaus and McAllister 1987; Kosmin and Lachman 1993; Miller and Stark 2002; de Vaus and McAllister 1987.

43. One practitioner offered these thoughts: "Culturally, feeling has been consigned to the domain of women. . . . With the movement of women into mainstream earning and career activity, it seems that as a group they are experiencing a lot more of the structural tensions in the culture. They see more, they feel more, even if they may not have stronger capacity for feeling, but I suspect they do in a lot of cases. So they are subjected to more of the structural stresses and break points it seems to me than are men. . . . I suspect that women are there [at religious centers] because they're positioned to see more of life. They raise children more consistently than men. They bear the responsibilities of life-death transitions more than men. In other words, they are showing up for more of life than men are forced to do."

44. The argument that women are more interconnected with others than are men was made by Gilligan (1982) and connected to research done by Nancy Chodorow (1978) and the Center for Research on Women at Wellesley College.

45. Gender as it relates to family responsibilities could also explain who comes to CIMC. Women, for example, might have fewer opportunities than men to meditate silently in their homes. Since the vast majority of practitioners do not have children, however, this is likely not the case.

46. A male researcher needs to investigate this possibility.

## Chapter Eight

1. The voluntary nature of religions practiced by post-1965 immigrants and of religion in general in the United States is often noted. See Warner 2000; Warner and Wittner 1998; Warner 1993.

2. Buddhism in some parts of Southeast Asia in the mid-twentieth century was going through its own process of modernization, although I do not trace these developments here. See chap. 2, n. 17, for related references.

3. Among immigrant Buddhist groups before 1965, this is made clear in Kashima 1977 and Tuck 1987; and since 1965, in Lin 1996; McLellan 1999; Nguyen and Barber 1998; Padgett 2002; Perreira 2002; and VanEsterik 1992. For evidence from a wide range of religious groups see Abusharaf 1998; Bankston and Zhou 2000; Ebaugh and Chafetz 2000; Kwon, Kim, and Warner 2001; Warner and Wittner 1998; Yang and Ebaugh 2001b. Hindu religious groups are an interesting exception to this general pattern; see Kurien 1998, 2001.

4. Warner 1994; Yang and Ebaugh 2001b.

5. There is variation in the extent to which ethnic activities are present in different religious organizations (Ebaugh and Chafetz 2000; Cadge and Sangdhanoo 2002).

6. See, for example, Min 1992; Kwon, Kim, and Warner 2001.

7. Yang and Ebaugh 2001a; Ebaugh and Chafetz 1999.

8. Despite its popularity, there is very little scholarly literature on yoga (see Lau 2000 for an exception). Relevant writing in the popular literature includes D'Antonio 1992; Lesser 1999; Ittner 2002.

9. For several examples, see Fields 1981; Hammond and Machacek 1999; Preston 1988; Fronsdal 1998a.

10. See Gussner and Berkowitz 1988. For discussions of baby boomers and their interest in specific religious practices, see Roof 1993; Wuthnow 1998a.

11. Denniston and McWilliams 1999; Garrett 2001.

12. Batchelor 1997.

13. Additional research is needed to assess systematically the extent to which these are Theravada Buddhist rather than simply Buddhist adaptations.

14. Gethin 1998; Mitchell 2002; Harvey 1990; Hallisey and Reynolds 1995.

15. Positive media and other cultural portrayals of Buddhist groups abound, and the American public tends to look quite favorably on Buddhism in comparison to other non-Western religious traditions. In a recent national survey, for example, close to 60 percent of people said they would welcome Buddhists' becoming a stronger presence in the United States. More respondents described Buddhism as peace-loving and fewer respondents described it as fanatical than other religious groups. Americans are also significantly more aware and supportive of Buddhism than of other non-Western religions in America such as Hinduism and Islam (Wuthnow 2003 (N = 2,910, weighted results); Wuthnow and Cadge, forthcoming.

16. Weber 1958, 62–63, 284–85. I agree with Queen (1999) that there is a recognizable American Buddhism developing that transcends the differences among groups with different ethnic backgrounds and histories.

17. Campbell 2003.

18. Herberg 1955.

19. Interview with Phra Rātchakittiwēthī, July 7, 2001.

20. Recent writings by young Buddhists point to the absence of young Buddhist practitioners at many convert centers (Loundon 2001).

21. See http://www.dharma.org/ims/youth_outreach.htm.

22. One-third of Thai temples in the United States currently have a parallel congregation or group of non-Thai, largely white people, who meet regularly in the temple, mainly for meditation instruction (Cadge and Sangdhanoo 2002).

23. The creation of an indigenous sangha is unlikely, at least among Thais, because most do not want their children to become monks for long periods of time (Perreira, forthcoming).

24. *IMS newsletter,* Fall 1999 (Goldstein 1998).

25. Cadge and Sangdhanoo 2002.

26. For example, see Goldstein 2002.

## Appendix A

1. See Cadge and Sangdhanoo 2002.

# REFERENCE LIST

Abusharaf, Rogaia Mustafa. "Structural Adaptations in an Immigrant Muslim Congregation in New York." In *Gatherings in Diaspora: Religious Communities and the New Immigration*, edited by R. Stephen Warner and Judith Wittner, 235–64. Philadelphia: Temple University Press, 1998.

Acker, Joan. "Gendering Organizational Theory." In *Gendering Organizational Analysis*, edited by Albert J. Mills and Peta Tancred, 248–60. Newbury Park: Sage Publications, 1992.

————. "Hierarchies, Jobs, Bodies: A Theory of Gendered Organizations." *Gender and Society* 4, no. 2 (1990): 139–58.

Adler, Jerry. "800,000 Hands Clapping." *Newsweek*, June 13, 1994, 46–47.

Albanese, Catherine. "Exchanging Selves, Exchanging Souls: Contact, Combination, and American Religious History." In *Retelling U.S. Religious History*, edited by Thomas Tweed, 200–226. Berkeley: University of California Press, 1997.

Amaro, Ajahn. "Just Another Thing in the Forest." *Tricycle* 8, no. 2 (1998): 78–83.

Ammerman, Nancy. *Bible Believers: Fundamentalists in the Modern World*. New Jersey: Rutgers University Press, 1987.

————. "Religious Practice in Everyday Life." Paper presented at the Society for the Scientific Study of Religion, Salt Lake City, UT (October 2002).

Arrighi, Giovanni. *The Long Twentieth Century: Money, Power, and the Origins of Our Times*. New York: Verso, 1994.

Asai, Senryo, and Duncan Ryūken Williams. "Japanese American Zen Temples: Cultural Identity and Economics." In *American Buddhism: Methods and Findings in Recent Scholarship*, edited by Duncan Ryūken Williams and Christopher S. Queen, 20–35. Surrey: Curzon Press, 1999.

Bankston, Carl L., III. "Bayou Lotus: Theravada Buddhism in Southwestern Louisiana." *Sociological Spectrum* 17, no. 4 (1997): 453–72.

Bankston, Carl L., III., and Min Zhou. "De Facto Congregationalism and Socioeconomic Mobility in Laotian and Vietnamese Immigrant Communities: A Study of Religious Institutions and Economic Change." *Review of Religious Research* 41, no. 4 (2000): 453–70.

Bareau, Andre. "Hinaya Buddhism." In *Encyclopedia of Religion*, edited by Mircea Eliade. New York: Macmillan, 1987.

Bartholomeusz, Tessa J. *Women under the Bo Tree: Buddhist Nuns in Sri Lanka.* Cambridge: Cambridge University Press, 1994.

————. "Southeast Asian Buddhism." In *Encyclopedia of Women and World Religion,* edited by Serinity Young. New York: Macmillan Reference, 1999.

Batchelor, Martine. *Walking on Lotus Flowers: Buddhist Women Living, Loving, and Meditating.* Edited by Gil Farrer-Halls. London: Thorsons, 1996.

Batchelor, Stephen. "A Thai Forest Tradition Grows in England." *Tricycle* 3, no. 4 (1994): 39–44.

————. *Buddhism without Beliefs: A Contemporary Guide to Awakening.* New York: Riverhead Books, 1997.

Baumann, Martin. "The Dharma Has Come West: A Survey of Recent Studies and Sources." *Journal of Buddhist Ethics* 4 (1997).

————. "Protective Amulets and Awareness Techniques, or How to Make Sense of Buddhism in the West." In *Westward Dharma: Buddhism beyond Asia,* edited by Charles S. Prebish and Martin Baumann, 51–65. Berkeley: University of California Press, 2002.

Bell, Sandra. "Being Creative with Tradition: Rooting Theravada Buddhism in Britain." *Journal of Global Buddhism* 1 (2000): 1–30.

Bellah, Robert N., et al. *Habits of the Heart: Individualism and Commitment in American Life.* Berkeley: University of California Press, 1985.

Berger, Peter L. *The Sacred Canopy: Elements of a Sociological Theory of Religion.* Garden City, NY: Anchor Books, 1967.

————. "Globalization and Religion." *The Hedgehog Review: Critical Reflections on Contemporary Culture* 4, no. 2 (2002): 7–20.

Berger, Peter L., and Samuel P. Huntington, eds. *Many Globalizations: Cultural Diversity in the Contemporary World.* New York: Oxford University Press, 2002.

Beyer, Peter. Introduction to *Religion in the Process of Globalization,* edited by Peter F. Beyer, i–xliv. Wurzburg, Germany: Ergon Verlag, 2001.

Blackburn, Anne. "The Evolution of Sinhalese Buddhist Identity: Reflections on Process." Senior Thesis, Department of Religion, Swarthmore College, 1987.

Blum, Linda M. *Between Feminism and Labor: The Significance of the Comparable Worth Movement.* Berkeley: University of California Press, 1991.

Bombardieri, Marcella. "Teens Take It Slow." *Boston Globe,* July 7, 2000.

Bond, George D. "The Buddha as Refuge in the Theravada Buddhist Tradition." In *The Threefold Refuge in the Theravada Buddhist Tradition,* edited by John Ross Carter, 16–32. Chambersburg, PA: Anima Publications, 1982.

————. *The Buddhist Revival in Sri Lanka: Religious Tradition, Reinterpretation, and Response.* Columbia: University of South Carolina Press, 1988.

Boorstein, Sylvia. *That's Funny, You Don't Look Buddhist: On Being a Faithful Jew and a Passionate Buddhist.* San Francisco: Harper San Francisco, 1997.

Boucher, Sandy. *Turning the Wheel: American Women Creating the New Buddhism.* Boston: Beacon Press, 1993.

————. *Opening the Lotus: A Woman's Guide to Buddhism.* Boston: Beacon Press, 1997.

————. *Discovering Kwan Yin, Buddhist Goddess of Compassion.* Boston: Beacon Press, 1999a.

————. "Women, Buddhism, and Vipassana Meditation." In *Asian Religions in America,* edited by Tom Tween and Stephen Prothero, 80–81. New York: Oxford University Press, 1999b.

Braude, Ann. "Women's History Is American Religious History." *Retelling U.S. Religious History*, edited by Thomas Tweed, 87–107. Berkeley: University of California Press, 1997.

Braudel, Fernand. *The Mediterranean and the Mediterranean World in the Age of Philip II*. 2 vols. New York: Harper and Row, 1972–1973.

——. *Afterthoughts on Material Civilization and Capitalism*. Baltimore: Johns Hopkins University Press, 1977.

Breyer, Chloe Anne. "Religious Liberty in Law and Practice: Vietnamese Home Temples and the First Amendment." *Journal of Church and State* 35 (1993): 367–401.

Brodey, Deborah Alexandra. "From Judaism to Buddhism: Jewish Women's Search for Identity." MA thesis, University of Toronto, 1997.

Brus, Eric. "Right Livelihood and Spiritual Practice." *Insight* (Spring 1996): 38.

Cabezon, Jose Ignacio, ed. *Buddhism, Sexuality, and Gender*. Albany: SUNY Press, 1992.

Cadge, Wendy. "Gendered Religious Organizations: The Case of Theravada Buddhism in America." *Gender and Society* 18, no. 6 (forthcoming).

Cadge, Wendy, and Lynn Davidman. "Ascription, Choice, and the Construction of Religious Identities in the Contemporary United States." Paper, Bowdoin College Department of Sociology and Anthropology, 2003.

Cadge, Wendy, and Sidhorn Sangdhanoo. "Thai Buddhism in America: A Historical and Contemporary Overview." Presented at the Society for the Scientific Study of Religion meetings, Salt Lake City, UT (October 2002).

Camerini, Michael. *Becoming the Buddha in L.A.* Boston: WGBH Educational Foundation, 1993.

Campbell, Dwayne. "Towering Faith to Take Shape." *Philadelphia Inquirer*, September 27, 2003.

Carter, John Ross. *Dhamma: Western Academic and Sinhalese Buddhist Interpretations, A Study of a Religious Concept*. Tokyo: Hokuseido Press, 1978.

——. "Dhamma as Refuge in the Theravada Buddhist Tradition." In *The Threefold Refuge in the Theravada Buddhist Tradition*, edited by John Ross Carter, 33–40. Chambersburg, VA: Anima Publications, 1982a.

——, ed. *The Threefold Refuge in the Theravada Buddhist Tradition*. Chambersburg, VA: Anima Publications, 1982b.

Casanova, Jose. "Globalizing Catholicism and Return to a 'Universal' Church." In *Transnational Religion and Fading States*, edited by Susanne Hoeber Rudolph and James Piscatori, 121–43. Boulder: Westview Press, 1997.

Chandler, Stuart. "Placing Palms Together: Religious and Cultural Dimensions of the Hsi Lai Temple Political Donations Controversy." In *American Buddhism: Methods and Findings in Recent Scholarship*, edited by Duncan Ryūken Williams and Christopher S. Queen, 36–56. Surrey: Curzon, 1999.

Charney, Michael W. "Burmese." In *American Immigrant Cultures: Builders of a Nation*, edited by David Levinson and Melvin Ember, 115–18. New York: Macmillan, 1997.

Chaves, Mark. *Ordaining Women: Culture and Conflict in Religious Organizations*. Cambridge: Harvard University Press, 1997.

Chayes, Bill, and Issac Solotaroff. *Jews and Buddhism: Belief Amended, Faith Revealed*. Video. Directed by Bill Chayes and Issac Solotaroff and produced in cooperation with the Judah L. Magnes Museum. New York: Filmakers Library, 1999.

Cheah, Joseph. "Adaptation of the Monastic and Popular Traditions of Burmese Buddhism by the Burmese Immigrant Communities in Los Angeles and the Bay Area." Presented at the American Academy of Religion Meetings, Toronto, November 2001.

———. "Cultural Identity and Burmese American Buddhists." *Peace Review* 14, no. 4 (2002): 415–19.

Chen, Carolyn. *Getting Saved in America: Taiwanese Immigrants Converting to Evangelical Christianity and Buddhism.* Princeton: Princeton University Press, forthcoming.

Chodorow, Nancy. *The Reproduction of Mothering: Psychoanalysis and the Sociology of Gender.* Berkeley: University of California Press, 1978.

Chodron, Bhiksuni Thubten. "Western Buddhist Nuns: A New Phenomenon in an Ancient Tradition." In *Women's Buddhism, Buddhism's Women,* edited by Ellison Banks Findly, 81–96. Boston: Wisdom Publications, 2000.

Clark, E. T. *The Psychology of Religious Awakening.* New York: Macmillan, 1929.

Cockburn, Cynthia. *In the Way of Women: Men's Resistance to Sex Equality in Organizations.* Ithaca: ILR Press, 1991.

Codman-Wilson, Mary Louise. "Thai Cultural and Religious Identity and Understanding of Well-Being in the United States: An Ethnographic Study of an Immigrant Church." PhD diss., Garrett-Evangelical Theological Seminary with Northwestern University, 1992.

Cohen, Steven M., and Arnold W. Eisen. *The Jew Within: Self, Family, and Community in America.* Bloomington: Indiana University Press, 2000.

Coleman, James William. *The New Buddhism: The Western Transformation of an Ancient Tradition.* New York: Oxford University Press, 2001.

Collins, Steven. *Selfless Persons: Imagery and Thought in Theravada Buddhism.* Cambridge: Cambridge University Press, 1982.

———. "What Are Buddhists Doing When They Deny the Self." *Religion and Practical Reason: New Essays in the Comparative Philosophy of Religions,* edited by Frank E. Reynolds and David Tracey, 59–86. Albany: SUNY Press, 1994.

Cox, Christopher. "Peaceful Weekend Retreat Leaves News Reporter Speechless." *Boston Herald,* March 7, 1995.

D'Antonio, Michael. *Heaven on Earth.* New York: Crown Publishers, 1992.

Davidman, Lynn. *Tradition in a Rootless World: Women Turn to Orthodox Judaism.* Berkeley: University of California Press, 1991.

Davie, Jody Shapiro. *Women in the Presence: Constructing Community and Seeking Spirituality in Mainline Protestantism.* Philadelphia: University of Pennsylvania Press, 1995.

Davis, Jake. "Strong Roots, Sweet Fruit: The Liberation Teachings of Mindfulness in the Land of the Free." Senior Thesis, Marlboro College, 2002.

de Vaus, David, and Ian McAllister. "Gender Differences in Religion: A Test of the Structural Location Theory." *American Sociological Review* 52, no. 4 (1987): 472–81.

DeMont, John. "Sunrise in the East." *Maclean's,* April 19, 1999, 112(16):60.

Denniston, Denise, and Peter McWilliams. "A TM Catechism (1975)." In *Asian Religions in America: A Documentary History,* edited by Thomas A. Tweed and Stephen Prothero, 241–44. New York: Oxford University Press, 1999.

Desbarats, Jacqueline. "Thai Migration to Los Angeles." *Geographical Review* 69, no. 3 (1979): 302–18.

DiMaggio, Paul. "Culture and Cognition." *Annual Review of Sociology* 23 (1997): 263–87.

———. "The Relevance of Organizational Theory to the Study of Religion." In *Sacred Companies: Organizational Aspects of Religion and Religious Aspects of Organizations,* edited by N. J. Demerath III, Peter Dobkin Hall, Terry Schmitt, and Rhys H. Williams, 7–23. New York: Oxford University Press, 1998.

Douglas, Thomas. "The Cross and the Lotus: Changing Religious Practices among Cambodian Immigrants in Seattle." In *Revealing the Sacred in Asian and Pacific America*, edited by Jane Naomi Iwamura and Paul Spickard, 159–75. New York: Routledge, 2003.

Dresser, Marianne, ed. *Buddhist Women on the Edge: Contemporary Perspectives from the Western Frontier.* Berkeley: North Atlantic Press, 1996.

Durkheim, Emile. *The Elementary Forms of the Religious Life.* New York: Macmillan, 1915.

Ebaugh, Helen Rose, and Janet Saltzman Chafetz. "Agents for Cultural Reproduction and Structural Change: The Ironic Role of Women in Immigrant Religious Institutions." *Social Forces* 78, no. 2 (1999): 585–612.

———. *Religion and the New Immigrants: Continuities and Adaptations in Immigrant Congregations.* Walnut Creek: AltaMira Press, 2000.

Eck, Diana. *On Common Ground: World Religions in America.* New York: Columbia University Press, 1997.

———. *A New Religious America: How a "Christian Country" Has Now Become the World's Most Religiously Diverse Nation.* San Francisco: Harper San Francisco, 2001.

Farber, Don. *Taking Refuge in LA: Life in a Vietnamese Buddhist Temple.* New York: Aperture, 1987.

Faure, Bernard. *The Power of Denial: Buddhism, Purity, and Gender.* Princeton: Princeton University Press, 2003.

Fausto-Sterling, Anne. *Sexing the Body: Gender Politics and the Construction of Sexuality.* New York: Basic Books, 2000.

Fenton, John Y. "Hinduism." In *Encyclopedia of the American Religious Experience: Studies of Traditions and Movements*, edited by Charles H. Lippy and Peter W. Williams. New York: Scribner and Sons, 1988.

Fields, Rick. *How the Swans Came to the Lake: A Narrative History of Buddhism in America.* New York: Shambhala Press, 1981.

———. "Divided Dharma: White Buddhists, Ethnic Buddhists, and Racism." In *The Faces of Buddhism in America*, edited by Charles S. Prebish and Kenneth K. Tanaka, 196–206. Berkeley: University of California Press, 1998.

Finney, Henry C. "American Zen's 'Japan Connection': A Critical Case Study of Zen Buddhism's Diffusion to the West." *Sociological Analysis* 52, no. 4 (1991): 379–96.

Fitzpatrick, Bridget. "Diversity in Practice: Placemaking among Sinhalese and Americans at the Washington Buddhist Vihara." PhD diss., American University, 2000.

Footrakoon, Orapan. "Lived Experiences of Thai War Brides in Mixed Thai-American Families in the United States." PhD diss., University of Minnesota, 1999.

Fraser, Kennedy. "Buddhism's Flowering in America: An Inside View." *New York Times*, November 3, 1997.

Frederick, Marla F. *Between Sundays: Black Women and Everyday Struggles of Faith.* Berkeley: University of California Press, 2003.

Friedman, Lenore, and Susan Moon, eds. *Being Bodies: Buddhist Women on the Paradox of Embodiment.* Boston: Shambhala, 1997.

Fronsdal, Egil. "Theravada Spirituality in the West." In *Buddhist Spirituality: Later China, Korea, Japan, and the Modern World*, edited by Takeuchi Yoshinori, 482–96. New York: Crossroads, 1999.

Fronsdal, Gil. "Insight Meditation in the United States: Life, Liberty and the Pursuit of Happiness." In *The Faces of Buddhism in America*, edited by Charles S. Prebish and Kenneth K. Tanaka, 163–82. Berkeley: University of California Press, 1998a.

————. "Theravada: The Path of Insight." In *The Complete Guide to Buddhist America*, edited by Don Morreale, 3–9. Boston: Shambhala, 1998b.

————. "Virtues without Rules: Ethics in the Insight Meditation Movement." In *Westward Dharma: Buddhism beyond Asia*, edited by Charles S. Prebish and Martin Baumann, 285–306. Berkeley: University of California Press, 2002.

Fung, Timothy. "The Vinaya of the Living Theravada Buddhist Tradition in the West." PhD diss., California Institute of Integral Studies, 1999.

Gallup, George, Jr. "Aggregate of Gallup Poll Religion Questions: Detailed Tabulations." Data provided by Gallup, Princeton, NJ, 2001.

Gallup, George, Jr., and Jim Castelli. *The People's Religion: American Faith in the 90's*. New York: Macmillan, 1989.

Gallup, George, Jr., and D. Michael Lindsay. *Surveying the Religious Landscape: Trends in U.S. Beliefs*. Harrisburg: Morehouse Publishing, 1999.

Gans, Herbert. "Symbolic Ethnicity and Symbolic Religiosity: Towards a Comparison of Ethnic and Religious Acculturation." *Ethnic and Racial Studies* 17, no. 4 (1994): 577–92.

Garrett, Catherine. "Transcendental Meditation, Reiki, and Yoga: Suffering, Ritual, and Self-Transformation." *Journal of Contemporary Religion* 16, no. 3 (2001): 329–42.

Geertz, Clifford. *The Interpretation of Cultures: Selected Essays*. New York: Basic Books, 1973.

Gethin, Rupert. *The Foundations of Buddhism*. New York: Oxford University Press, 1998.

Gilligan, Carol. *In a Different Voice: Psychological Theory and Women's Development*. Cambridge: Harvard University Press, 1982.

Goenka, S. N. *The Art of Living: Vipassana Meditation*. Pamphlet, n.d.

Goenka, S. N. "Superscience: An Interview by Helen Tworkov." *Tricycle* 10, no. 2 (2000): 44–50.

Goldstein, Joseph. "To the Forest for Refuge: An Interview with Joseph Goldstein." *Insight* (Fall 1998): 3–5.

————. "How Amazing! An Interview with Amy Gross." *Tricycle* 8, no. 4 (1999): 30–37.

————. *One Dharma: The Emerging Western Buddhism*. San Francisco: Harper San Francisco, 2002.

Gombrich, Richard F. *Theravada Buddhism: A Social History from Ancient Benares to Modern Colombo*. New York: Routledge, 1988.

Gordon, Linda. "Southeast Asian Refugee Migration to the United States." In *Pacific Bridges: The New Immigration from Asia and the Pacific Islands*, edited by James T. Fawcett and Benjamin V. Carino, 153–73. New York: Center for Migration Studies, 1987.

Gould, Rebecca Kneale. "Getting (Not Too) Close to Nature: Modern Homesteading as Lived Religion in America." In *Lived Religion: Toward a History of Practice*, edited by David D. Hall, 217–42. Princeton: Princeton University Press, 1997.

Grady, Michael Liebenson. "Waking Up in Relationships." *Insight* (Fall 2000): 43.

Grady, Narayan Liebenson. "What Can I Learn from This? An Interview with Narayan Liebenson Grady." *Insight* (Fall 1995): 3–5.

————. "Refuge in the Sangha." In *Voices of Insight*, edited by Sharon Salzberg, 195–205. Boston: Shambhala Press, 2001.

————. *When Singing Just Sing: Life as Meditation*. Wellesley, MA: Ruby Shoes Studio, n.d.

Gregory, Peter. "Describing the Elephant: Buddhism in America." *Religion and American Culture* 11, no. 2 (2001): 233–63.

Griffith, R. Marie. *God's Daughters: Evangelical Women and the Power of Submission.* Berkeley: University of California Press, 1997.

Gross, Rita. *Buddhism after Patriarchy: A Feminist History, Analysis, and Reconstruction of Buddhism.* Albany: SUNY Press, 1993.

Guillen, Mauro F. "Is Globalization Civilizing, Destructive, or Feeble? A Critique of Five Key Debates in the Social Science Literature." *Annual Review of Sociology* 27 (2001): 235–60.

Gunaratana, Ven. Henepola. "Growth and Development of Buddhist Organizations: An Organic Process of Cooperation." Paper given at the International Monastic Seminar in Toronto, September 29, 1998; available at http://www.bhavanasociety.org/articles/seminar.htm.

Gussner, R. E., and S. D. Berkowitz. "Scholars, Sects, and Sanghas, I: Recruitment to Asian-Based Meditation Groups in North America." *Sociological Analysis* 49, no. 2 (1988): 136–70.

Hall, David D., ed. *Lived Religion in America: Toward a History of Practice.* Princeton: Princeton University Press, 1997.

Hallisey, Charles, and Anne Hansen. "Narrative, Sub-Ethics, and the Moral Life: Some Evidence from Theravada Buddhism." *Journal of Religious Ethics* 24, no. 2 (1996): 305–27.

Hallisey, Charles, and Frank Reynolds. "Buddhism: An Overview." In *The Encyclopedia of Religion,* edited by Mircea Eliade, 334–50. New York: Macmillan Library Reference, 1995.

Hammond, Phillip E., and David W. Machacek. *Soka Gakkai in America: Accommodation and Conversion.* New York: Oxford University Press, 1999.

Hammond, Phillip E., and Kee Warner. "Religion and Ethnicity in Late Twentieth Century America." *Annals of the American Academy of Political and Social Science* 527 (May 1993): 55–66.

Handlin, Oscar. *The Uprooted: The Epic Story of the Great Migrations That Made the American People.* Boston: Little Brown and Co., 1951.

Harris, Elizabeth. "The Female in Buddhism." In *Buddhist Women across Cultures: Realizations,* edited by Karma Lekshe Tsomo, 49–65. Albany: SUNY Press, 1999.

Harvey, Peter. *An Introduction to Buddhism: Teachings, History, and Practices.* New York: Cambridge University Press, 1990.

Heikkila-Horn, Marja-Leena. "Two Paths to Revivalism in Thai Buddhism: The Dhammakaya and Santi Asoke Movements." *Temenos* 32 (1996): 93–111.

Hein, Jeremy. *From Vietnam, Laos, and Cambodia: A Refugee Experience in the United States.* New York: Twayne Publishers, 1995.

Held, David, et al. *Global Transformations: Politics, Economics, and Culture.* Stanford: Stanford University Press, 1999.

Helm, Chris. "One Tough Lama." *Harper's,* August 1996, 11–12.

Herberg, Will. *Protestant-Catholic-Jew: An Essay in American Religious Sociology.* Garden City: Doubleday, 1955.

Ho, Manli. "Meditation Group Buys Barre Novitiate." *Boston Globe,* December 31, 1975.

Hopewell, James F.. *Congregations: Stories and Structures.* Edited by Barbara G. Wheeler. Philadelphia: Fortress Press, 1987.

Hopkins, Dwight N., et al., eds. *Religions/Globalizations: Theories and Cases.* Durham: Duke University Press, 2001.

Hori, G. Victor Sogen. "Japanese Zen in America: Americanizing the Face in the Mirror." In *The Faces of Buddhism in America*, edited by Charles S. Prebish and Kenneth K. Tanaka. Berkeley: University of California Press, 1998.

Hudson, Abhi. "IMS Turns Twenty: A Guest Reflects on the Celebration." *Insight* (Fall 1996).

"Insight Meditation Society." *Insight* (Spring 1996): 8.

INS (Immigration and Naturalization Service). *Annual Report.* Washington, D.C.: U.S. Government Printing Office, 1969, 1970, 1971, 1972, 1973, 1974, 1975, 1976, and 1977.

"Intensive Meditation." *Bucksport (ME) Free Press*, September 18, 1975.

Ishi, Yoneo. *Sangha, State, and Society: Thai Buddhism in History.* Honolulu: University of Hawaii Press, 1986.

Ittner, John. *Lighting the Lamp of Wisdom: A Week inside a Yoga Ashram.* Woodstock, Vt.: SkyLight Paths Pubs., 2002.

Jacobson, Jessica. "Religion and Ethnicity: Dual and Alternative Sources of Identity among Young British Pakistanis." *Ethnic and Racial Studies* 20, no. 2 (1997): 238–56.

Jasso, Guillermina, et al. "Exploring the Religious Preference of Recent Immigrants to the United States: Evidence from the New Immigrant Survey Pilot." In *Religion and Immigration: Christian, Jewish, and Muslim Experiences in the United States*, edited by Yvonne Haddad et al. Walnut Creek, AltaMira Press, 2003.

Jenkins, Philip. *The Next Christendom: The Coming of Global Christianity.* New York: Oxford University Press, 2002.

Kabat-Zinn, Jon. *Wherever You Go, There You Are: Mindfulness Meditation in Everyday Life.* New York: Hyperion, 1995.

Kabilsingh, Chatsumarn. *Thai Women in Buddhism.* Berkeley: Parallax Press, 1991.

Kamenetz, Rodger. "Robert Thurman Doesn't Look Buddhist." *New York Times Magazine*, May 5, 1996, 46–49.

———. *The Jew in the Lotus: A Poet's Rediscovery of Jewish Identity in Buddhist India.* San Francisco: Harper San Francisco, 1994.

Kanter, Rosabeth Moss. *Men and Women of the Corporation.* New York: Basic Books, 1977.

Kashima, Tetsuden. *Buddhism in America: The Social Organization of an Ethnic Religious Institution.* Westport, CT: Greenwood Press, 1977.

Kelly, Lynn. "Dharma Leader: An Interview with James Baraz." *Awakening Mind: Insight Meditation Community of Washington* (Summer/Fall 2000).

Kelly, Mary. "The Dalai Lama Visits the Insight Meditation Center." *Barre Gazette*, October 17, 1979.

Keyes, Charles. "Mother or Mistress but Never a Monk: Culture of Gender and Rural Women in Buddhist Thailand." *American Ethnologist* 11, no. 2 (1984): 223–41.

Kim, Bok-Lim C., et al. *Women in Shadows: A Handbook for Service Providers Working with Asian Wives of U.S. Military Personnel.* La Jolla: National Committee Concerned with Asian Wives of U.S. Servicemen, 1981.

King, Winston. "Contemporary Burmese Buddhism." In *Buddhism in the Modern World*, edited by Heinrich Dumoulin, 81–98. New York: Macmillan, 1976.

———. *Theravada Meditation: The Buddhist Transformation of Yoga.* University Park: Penn State University Press, 1980.

Kirsch, Thomas. "Buddhism, Sex Roles, and the Thai Economy." In *Women of Southeast Asia*, edited by Penny Van Esterik. DeKalb: Northern Illinois University Center for

South and Southeast Asian Studies, Monograph Series on Southeast Asia, occasional paper 9, 1982.

Klassen, Pamela E. *Blessed Events: Religion and Home Birth in America.* Princeton: Princeton University Press, 2001.

Kornfield, Jack. *A Path with a Heart: A Guide through the Perils and Promises of Spiritual Life.* New York: Bantam Books, 1993.

———. "Domains of Consciousness: An Interview with Jack Kornfield." *Tricycle* 6, no. 1 (1996): 34–40.

———. "American Buddhism." In *The Complete Guide to Buddhist America*, edited by Don Morreale, xxi–xxx. Boston: Shambhala, 1998.

———. "The Sure Heart's Release: An Interview with Jack Kornfield." *Tricycle* 9, no. 4 (2000): 37–44.

Kosmin, Barry A., and Seymour P. Lachman. *One Nation under God: Religion in Contemporary American Society.* New York: Harmony Books, 1993.

Kuoch, Theanvy. "Buddhism and Mental Health among Cambodian Refuges." In *Women's Buddhism, Buddhism's Women*, edited by Ellison Banks Findlay, 425–32. Boston: Wisdom Publications, 2000.

Kurien, Prema. "Becoming American by Becoming Hindu: Indian Americans Take Their Place at the Multicultural Table." In *Gatherings in Diaspora: Religious Communities and the New Immigration*, edited by R. Stephen Warner and Judith Wittner, 37–70. Philadelphia: Temple University Press, 1998.

———. "Gendered Ethnicity: Creating a Hindu Indian Identity in the United States." *American Behavioral Scientist* 42, no. 4 (1999): 648–70.

———. " 'We Are Better Hindus Here': Religion and Ethnicity among Indian Americans." In *Religions in Asian America: Building Faith Communities*, edited by Pyong Gap Min and Jung Ha Kim, 99–120. Walnut Creek: AltaMira Press, 2001.

Kwon, Ho-Youn, Kwang Chung Kim, and R. Stephen Warner. *Korean Americans and Their Religions: Pilgrims and Missionaries from a Different Shore.* University Park: Pennsylvania State University Press, 2001.

Lang, Kurt, and Gladys Engel Lang. *Collective Dynamics.* New York: Crowell, 1961.

Larsen, Wanwadee. *Confessions of a Mail Order Bride: American Life through Thai Eyes.* Far Hills, NJ: New Horizon Press, 1989.

Lau, Kimberly J. *New Age Capitalism: Making Money East of Eden.* Philadelphia: University of Pennsylvania Press, 2000.

Lavine, Amy. "Tibetan Buddhism in America: The Development of American Vajrayana." In *The Faces of Buddhism in America*, edited by Charles S. Prebish and Kenneth K. Tanaka. Berkeley: University of California, 1998.

Layman, Emma McCloy. *Buddhism in America.* Chicago: Nelson Hall, 1976.

Lefferts, H. Leedom, Jr. "Buddhist Action: Lay Women and Thai Monks." In *Women's Buddhism, Buddhism's Women*, edited by Ellison Banks Findly, 63–80. Boston: Wisdom, 2000.

Lesser, Elizabeth. *The Seeker's Guide: Making Your Life a Spiritual Adventure.* New York: Villard, 1999.

Levitt, Peggy. "Social Remittances: Migration Driven Local Level Forms of Cultural Diffusion." *International Migration Review* 32, no. 4 (1998): 926–48.

———. "They Prayed in Boston and It Rained in Brazil: Toward a Map of Transnational

Religious Life." Paper presented at the Society for the Scientific Study of Religion Meetings (October 2000).

————."Between God, Ethnicity, and Country: An Approach to the Study of Transnational Religion." Working paper #01–06, Center for Migration and Development, Princeton University, 2001a.

————. *The Transnational Villagers*. Berkeley: University of California Press, 2001b.

————. " 'You Know, Abraham Was Really the First Immigrant': Religion and Transnational Migration." *International Migration Review* (forthcoming).

Lewis, Nantawan Boonprasat. "Thai." In *American Immigrant Cultures: Builders of a Nation*, edited by David Levinson and Melvin Ember, 883–87. New York: Macmillan, 1997.

Lin, Irene. "Journey to the Far West: Chinese Buddhism in America." *Amerasia Journal* 22, no. 1 (1996): 107–32.

Ling, Paul Kimberley. "The Intensive Buddhist Meditation Retreat and the Self: Psychological and Theravadin Considerations." PhD diss., Boston University, 1981.

Linton, Ralph. *The Study of Man: An Introduction*. New York: D. Appleton-Century Co., 1936.

Lopez, Donald S., *Prisoners of Shangri-La: Tibetan Buddhism and the West*. Chicago: University of Chicago Press, 1998.

Loundon, Sumi, ed. *Blue Jean Buddha: Voices of Young Buddhists*. Boston: Wisdom Publications, 2001.

Madihe Pannasiha Maha Nayaka Thera. "Bringing the Dhamma to America: The View of the Founder." In *Twenty-fifth Anniversary Book of the Washington Buddhist Vihara*, 1–2. Washington, D.C., 1991.

Magness, T. *Samma Samadhi: The Method of Right Insight*. Bangkok: Graphic Arts Research Center, 1988.

McLellan, Janet. *Many Petals of the Lotus: Five Asian Buddhist Communities in Toronto*. Toronto: University of Toronto Press, 1999.

Malmgren, Jeanne. "Noble Silence." *St. Petersburg Times*, November 16, 1991.

Mayhew, Leon H., ed. *Talcott Parsons on Institutions and Social Evolution: Selected Writings*. Chicago: University of Chicago Press, 1982.

Melton, J. Gordon. *Encyclopedia of American Religions*, 4th ed. Detroit: Gale Research, 1993.

Menjivar, Cecilia. "Religious Institutions and Transnationalism: A Case Study of Catholic and Evangelical Salvadoran Immigrants." *International Journal of Politics, Culture, and Society* 12, no. 4 (1999): 589–612.

Metcalf, Franz Aubrey. "Why Do Americans Practice Zen Buddhism?" Presented at a conference at Harvard Divinity School, 1997.

————. "The Encounter of Buddhism and Psychology." In *Westward Dharma: Buddhism beyond Asia*, edited by Charles S. Prebish and Martin Baumann, 348–64. Berkeley: University of California Press, 2002.

Miller, Alan, and Rodney Stark. "Gender and Religiousness: Can Socialization Explanations Be Saved?" *American Journal of Sociology* 107, no. 6 (2002): 1399–423.

Min, Pyong Gap. "The Structure and Social Function of Korean Immigrant Churches in the United States." *International Migration Review* 26, no. 4 (1992): 1370–94.

Minocha, Urmil. "South Asian Immigrants: Trends and Impacts on the Sending and Receiving Societies." In *Pacific Bridges: The New Immigration from Asia and the Pacific Islands*, edited by James T. Fawcett and Benjamin V. Cariño, 347–73. New York: Center for Migration Studies, 1987.

Mitchell, Donald W. *Buddhism: Introducing the Buddhist Experience.* New York: Oxford University Press, 2002.

Moraine, Meredith, and Jerry Steward, "The Story So Far . . ." *Spirit Rock Newspaper,* September 1995–January 1996.

Morreale, Don, ed.. *The Complete Guide to Buddhist America.* Boston: Shambhala Press, 1998.

Mortland, Carol. "Khmer Buddhists in the United States: Ultimate Questions." In *Cambodian Culture since 1975: Homeland and Exile,* edited by May M. Ebihara, Carol A. Mortland, and Judy Ledgerwood, 72–90. Ithaca: Cornell University Press, 1994.

Muecke, Marjorie. "Resettled Refugees' Reconstruction of Identity: Lao in Seattle." *Urban Anthropology* 16, nos. 3–4 (1987): 273–89.

Mullen, Eve Louise. "Tibetan Buddhism, American Interests: Influences upon the Lay and Monastic Relationship in New York's Tibetan Buddhist Immigrant Community." PhD diss., Temple University, 1999.

Murcott, Susan. *The First Buddhist Women: Translations and Commentary on the Therigatha.* Berkeley: Parallax Press, 1991.

Nattier, Jan. "Who Is a Buddhist? Charting the Landscape of Buddhist America." In *The Faces of Buddhism in America,* edited by Charles S. Prebish and Kenneth K. Tanaka, 183–95. Berkeley: University of California Press, 1998.

Nguyen, Cuong Tu, and A. W. Barber. "Vietnamese Buddhism in North America." In *The Faces of Buddhism in America,* edited by Charles S. Prebish and Kenneth K. Tanaka, 129–46. Berkeley: University of California Press, 1998.

Nock, A. D. *Conversion.* New York: Oxford University Press, 1933.

Numrich, Paul David. "Vinaya in Theravada Temples in the United States." *Journal of Buddhist Ethics* 1 (1994).

———. *Old Wisdom in the New World: Americanization in Two Immigrant Theravada Buddhist Temples.* Knoxville: University of Tennessee Press, 1996.

———. "Theravada Buddhism in America: Prospects for the Sangha." In *The Faces of Buddhism in America,* edited by Charles S. Prebish and Kenneth K. Tanaka, 147–62. Berkeley: University of California, 1998.

———. "Local Inter-Buddhist Associations in North America." In *American Buddhism: Methods and Findings in Recent Scholarship,* edited by Duncan Ryūken Williams and Christopher S. Queen. Surrey: Curzon, 1999.

———. "How the Swans Came to Lake Michigan: The Social Organization of Buddhist Chicago." *Journal for the Scientific Study of Religion* 39, no. 2 (2000a): 189–203.

———. "The Numbers Questioned: Thoughts for Pew's Religion and New Immigrants Research Initiative." (2000b). Available at http://newimmigrants.org/classroom/research/numrich-09052000.php3.

Obadia, Lionel. "Buddha in the Promised Land: Outlines of the Buddhist Settlement in Israel." In *Westward Dharma: Buddhism beyond Asia,* edited by Charles S. Prebish and Martin Baumann, 177–88. Berkeley: University of California Press, 2002.

Oh, Young Bong. "Buddhism in America: Can It Blend with Our Philosophy and Culture?" *USA Today* magazine 118, no. 2530 (July 1989): 84–85.

Olendzki, Andrew. "Buddhist Psychology: Classical Texts in Contemporary Perspective." *Insight* (1997): 32–36.

Orsi, Robert. *Thank You, St. Jude: Women's Devotion to the Patron Saint of Hopeless Causes.* New Haven: Yale University Press, 1996.

————. "Everyday Miracles: The Study of Lived Religion." In *Lived Religion in America: Toward a History of Practice*, edited by David D. Hall, 3–21. Princeton: Princeton University Press, 1997.

————. "Is the Study of Lived Religion Irrelevant to the World We Live In?" Special Presidential Plenary Address, Society for the Scientific Study of Religion. *Journal for the Scientific Study of Religion* 42, no. 2 (2003): 169–74.

Padgett, Douglas W. " 'Americans Need Something to Sit On,' or Zen Meditation Materials and Buddhist Diversity in North America." *Journal of Global Buddhism* 1 (2000): 31–60.

————. "The Translating Temple: Diasporic Buddhism in Florida." In *Westward Dharma: Buddhism beyond Asia*, edited by Charles S. Prebish and Martin Baumann, 201–17. Berkeley: University of California Press, 2002.

Paisano, Edna, et al. *We the Americans: Asians.* Washington, D.C.: U.S. Department of Commerce, 1993.

Payutto, P. A. (Ven. Phra Dhammapitaka). *Thai Buddhism in the Buddhist World.* Bangkok: Saha Dhammika, 1999.

Perreira, Todd LeRoy. "Thais That Bind: A Middle-Way between 'Cradle' and 'Convert.' " Presented at the Society for the Scientific Study of Religion, Salt Lake City, UT (October 2002).

————. "Sassana Sakon and the New Asian American: Intermarriage and Identity at a Thai Buddhist Temple in Silicon Valley." In *Asian American Religions: Borders and Boundaries*, edited by Tony Carnes and Fenggang Yang. New York: New York University Press, forthcoming.

Philips, Judy. "Dharma as Dana: An Interview with Judy Phillips." *Insight* (Fall 2000): 30–32.

Piyananda, Walpola. "The History of Dharma Vijaya Buddhist Vihara." *Dharma Vijaya Magazine* (August 1990): 4–10.

————. *Saffron Days in L.A.: Tales of a Buddhist Monk in America.* Boston: Shambhala, 2001.

Porterfield, Amanda. *The Transformation of American Religion: The Story of a Late-Twentieth-Century Awakening.* New York: Oxford University Press, 2001.

Portes, Alejandro, and Ruben G. Rumbaut. *Immigrant America: A Portrait*, 2nd ed. Berkeley: University of California Press, 1996.

Prebish, Charles S. *American Buddhism.* North Scituate, MA: Duxbury Press, 1979.

————. "The Academic Study of Buddhism in America: A Silent Sangha." In *American Buddhism: Methods and Findings in Recent Scholarship*, edited by Duncan Ryūken Williams and Christopher S. Queen, 183–214. Surrey: Curzon, 1999a.

————. *Luminous Passage: The Practice and Study of Buddhism in America.* Berkeley: University of California Press, 1999b.

————. "Varying the Vinaya: Creative Responses to Modernity." In *Buddhism in the Modern World: Adaptations of an Ancient Tradition*, ed. Steven Heine and Charles Prebish. New York: Oxford University Press, 2003.

Prebish, Charles S., and Martin Baumann. *Westward Dharma: Buddhism beyond Asia.* Berkeley: University of California Press, 2002.

Prebish, Charles S., and Kenneth K. Tanaka, eds. *The Faces of Buddhism in America.* Berkeley: University of California Press, 1998.

Preston, David L. *The Social Organization of Zen Practice: Constructing Transcultural Reality.* New York: Cambridge University Press, 1988.

Proschan, Frank. "Lao." In *American Immigrant Cultures: Builders of a Nation,* edited by David Levinson and Melvin Ember, 565–73. New York: Macmillan, 1997.

Putnam, Robert. *Bowling Alone: The Collapse and Revival of American Community.* New York: Simon and Schuster, 2000.

Queen, Christopher S. Introduction to *American Buddhism: Methods and Findings in Recent Scholarship,* edited by Duncan Ryūken Williams and Christopher S. Queen, xiv–xxxvii. Surrey: Curzon Press, 1999.

———, ed. *Engaged Buddhism in the West.* Boston: Wisdom Publications, 2000.

Rahula, Walpola. *What the Buddha Taught.* New York: Grove Press, 1974.

Rayaprol, Aparna. *Negotiating Identities: Women in the Indian Diaspora.* New York: Oxford University Press, 1997.

Reed, Barbara. "The Gender Symbolism of Kuan-Yin Bodhisattva." In *Buddhism, Sexuality, and Gender,* edited by Jose Ignacio Cabezon, 159–80. Albany: SUNY Press, 1992.

*Religion and Ethics Newsweekly.* "Tensions in American Buddhism." Web page, 2001. Available at http://www.pbs.org/wnet/religionandethics/week445/cover.html.

Reynolds, Frank, and Donald Capps, eds. *The Biographical Process: Studies in the History and Psychology of Religion.* The Hague: Mouton, 1976.

Robinson, Richard H., and Willard L. Johnson. *The Buddhist Religion: A Historical Introduction.* Belmont, CA: Wadsworth, 1997.

Roehm, Michael. "A Few Fragments from the Vihara's Twenty-Five Year Chronology." In *Twenty-fifth Anniversary Book of the Washington Buddhist Vihara,* 9–22. Washington, D.C., 1991.

Roether, Barbara. "Exile Spirit: Barbara Roether Profiles Thanissaro Bhikkhu and the Metta Forest Monastery." *Tricycle* 5, no. 2 (1995): 77–83.

Rogers, Everett M. *Diffusion of Innovations.* New York: Free Press, 1995.

Roof, Wade Clark. *A Generation of Seekers: The Spiritual Journeys of the Baby Boom Generation.* San Francisco: Harper San Francisco, 1993.

Rosenberg, Larry. "Communication Styles and Student Learning: A Factor Analytic Study of Teacher-Student Interaction." PhD diss., University of Chicago, 1961.

———. "Breathing Lessons: An Interview with David Guy." *Sun,* no. 248 (1996): 4–9.

———. "The Art of Doing Nothing: An Interview by Amy Gross." *Tricycle* 7, no. 3 (1998): 40–47.

———. "The Wisdom of the Ordinary Mind: An Interview." *Insight* (1999): 3–6.

———. "Body People, Mind People." *Insight* (2001): 43.

Rosenberg, Larry, with David Guy. *Breath by Breath: The Liberating Practice of Insight Meditation.* Boston: Shambhala, 1998.

Rumbaut, Ruben G. "Cambodians." In *American Immigrant Cultures: Builders of a Nation,* edited by David Levinson and Melvin Ember, 123–32. New York: Macmillan, 1997.

Salzberg, Sharon. *Lovingkindness: The Revolutionary Art of Happiness.* Boston: Shambhala, 1995.

———. *Voices of Insight.* Boston: Shambhala, 2001.

———. *Faith: Trusting Your Own Deepest Experience.* New York: Riverhead Books, 2002.

Scott, Joan. "Gender: A Useful Category of Analysis." *American Historical Review* 91, no. 5 (1986).

Seager, Richard Hughes. *The World's Parliament of Religions: The East/West Encounter, Chicago, 1893.* Bloomington: Indiana University Press, 1995.

———. *Buddhism in America.* New York: Columbia University Press, 1999.

Seneviratne, H. L. "Sri Lankans." In *American Immigrant Cultures: Builders of a Nation*, edited by David Levison and Melvin Ember, 842–45. New York: Macmillan, 1997.

Shanti, Havanpola, and Anura Senanayake, "A Biographical Sketch of Venerable Doctor Havanpola Ratanasara Nayake Maha Thera." Special issue, *Dharma Vijaya Magazine*, February 1999.

Shattuck, Cybelle. *Dharma in the Golden State: South Asian Religious Traditions in California*. Santa Barbara: Fithian Press, 1996.

Shaw, Miranda. *Passionate Enlightenment: Women in Tantric Buddhism*. Princeton: Princeton University Press, 1994.

Sherkat, Darren, and Christopher Ellison. "Recent Developments and Current Controversies in the Sociology of Religion." *Annual Review of Sociology* 25 (1999): 363–94.

Siegel, Taggart. *Blue Collar and Buddha*. San Francisco: CrossCurrent Media, NAATA, 1987.

Smith, Christian. *American Evangelicalism: Embattled and Thriving*. Chicago: University of Chicago Press, 1998.

Smith, Tom W. "Religious Diversity in America: The Emergence of Muslims, Buddhists, Hindus, and Others." *Journal for the Scientific Study of Religion* 41, no. 3 (2002): 577–85.

Smith-Hefner, Nancy J. *Khmer American: Identity and Moral Education in a Diasporic Community*. Berkeley: University of California Press, 1999.

Snow, David, and Richard Machalek. "The Sociology of Conversion." *Annual Review of Sociology* 10 (1984): 167–90.

Soeng, Mu. "Korean Buddhism in America: A New Style of Zen." In *The Faces of Buddhism in America*, edited by Charles S. Prebish and Kenneth K. Tanaka, 117–28. Berkeley: University of California Press, 1998.

Sponberg, Alan. "Attitudes toward Women and the Feminine in Early Buddhism." In *Buddhism, Sexuality, and Gender*, edited by Jose Ignacio Cabezon. Albany: SUNY Press, 1992.

Strang, David, and Sarah A. Soule. "Diffusion in Organizations and Social Movements: From Hybrid Corn to Poison Pills." *Annual Review of Sociology* 24 (1998): 265–90.

Strong, John S. *The Experience of Buddhism: Sources and Interpretations*. Belmont, CA: Wadsworth Publishing, 1995.

Sucitto, Ajahn, and Amaravati Sangha. "Amaravati and the Teachings of Ajahn Sumedho." *Insight* (Spring 1993): 1.

Suskind, Ron. "Silent Treatment: Our Reporter Tries the Meditative Life." *Wall Street Journal*, November 16, 1984.

Swearer, Donald K. "Fundamentalistic Movements in Theravada Buddhism." In *Fundamentalisms Observed*, edited by Martin Marty and R. Scott Appleby, 628–90. Chicago: University of Chicago Press, 1991.

———. *The Buddhist World of Southeast Asia*. Albany: SUNY Press, 1995.

———. "The Worldliness of Buddhism." *Wilson Quarterly* 21 (1999).

Swidler, Ann. "Culture in Action: Symbols and Strategies." *American Sociological Review* 51, no. 2 (1986): 273–86.

Tambiah, Stanley J. *Buddhism and Spirit Cults in North-East Thailand*. Cambridge: Cambridge University Press, 1970.

———. *World Conqueror and World Renouncer: A Study of Buddhism and Polity in Thailand against a Historical Background*. New York: Cambridge University Press, 1976.

Tanaka, Kenneth K. "Epilogue: The Colors and Contours of American Buddhism." In *The Faces of Buddhism in America*, edited by Charles S. Prebish and Kenneth K. Tanaka, 287–98. Berkeley: University of California Press, 1998.

———. "Issues of Ethnicity in the Buddhist Churches of America." In *American Buddhism: Methods and Findings in Recent Scholarship*, edited by Duncan Ryūken Williams and Christopher S. Queen, 3–19. Surrey: Curzon Press, 1999.

Thanissaro Bhikkhu, *Refuge: An Introduction to the Buddha, Dhamma, and Sangha.* N.p.: Dhammayut Order in the United States, 1996a.

———. "An Interview with Thanissaro Bhikkhu: A Question of Skill." *Insight* (Spring 2000).

———. "Romancing the Buddha." *Tricycle* (2002): 45–47.

———, trans. *The Buddhist Monastic Code: The Patimokkha Training Rules.* N.p., 1996b.

———, trans. *The Buddhist Monastic Code II: The Khandhaka Rules.* N.p., 2001.

Thomas, Edward J. *The Life of Buddha as Legend and History.* Mineola, NY: Dover Publications, 2000.

Tipton, Steven M. *Getting Saved from the Sixties: Moral Meaning in Conversion and Cultural Change.* Berkeley: University of California Press, 1982.

Tiyavanich, Kamala. *Forest Recollections: Wandering Monks in Twentieth-Century Thailand.* Honolulu: University of Hawaii Press, 1997.

Tocqueville, Alexis de. *Democracy in America.* 2 vols. New York: Anchor, 1945.

Tsomo, Karma Lekshe, ed. *Buddhist Women across Cultures: Realizations.* Albany: SUNY Press, 1999.

Tuck, Donald. *Buddhist Churches of America: Jodo Shinshu.* Lewiston, NY: Edwin Mellen Press, 1987.

Tweed, Thomas A. *The American Encounter with Buddhism, 1844–1912: Victorian Culture and the Limits of Dissent.* Bloomington: Indiana University Press, 1992.

———. "Night-Stand Buddhists and Other Creatures: Sympathizers, Adherents, and the Study of Religion." In *American Buddhism: Methods and Findings in Recent Scholarship*, edited by Duncan Ryūken Williams and Christopher S. Queen, 71–90. Surrey: Curzon, 1999.

Tworkov, Helen. "Going Upstream: An Interview with Bhante Henepola Gunaratana." *Tricycle* 4, no. 3 (1995): 37–41.

Uchiyama, Kosho. *Opening the Hand of Thought: Approaches to Zen.* New York: Arkana, 1993.

Upasak, Chandrika S. *Dictionary of Early Buddhist Monastic Terms Based on Pali Literature.* Varanasi: Bharati Prakashan, 1975.

Van Biema, David. "Buddhism in America." *Time*, October 13, 1997, 72ff.

Van Dusen, Caitlin. "Dana Works: Dharma Seed Archival Center." *Tricycle* (Winter 2002): 85.

VanEsterik, Penny. "Laywomen in Theravada Buddhism." In *Women of Southeast Asia*, edited by Penny VanEsterik. DeKalb: Northern Illinois University Center for South and Southeast Asian Studies, Monograph Series on Southeast Asia, occasional paper 9, 1982.

———. *Taking Refuge: Lao Buddhists in North America.* Tempe: Arizona State University, 1992.

———. "Ritual and the Performance of Buddhist Identity among Lao Buddhists in North America." In *American Buddhism: Methods and Findings in Recent Scholarship*, edited by Duncan Ryūken Williams and Christopher S. Queen. Surrey: Curzon, 1999.

Verhoeven, Martin John. " 'Americanizing the Buddha: The World Parliament of Religions, Paul Carus, and the Making of Modern Buddhism." PhD diss., University of Wisconsin–Madison, 1997.

Wallace, B. Alan. "The Spectrum of Buddhist Practice in the West." In *Westward Dharma: Buddhism beyond Asia*, edited by Charles S. Prebish and Martin Baumann, 34–50. Berkeley: University of California Press, 2002.

Wallerstein, Immanuel. *The Modern World System I: Capitalist Agriculture and the Origins of the European World-Economy in the Sixteenth Century*. New York: Academic Press, 1974.

———. *The Modern World System II: Mercantilism and the Consolidation of the European World-Economy, 1600–1750*. New York: Academic Press, 1980.

———. *The Modern World System III: The Second Era of Great Expansion of the Capitalist World-Economy, 1730s–1840s*. New York: Academic Press, 1988.

Warner, R. Stephen. "Work in Progress: Toward a New Paradigm for the Sociological Study of Religion in the United States." *American Journal of Sociology* 98, no. 5 (1993): 1044–93.

———. "The Place of Congregation in the Contemporary American Religious Configuration." In *American Congregations: New Perspectives in the Study of Congregation*, vol. 2, edited by James P. Wind and James M. Lewis, 54–100. Chicago: University of Chicago Press, 1994.

———. "Religion and New (Post-1965) Immigrants: Some Principles Drawn from Field Research." *American Studies* 41, no. 2/3 (2000): 267–86.

Warner, R. Stephen, and Judith Wittner. *Gatherings in Diaspora: Religious Communities and the New Immigration*. Philadelphia: Temple University Press, 1998.

Warren, Jonathan Dean. "Vipassana in the Pacific Northwest: Seeking the Moment in a Sea of Metaphors." Thesis presented to the Division of Philosophy, Religion, and Psychology, Reed College, 2002.

Waters, Malcolm. *Globalization*. New York: Routledge, 1995.

Weber, Max. "The Social Psychology of the World Religions." In *From Max Weber: Essays in Sociology*, edited by H. H. Gerth and C. Wright Mills, 267–301. New York: Oxford University Press, 1958.

West, Candace, and Don H. Zimmerman. "Doing Gender." *Gender and Society* 1, no. 2 (1987): 125–51.

White, Jeanne. "How Can I Make It Here? The Adaptation to Rural American Life by Lao Refugee Women." PhD diss., University of Georgia, 2000.

Wijayasundara, Senarat. "Restoring the Order of Nuns to the Theravadin Tradition." In *Buddhist Women across Cultures: Realizations*, edited by Karma Lekshe Tsomo, 79–87. Albany: SUNY Press, 1999.

Williams, Duncan Ryūken, and Christopher S. Queen, eds. *American Buddhism: Methods and Findings in Recent Scholarship*. Surrey: Curzon Press, 1999.

Wind, James P., and James W. Lewis, eds. *American Congregations: New Perspectives in the Study of Congregations*. Chicago: University of Chicago Press, 1994.

Wuthnow, Robert. *Meaning and Moral Order: Explorations in Cultural Analysis*. Berkeley: University of California Press, 1987.

———. *Sharing the Journey: Support Groups and America's New Quest for Community*. New York: Free Press, 1994.

———. *Poor Richard's Principle: Recovering the American Dream through the Moral Dimension of Work, Business, and Money*. Princeton: Princeton University Press, 1996.

———. *After Heaven: Spirituality in America since the 1950s*. Berkeley: University of California Press, 1998a.

———. *Loose Connections: Joining Together in America's Fragmented Communities*. Cambridge: Harvard University Press, 1998b.

————. "Religion and Diversity Survey Codebook. Machine Readable Data File." Princeton University Department of Sociology, 2003.

Wuthnow, Robert, and Wendy Cadge. "Buddhists and Buddhism in the United States: Accounting for Americans' Receptivity." *Journal for the Scientific Study of Religion* 43, no. 3 (forthcoming).

Yang, Fenggang, and Helen Rose Ebaugh. "Religion and Ethnicity among New Immigrants: The Impact of Majority/Minority Status in Home and Host Countries." *Journal for the Scientific Study of Religion* 40, no. 3 (2001a): 367–78.

————. "Transformations in New Immigrant Religions and Their Global Implications." *American Sociological Review* 66, no. 2 (2001b): 269–88.

Zhou, Min, Carl L. Bankston III, and Rebecca Kim. "Rebuilding Spiritual Lives in the New Land: Religious Practices among Southeast Asian Refugees in the United States." In *Religions in Asian America: Building Faith Communities*, edited by Pyong Gap Min and Jung Ha Kim, 37–70. Walnut Creek: AltaMira Press, 2001.

# INDEX